THE ART OF
JEAN
RACINE

THE ART

OF JEAN RACINE

BERNARD WEINBERG

THE UNIVERSITY OF CHICAGO PRESS

CHICAGO AND LONDON

Library of Congress Catalog Card Number: 63-20900
THE UNIVERSITY OF CHICAGO PRESS, CHICAGO & LONDON
The University of Toronto Press, Toronto 5, Canada
© *1963 by The University of Chicago. All rights reserved. Published 1963*
Printed in the United States of America

To the Memory of
My Mother

Introduction

In the chapters that follow—there will be eleven of them, one for each of Racine's tragedies, arranged in chronological order—I mean to seek some answers to a very simple question: How did Racine's art of the serious drama evolve and develop from the earliest through the last of his tragedies? This will resolve itself, in each chapter, into a set of constitutive questions: What successful solutions has he already found, and how will he improve upon them? What failings are apparent, and how will he attempt to correct or eliminate them? Through what new ways of posing the problem of dramatic structure will he arrive at better achievements? What failings persist or reappear? In what areas is there constant improvement?

Every artist, as he works toward the perfection of his art, must consider each completed piece as an apprentice piece for the next. And while he may feel, for many reasons, that he can go no farther with the particular poem, he nevertheless may see the possibility, in the poem about to be undertaken, of making it better than the last—of taking another step forward in the perfecting of his artistic techniques. He may see this possibility realized through a fresh way of thinking of the total poetic structure or through the discovery of other devices for exploiting it or through the avoidance of technical errors that made the last poem less satisfactory than it might have been. As an artist, he considers his art the constant element, the continuum, that links each of his works to all the others; and the perfecting of his art remains the general goal that he pursues in each of his particular poems.

The questions that I shall ask about Racine presuppose some such relationship of the artist to his art. I shall assume that his continuous preoccupation with the form of tragedy was a reflection of his continuous wish to write better tragedies; that he worried about imperfections of one sort or another in each of his tragedies and tried to avoid them in the next; that he gloried in such successes as he achieved and tried to multiply them.

The very nature of the questions raised determines and delimits the method that will be useful in answering them. The only useful documents are the tragedies themselves. The only useful method is an analytical one, one which will permit the asking of the same questions about each of the plays. I shall therefore consult no documents other than the tragedies, make no inquiries other than those relevant to the structure of each tragedy.

But since I have spoken of failures and successes in the writing of serious drama, since I have alluded to the perfecting of an artist's art, it is clear that I shall constantly be involved with matters of better and worse, with evaluations of plays and of parts of plays, with notches along a scale of perfection. This means that I shall constantly be applying criteria and, in so doing, that I shall always have in mind some standard of judging the dramatic form as a whole. I wish now to distinguish this standard from the conventions, the traditions, the historical considerations, the "images" and the "ideals" that have so long been associated with tragedy.

If the standard is not a double one, at least it may be applied equally well—and alternatively—to two aspects of the work of art: to the effect that it is capable of producing upon a qualified audience, and to the elements of its structure that constitute the potential for that effect. More simply put, the effect is a product of the form, and the same standard may be applied to both. If a genre such as tragedy is capable of a certain range of emotional effects upon an audience, then a particular tragedy will produce an emotion that falls within that range. It will produce this emotion more or less well depending upon how it has been built as a tragedy, how the parts of which it is made have been organized into an artistic whole. The effect of any given poem being unique and peculiar to itself, its form will be a unique organization of the poetic parts of which it is composed.

Perhaps the relationship of form to effect is even more apparent in the dramatic than in the non-dramatic genres. For in a dramatic work the effect results more clearly and more immediately from the way in which the form is represented to its "public" audience than from the actual, intrinsic nature of the form itself. Let me explain what I mean by this. If we think of the literary work as an instrument carefully and deliberately contrived by the poet in such a way as to affect its audience as he wishes, then the dramatic instrument will depend in a special way upon such factors as the order of presentation of its parts (relative and absolute order), upon its timing, upon the progressive creation of the emotional potential. This is true, of course, of any work of art that operates in time. But in a dramatic work, where the audience is present and in a sense remote, where it is present presumably only once and must be moved immediately and relatively quickly, where it is present for only a short time, it is imperative that each contribution to the total effect be made surely and at the right time. The audience can neither backtrack nor refer ahead. It must be given each piece of information, it must be made aware of each change in the state of affairs or in the action, at exactly the right moment. And all this must be done through the speeches and the actions of the persons participating in the drama.

The example of Sophocles' *Oedipus Rex* may help to clarify this distinction. Let us say that the *Oedipus Rex* is the story of a man who, having determined to discover and punish the criminal responsible for his country's plight, pursues the inquiry (over all objections) until he discovers that he himself is the criminal and punishes himself. This "story," like any other story, might have been told in a multitude of ways. A narrative poet might well have begun his tale at the beginning (say, the prophecies relative to Oedipus), have told each episode in succession, have pursued a straight line to the end; he would have told a different story and produced a different effect in his reader. Another might have chosen a point midway through the sequence of events, gone back to summarize the antecedent events, gone forward to the denouement; his story might have been the same, the effect would have been different. Any change in the order of presentation necessarily involves a change in the way that the emotional response is elicited. Sophocles' particular procedure involved, first, the selection or the "invention" of a particular segment of the legendary materials (using the rest only as explanatory or causal) and, second, the choice of an order of representation of the events. He chose to develop three lines of action simultaneously, which, as their interrelationship became progressively clearer to the audience, made up a single line of action and produced a single —and highly effective—emotional response: the successive revelation of past events in reply to Oedipus' reiterated question; the gradual discovery by others (Jocasta and Creon especially) that Oedipus was the guilty one, and their attempts to dissuade him from the inquiry; and Oedipus' own movement toward that final discovery. This is a unique handling of the Oedipus materials, depending in considerable part upon the exact moment when each event occurs on the stage, and the total effect is a function of the dual development of story and presentation.

For Racine, working in the area of serious drama, the problem must have been the same with each successive tragedy. He needed first to find a "subject"; and this was usually found in existing legendary or historical or literary materials. He needed next to carve out of that "subject" a "story" or an "action" or a "plot"; and this was in a sense the first truly artistic part of the procedure, since it meant conceiving the whole of the dramatic action as a unity and an entity capable of producing the desired emotional effect. He needed then (although I do not insist upon this chronology in the creative process) to give to each of the persons involved in the drama the kind of character that would make it possible for him to do what he needed to do in the drama, and to provide each person with useful passions and ideas. At some point in the process, finally, he needed to decide upon how he would order and present the materials—upon how he would convert the story into a play—and to determine in great detail precisely the order of staging the materials that he would adopt.

"Success" or "failure" would be a measure of the degree to which he achieved, in each play, not his intentions with respect to the play (we never know anything about intentions), but rather that kind of total dramatic form that might produce a sure, clear, and properly forceful emotional effect in the qualified audience. The criterion might then here be stated in terms of the total effect, of the degree to which there existed in the play a potential for an emotional response that would be appropriate to the action and the persons, that would be properly centered upon the protagonist, that would be unambiguous, that would be neither deficient nor excessive in degree. If the decisions of which I have spoken had been correctly made, if the play had then been devised and each of its parts produced in a way to bring about this effect, the play would be successful. Looked at in the other manner, from the point of view of the form or the structure itself, the criterion might be stated in terms of total structural excellence: of the degree to which a total and unified form was achieved, to which each needed part was present and no unnecessary part intruded, to which each part was present at the proper place and developed to the proper extent. This is, in a sense, the single and universal poetic criterion. To it one might add another (really contained within the first): the extent to which all the potentials of the subject, both structural and emotional, have been fully realized; this is the criterion of "richness."

We may then speak of success or failure in terms of the individual work of art alone, referring to the work itself for a body of judgments upon the whole and its parts; to this extent the work is self-judging, provides its own criteria. But these criteria, in turn, are known to us and useful to us only in so far as we derive them from broader and more general criteria relevant to the art as a whole and to our conception of the nature of poetic or dramatic structures. We may thus also speak of success or failure in terms of the universal possibilities of the art, relating the individual work to broader notions of poetics and aesthetics.

This is a far cry, of course, from judging works in terms of conventions or traditions or historical considerations. Indeed, I might go so far as to say that such "judgments" do not exist: from history, from tradition, we get no more than the bases for comparative statements, and these statements bear upon material rather than upon "formal" elements. From conventions we get such statements as relate to superficial form—to prosody and to external organization—or we get statements about the conformity or the non-conformity of a particular work to what was done in other works in the past. We may accept or resist the temptation to equate good with conformity and bad with non-conformity; if we yield to this temptation, we commit ourselves to the kind of "judging by the rules" that was practiced by Racine's own contemporaries and that gave conventional rather than artistic judgments. The kind of reading that I am proposing makes no reference to rules or conventions. It takes the poem itself as a point of departure and as a point of arrival; it goes outside the poem only for general notions about the nature of the poetic art and for the criteria that are generated by these notions.

The "perfecting of an artist's art" may then also be seen by remaining within the context of his works. Each work constitutes the solution to an artistic problem; the problem is set by the poet and solved by the poet; the poet is at once artist and critic. Each solution is satisfactory or unsatisfactory depending upon whether the poet-critic, as he judges the work of the poet-artist, finds that it is or is not perfect within the powers and limiations of the art. We may assume, I think, that the critic never finds the work of the artist absolutely perfect, that he always believes in the possibility of a better performance next time. The artist accepts this self-judgment and tries to arrive nearer to perfection in the next work. He sets a different problem, tries alternative means of solution. And if he is successful in this progressive sequence, each work brings him a greater command of his art, a greater mastery over its techniques and its tricks—a step closer to perfection.

I shall be looking at the eleven tragedies of Racine with these questions, these techniques of reading and judging, in mind. I shall try to see them as the artist himself might have seen them, not because I have any illusions about re-creating the artistic process or any wish to do so, but because I believe that these plays, as we have them, speak for themselves as solutions to artistic problems. By seeing the problem as the artist may have seen it, we may learn something about the plays that will be useful for their understanding and appreciation; by judging the solutions as the poet-critic may have judged them, we may learn something about the ways in which he sought to improve his art.

There are two areas in which a reference to historical considerations may be helpful to us. First, in the matter of the conventions of the tragic form during Racine's time. By considering these occasionally, we may find explanations—but not justifications or judgments—of why Racine did certain things as he did, of why he was led into certain errors or certain felicitous solutions. Second, in the history of French tragedy before Racine. This might be thought of as adding Racine's problems and solutions, his trials and errors, to those of his predecessors. In a way, the whole of an art grows in a way much like that of a single artist, and the point at which a given poet takes up the general problem is extremely important for him. Racine's problem was different from Corneille's, Corneille's from Montchrestien's, Montchrestien's from Jodelle's. Each could profit from the experience of his predecessors, as each built upon their achievements. Had Racine not had the example of Corneille before him, his whole struggle with the art of tragedy would have been different. It might have been more difficult, it might have been easier; he might have avoided certain mistakes, while missing certain successes to which Corneille's experience led him.

I do not mean at all to trace this history. But an infrequent reference to it may help us to see how and why Racine raised certain problems and found certain solutions, how and why the perfecting of his art of the serious drama took the course that it did.

THE TEXT

Passages from Racine are quoted from the edition of Paul Mesnard, *Œuvres de J. Racine,* in the series "Les Grands Écrivains de la France" (2d edition; Paris: Hachette). I have modified the spelling slightly, especially in the *-ois* verb endings, and have in some cases modernized the accentuation. I have removed a number of capital letters where current usage would not justify them. Although I have largely retained the punctuation of the edition cited, at some points I have thought it useful to repunctuate in order to clarify the readings.

Contents

I

La Thébaïde ou Les Frères Ennemis

RACINE wrote his first dramatic piece, *La Thébaïde ou Les Frères Ennemis,* in 1663; it was produced and published in 1664. For this first work in the dramatic manner, he chose a subject from Greek antiquity, one which, ever since Aeschylus' *Seven against Thebes,* had many times been exploited in Greek, in Latin, and in French.

Faced with this rich source of historical or legendary material, his first problem as a poet was to decide which ones of the many traditional events he would select as a basis for his own tragedy and what new episodes he would have to invent. The play as we have it shows that he chose to include the following materials:

1. First and foremost, the attempts by various persons, especially Jocaste and Antigone, to prevent the two rival brothers (the "frères ennemis" struggling for the domination of Thebes) from doing battle against each other. These attempts must of course fail and the battle had to be done. This line of action could therefore not provide a useful denouement, and moreover it was insufficient to occupy the extent of an entire tragedy. Other materials must be added to expand and enrich the subject.

2. The main item added to provide the denouement was the oracle, saying (in its necessarily ambiguous way) that Thebes could not be free of war until the "last of the royal blood" was

1

shed. This made it possible for the personages to entertain a false hope of peace when Ménecée, second son of Créon and the "last" member of the royal family because he was the youngest, killed himself in order to accomplish the oracle. It also made it necessary for all members of the royal family—Jocaste, Étéocle, Polynice, Créon, Hémon, and Antigone—to die before the oracle was completely fulfilled.

3. In order that some of these persons might die, however, additional lines of action must be introduced. Jocaste, principal actor in the effort to separate the two brothers, must decide early in the play that if she does not succeed she will die. Hémon and Antigone must share a hopeless love, in order that Hémon, for love of Antigone, will intercede between the two brothers (and be killed) and that Antigone, for love of Hémon, will die rather than marry another.

4. Especially, a complex and varied action must be provided for Créon. As brother to Jocaste, he will succeed to the throne if his two nephews die; hence he will constantly oppose Jocaste's efforts toward peace and attempt to precipitate the final battle. His love for Antigone will result, on the one hand, in her more immediate suicide and, on the other hand, in his own death after she dies.

5. Finally, the "frères ennemis," Étéocle and Polynice, are put into a situation where reconciliation is impossible, and their mutual hatred must lead to their killing each other.

It is apparent from this enumeration of the component actions of *La Thébaïde* that Racine's first solution to the problem of dramatic structure was the multiplication of lines of action. The central and basic situation of the two brothers' struggle for domination of Thebes, along with the unsuccessful attempts by others to keep them from armed battle, did not contain within itself sufficient stuff for a full-length tragedy; nor, probably, did it contain the potential that Racine wished for the emotional effect of his play. He therefore "invented," as elements related to the story of the two brothers, the lines of Jocaste, of Créon, of Antigone and

Hémon, of Ménecée. He was evidently satisfied that these lines could be woven into a single line of action and give rise to a single emotional effect; I shall inquire later into the success or failure of this attempt.

One of the results of this multiplication of lines was that the personages of the drama and their interests tended to fall into separate camps. We may see, on the one hand, a group of people determined that the war should go on and that the pitched battle or the single combat should take place: Étéocle and Polynice directly and overtly, Créon indirectly and in an underhanded fashion. On the other hand, those people who try to prevent battle and combat: Jocaste, because of her motherly love, attempts to dissuade the brothers separately and together; Antigone intervenes directly, using a sister's love, and indirectly through Hémon, who follows her orders; Ménecée dies through patriotism, believing that his suicide will put an end to the struggle. The general order of events will thus be an attempt by a person or persons wishing to prevent the war, followed by a failure because of the activity of a person or persons wishing to continue the war, followed by another attempt. This division of the persons, of their interests and activities, leads to the possibility of a pattern for the general organization of the plot, a pattern of attempt and failure which does not, however, necessarily determine the specific order of the attempts.

We shall be able to see how Racine ordered these attempts if we look at the content of each successive act; at the same time, we shall be able to discover how the emotional effect was built and developed.

Act I. The first act contains, at the very outset, Jocaste's statement of her intention to enlist the aid of Antigone and to speak to the embattled brothers:

> Que l'on coure avertir et hâter la princesse ...   (15)

> Allons, chère Antigone, et courons de ce pas
> Arrêter, s'il se peut, leur parricide bras.   (37–38)

The visit is rendered unnecessary, however, by the arrival of Étéocle. The first attempt takes place, therefore, in a long scene (scene 3) in which Jocaste places before Étéocle a series of arguments why he should desist; but Étéocle counters with his own arguments, refuses to be swayed by those of his mother, and the attempt fails. The way is prepared for a second attempt when Étéocle offers to allow Polynice to visit his mother within the city. He is confident that if the Thebans are allowed to choose their king, he himself rather than Polynice will be victorious. This act also contains, with relation to the other lines of action, a statement by Jocaste that she recognizes Créon's ambitions and the reasons for his behavior, along with Créon's denial; Créon's expression of his hatred for his son, Hémon, who has espoused the cause of Polynice; and allusions to the love of Antigone for Hémon and of Créon for Antigone. These other lines are not yet set in motion (except perhaps for Antigone's defense of Hémon), but the basic situation is stated.

As for the initial steps in the arousing of the spectator's emotions, Act I is already very complex. It is noteworthy that the first speaker is Jocaste and that the first emotions evoked are her sorrow and her despair; these emotions continue to be stressed throughout the act:

> Ah! mortelles douleurs!
> Qu'un moment de repos me va coûter de pleurs!   (1–2)

> Mes yeux ... ouverts aux larmes,
>   ... de telles alarmes?   (3–4)

> Nous voici donc, hélas! à ce jour détestable
> Dont la seule frayeur me rendait misérable!   (19–20)

> Ma fille, avez-vous su l'excès de nos misères?   (35)

>   ... ma douleur est extrême.   (44)

> Seconde mes soupirs, donne force à mes pleurs,
> Et comme il faut, enfin, fais parler mes douleurs.   (301–2)

The reader's initial favorable disposition toward Jocaste's purely maternal feelings is enhanced by the kinds of arguments she sets forth in her exchanges with Étéocle and Créon; she is invariably on the side that is presented, from the beginning, as the right side. She is for the natural affections, against the unnatural affections of her sons:

> Vous pourriez d'un tel sang, ô ciel! souiller vos armes?
> La couronne pour vous a-t-elle tant de charmes?
> Si par un parricide il la fallait gagner,
> Ah! mon fils, à ce prix voudriez-vous régner?   (71–74)

She is for honor and peace:

> Mais il ne tient qu'à vous, si l'honneur vous anime,
> De nous donner la paix sans le secours d'un crime.   (75–76)

She is for justice and hereditary rights:

> Vous le savez, mon fils, la justice et le sang
> Lui donnent, comme à vous, sa part à ce haut rang. (81–82)

She is for greatness of action and soul:

> Les peuples, admirant cette vertu sublime,
> Voudront toujours pour prince un roi si magnanime.
>
>   (139–40)

In her conversation with Créon, she shows herself to be perspicacious, confident of her sons' capacity to agree, equitable in her judgments, firm in her condemnation of Créon's duplicity. All the feelings attributed to her are, thus, such as would further dispose the audience in her favor.

The same effect is augmented by the establishment of attitudes of condemnation toward the other principal personages, especially Étéocle and Polynice but also Créon. In her very first speech, Jocaste refers to the brothers' battle as "le plus noir des forfaits" (6), and she accumulates such epithets as "ces inhumains" (17), "ces monstres" (27), "les crimes de mes fils" (29), "perfides" (31), "méchants, parricides" (32), "leur parricide bras" (38), "leur noire fureur" (41). Speaking to Étéocle, she calls him a "cœur ingrat et farouche" (111) and accuses him thus:

> ... le crime tout seul a pour vous des appas.   (114)

Créon establishes his position—against peace and for the continuation of the struggle—in his earliest appearances, both through his reproaches to Étéocle and in his replies to Jocaste. But it is Jocaste who turns the spectator against Créon:

> Mais avouez, Créon, que toute votre peine
> C'est de voir que la paix rend votre attente vaine,
> Qu'elle assure à mes fils le trône où vous tendez,
> Et va rompre le piège où vous les attendez.   (223–26)

> Vous inspirez au roi vos conseils dangereux,
> Et vous en servez un pour les perdre tous deux.   (233–34)

When Créon disowns his own son, our attitude toward him is completed and solidified:

> Je le dois, en effet, distinguer du commun,
> Mais c'est pour le haïr encor plus que pas un;
> Et je souhaiterais, dans ma juste colère,
> Que chacun le haït comme le hait son père.   (253–56)

The net effect of the speeches by and about various persons is to direct the audience's reactions, in the surest way, in favor of some of these persons and against others. We are immediately favorably disposed to Jocaste, and she becomes our first candidate for protagonist of the tragedy; we see in her somebody about whom our pity might center. As Act I develops, the same sympathy attaches to Antigone and Hémon, who are allied with Jocaste. Contrariwise, our antipathy to Étéocle, Polynice, and Créon is given a firm basis and considerable substance. The speeches of Étéocle, in this connection, are worthy of special notice. He uses good arguments to distinguish himself from his brother, to justify his own actions as corresponding to the wishes of the people of Thebes, and to condemn Polynice's as traitorous and contrary to the interests of Thebes. To this extent we approve of him. We also approve of his arrangements for Polynice's visit, of his courage and determination. But these positive qualities are counterbalanced by his haughtiness—

> Que je la quitte ou non, ne vous tourmentez pas;
> Faites ce que j'ordonne, et venez sur mes pas—   (185–86)

and by his refusal to accede to his mother's wishes. We are left in an ambivalent attitude. Probably the total result of his appearance in Act I is to make him preferable, as far as we are concerned, to Polynice, to cast additional discredit upon Polynice, and to confirm Jocaste's characterization of both brothers as "inhumains." Neither brother, as a result of this act, could command sufficient sympathy from us to qualify as a protagonist.

The first act thus sets in motion what seems to be the principal line of action, the attempts by Jocaste and others to prevent the bloody combat between the brothers. It also points to the possibility of auxiliary actions. It seems to present Jocaste as the protagonist, organizes our feelings in favor of her and of those who will second her attempts, arouses our aversion to those in the opposite camp. So far as we can see at this point, it also establishes a pattern for the future development of the play.

Act II. The second act, beginning with a long scene between Antigone and Hémon, seems not to continue directly the action of Act I. Scene 2 prolongs the same conversation, introducing the oracle and the interpretations by the two lovers. It is not until later that we realize that the first scene exists as a preparation for another "attempt" and that the second scene looks forward to later developments in the play. The main line of action moves ahead with this new attempt, in which Jocaste, Antigone, and Hémon all try to prevail upon Polynice, if not to desist from further efforts to regain the throne, at least to prolong the truce now in effect. The attempt fails, not because of Polynice's resistance, but because the truce is broken by the opposing forces.

As related to this attempt, scene 1 presents various reasons why an intercession on the part of Antigone and Hémon should stand

some chance of success. Their love, alluded to in Act I, is now
fully expressed; it becomes the basis for Hémon's original allegiance to Polynice—

> J'ai suivi Polynice, et vous l'avez voulu:
> Vous me l'avez prescrit par un ordre absolu—   (357–58)

and for his willingness, later, again to do Antigone's bidding. The
mere fact that Hémon has long been a faithful partisan of Polynice (and has even abandoned Antigone for him) will increase
his credit with the dispossessed brother. Antigone, we learn in
scene 1, had long preferred Polynice to Étéocle:

> Il m'était cher alors comme il est aujourd'hui,
>
> . . . .
>
> Nous nous aimions tous deux dès la plus tendre enfance,
> Et j'avais sur son cœur une entière puissance;
> Je trouvais à lui plaire une extrême douceur,
> Et les chagrins du frère étaient ceux de la sœur.   (365–70)

Moreover, as Hémon speaks of Polynice's distaste for war, he
raises some hope that Polynice may yield to persuasion; but
Antigone has doubts:

> Je les connais tous deux, et je répondrais bien
> Que leur cœur, cher Hémon, est plus dur que le mien.
>   (385–86)

The oracle reported in scene 2, like all such supernatural elements, introduces a disturbing factor into the development of the
main line of action. For in a way it negates the possibility that,
through a natural course of events, the "attempts" might be successful; it also makes the audience wonder if it is worth while
for Jocaste and her allies to continue, since it predicts:

> «Thébains, pour n'avoir plus de guerres,
> Il faut, par un ordre fatal,
> Que le dernier du sang royal
> Par son trépas ensanglante vos terres.»   (393–96)

But its most damaging effect is to suggest the possibility that the line of action will not be the one hitherto discerned, but rather one involving a larger number of people. "Le dernier du sang royal" is wilfully ambiguous; it could be taken as excluding the two brothers (this is the interpretation put upon it shortly by Ménecée), or as including all members of the royal family. If the latter is the case, all the principal actors in the tragedy will ultimately have to die; and they do. This is the way that Antigone and Hémon interpret the oracle in scene 2. "Tout notre sang," asks Antigone, "doit-il sentir votre colère?" (400). She fears both for herself and for Hémon, rather than for the brothers, and in so doing she turns our attention away from the two brothers and Jocaste's task of reconciliation and peace. The problem now becomes rather to know which of the two interpretations is correct and, if it is the second, how the royal family will be extinguished.

The interview with Polynice (scene 3) had been projected in Act I, as a proper sequel to the interview with Étéocle; it had, as we have seen, been further prepared in the early parts of Act II. It constitutes the second attempt. It divides into three parts, as Jocaste, Antigone, and Hémon in turn make representations to Polynice. It is a failure from the beginning, since Polynice counters with determined and unwavering arguments; it is a failure at the end when a soldier, arriving from the field of battle, announces that the truce has been broken, and Polynice leaves.

Act II continues the development of the emotions begun in Act I; but just as there is a misdirecting of the action, so there comes to be an ambivalence with respect to the passions. The relatively simple attitudes of "sympathy" for Jocaste and her allies and of "antipathy" for the brothers and Créon no longer prevail or, at least, they are mitigated by other feelings. First of these is the response to the love of Antigone and Hémon which, if it may be necessary to justify later actions, at this point diverts the audience from the passions aroused previously. Hémon (as a true "Brutus galant") speaks of the charms of his beloved and of the anguish of absence; but the spectator, resenting the turn to a new passion and a new situation, remains unconvinced. Antigone's speeches relate more directly to the effects of the war upon her love and hence seem to continue more successfully the feelings of Act I. In any case, both lovers, as they speak of Polynice, improve our feelings toward him, and when he appears in scene 3 his credit with us is roughly that of Étéocle.

Meanwhile, in the second scene, the reporting of the oracle tends again to dissipate the emotions. To the sense of coming catastrophe is added an increased concern, not for the brothers or Jocaste, but for the fate of Antigone and Hémon. Antigone epitomizes this concern:

> Fille d'Œdipe, il faut que je meure pour lui.
> Je l'attends, cette mort, et je l'attends sans plainte;
> Et, s'il faut avouer le sujet de ma crainte,
> C'est pour vous que je crains; oui, cher Hémon, pour vous.
> De ce sang malheureux vous sortez comme nous;
> Et je ne vois que trop que le courroux céleste
> Vous rendra, comme à nous, cet honneur bien funeste,
> Et fera regretter aux princes des Thébains
> De n'être pas sortis du dernier des humains.   (406–14)

The willingness of both lovers to die and the virtuous sentiments they express in support of this willingness increase our admiration for them and, incidentally, for Jocaste's camp. Yet we feel that, instead of being reinforced, our initial sympathies and antipathies have been diluted; even the more favorable situation of Polynice contributes to this effect, since the lines are less clearly drawn. The new basis for a vague and indefinite suspense, related to the loss of identity of the original protagonist, tends to be confusing.

Scene 3 introduces Polynice. He conforms immediately to his mother's description of him: he is haughty, disdainful of the people, calls his brother a tyrant and a slave, denies all blame for the war. Antigone characterizes him well:

La nature pour lui n'est plus qu'une chimère;
Il méconnaît sa sœur, il méprise sa mère;
Et l'ingrat, en l'état où son orgueil l'a mis,
Nous croit des étrangers, ou bien des ennemis.   (515–18)

He is, she says, "inexorable" (525); she goes so far as to tell him that Étéocle is less intractable, more human than himself (555–58). We thus return to our original estimate of the situation, seeing right and justice in the cause of Jocaste and Antigone, wrong and injustice in that of the brothers. Nor does scene 4 in any way change our appraisal; for before Polynice can reply to the multiple appeal for a continuation of the truce (possibly betraying more human sentiments), word comes that the truce is broken, and he leaves. Jocaste may once again, at the end of the act, call him a "barbare" (575).

At the end of Act II, we feel that the main line of action (as originally distinguished) has moved forward through the making and failure of the second "attempt"; that at least one alternative line of action has been set in motion; that the original clarity of the situation has been disturbed. Our earlier feelings with respect to the two camps have been reconfirmed and possibly enhanced, except that some new emotions and interests have been added. We do not feel, therefore, that our original emotions have become clearer or more powerful.

Act III. The function of Act III, relative to the actions under way, is triple. Through the patriotic suicide of Ménecée the oracle seems to be fulfilled, and an apparent denouement is reached. Jocaste exploits Ménecée's death as an argument for peace in her third "attempt" to separate the brothers. And a fourth "attempt," consisting in a confrontation of the two brothers, is prepared when Polynice requests an interview and Étéocle accords it; besides, the failure of this attempt is foreseen in Créon's declaration of his motives for supporting it.

Scenes 1 and 2 are instrumental, serving to make possible Antigone's report to Jocaste in scene 3. (We shall see at a later point what other function is given to scene 2.) That report, introduced by Antigone's

> Ah! Madame, en effet
> L'oracle est accompli, le ciel est satisfait, (617–18)

persuades us, temporarily at least, that the dominant action will be the one concerning the oracle; in so far as the oracle is now "accomplished," that action should now be completed. But there remains the possibility of the other interpretation. It is necessary, to keep this possibility alive, that Jocaste make the following speech, which links the two actions together and recalls to us the predominance of the first line of action:

> S'il [le ciel] me flatte aussitôt de quelque espoir de paix,
> Un oracle cruel me l'ôte pour jamais.
> Il m'amène mon fils; il veut que je le voie;
> Mais, hélas! combien cher me vend-il cette joie!
> Ce fils est insensible et ne m'écoute pas;
> Et soudain il me l'ôte et l'engage aux combats.
> Ainsi, toujours cruel, et toujours en colère,
> Il feint de s'apaiser, et devient plus sévère;
> Il n'interrompt ses coups que pour les redoubler,
> Et retire son bras pour me mieux accabler. (681–90)

Racine here uses a device that will become a favorite of his in later plays, that of informing the spectator, through a kind of summation or epitome, of what the principal line of action is and of the present state of affairs. Here, Jocaste doubts that Ménecée's suicide can really end her overriding preoccupation.

The fourth scene returns Étéocle and Créon to the stage. After a brief reproach to Étéocle for having broken the truce (which he denies), Jocaste tries to use the example of Ménecée as an argument for peace. Surprisingly enough (we remember his earlier positions), Créon joins in the same effort, using his paternal love as an explanation. But Étéocle remains firm. Perhaps, however, their urgings have some effect, since when (in scene 5) Attale requests an interview for Polynice, Étéocle grants it—albeit with some irritation. The meeting will take place "dans ces lieux," and we may look forward to another attempt at peace by Jocaste and those of her party.

Scene 6 has as its purpose to reveal the role of Créon in the conduct to this point of the main action, and to prepare his future interventions. Through his ambition, it now appears, he has set the brothers against each other, initiating the rivalry for the throne:

> D'Étéocle d'abord j'appuyai l'injustice;
> Je lui fis refuser le trône à Polynice.
> Tu sais que je pensais dès lors à m'y placer;
> Et je l'y mis, Attale, afin de l'en chasser.   (851–54)

It is he (not Étéocle) who has caused the truce to be broken:

> Enfin, ce même jour, je fais rompre la trêve,
> J'excite le soldat, tout le camp se soulève.   (867–68)

If he now seems to favor peace, if he wishes to bring the brothers together, it is because he realizes the full consequences of such a meeting:

> Ne t'étonne donc plus si je veux qu'ils se voient:
> Je veux qu'en se voyant leurs fureurs se déploient,
> Que rappelant leur haine, au lieu de la chasser,
> Ils s'étouffent, Attale, en voulant s'embrasser.   (887–90)

As for the future, his dual ambition now becomes patent: he wishes to obtain the throne and to place Antigone upon it as his queen.

Whereas Créon's role had heretofore been relatively minor, he now emerges as a much more prominent personage in the tragedy. Indeed, the importance of his past actions, the possible consequences of his current maneuvers, and the extent of his future ambitions make of him one of the predominant actors in the play. I do not think that he becomes a rival of Jocaste for the position of protagonist; but at the end of Act III he tends to become a center of interest and thus, possibly, to distract our attention from the main line of action. Once again, the directions of the action become confused; just as, in Act II, the whole matter of the oracle had become a complicating and disturbing factor, so now the new emphasis upon Créon raises doubts about what the real tendency of the action is supposed to be.

Consequently, Act III also produces curious results in the area of the effect upon the audience's passions. I think we might say that very little, if anything, happens to our fundamental feelings about the persons in the two opposed camps; our attitudes toward Jocaste, Antigone, and Hémon, toward Étéocle and Polynice, remain about the same. Not that they should change; but so long as they do not develop and grow, so long as they remain fairly static, we are apt to feel that they diminish and disappear. This feeling is increased, in the present case, by the scope given to two other passions affecting Jocaste and Créon. In scene 2, Jocaste speaks again of her maternal sorrow; but she also speaks of all her present troubles and sorrows as a punishment visited upon her by the gods for her past crimes: her marriage with her son Oedipus and her bearing of children to him:

> Tu ne l'ignores pas, depuis le jour infâme
> Où de mon propre fils je me trouvai la femme,
> Le moindre des tourments que mon cœur a soufferts
> Egale tous les maux que l'on souffre aux enfers.   (599–602)

Instead of increasing our pity for Jocaste, this declaration tends to do two other things: to make us blame and condemn the gods for their injustice to her, and to make us regard the present sorrows as not quite so bad as others she had previously undergone. The behavior of her sons becomes less unnatural—especially if the gods and not they are responsible for it—and she herself loses something of the role of protagonist merely because she loses will and initiative. I do not think that Racine intended the declaration to have this effect; he wanted, rather, to make clearer the motivation for Jocaste's suicide reported in Act V, brought about by her utter despair and by her conviction that God and the fates were against her. But the damage to the passions central to this tragic action seems to me to be clear.

That is also true of our feelings about Créon in scene 6. We had, of course, early put him in the camp of the antipathetic characters, when we realized that he was following his own ambitions and doing whatever he could to promote strife between the brothers; Jocaste has early accused him of these doings. But now he becomes a villain, adding duplicity and unscrupulousness to his traits. We come to hate him in his own right, not only as a member of a group of men to whom we are opposed, and to a degree that exceeds our antipathy for Étéocle and Polynice. As a result, Créon achieves an existence apart from this group, and a separate passion attaches to him.

Both these feelings are essentially disruptive. They make of Act III a continuation of Act II in the sense that both the internal action and our feelings toward it tend to become dispersed. We feel that we are losing our hold upon the action of the tragedy—and it upon us.

Act IV. The fourth act is devoted almost exclusively to the fourth "attempt." After having appealed individually to the two brothers, once to Polynice and twice to Étéocle, Jocaste finally succeeds in bringing them together before her, enabling her to try for a reconciliation and to use new arguments to which the two, now together, might be susceptible. When the attempt fails, Jocaste must realize her total failure; there is nothing left for her to do but to die.

The initial scene of the act, between Étéocle and Créon, prepares for the failure of the attempt. Étéocle reiterates his own hatred for Polynice, traces its history, and predicts a similar intransigence from Polynice. Créon incites Étéocle to continue the struggle:

> Et puisque la raison ne peut rien sur son cœur,
> Eprouvez ce que peut un bras toujours vainqueur. (949–50)

He also encourages Étéocle to use his own kind of duplicity. The procedures and the outcome of the interview are thus evident in advance. The second scene, announcing the approach of the others, gives Créon another opportunity to predict what will happen:

> Fortune, achève mon ouvrage,
> Et livre-les tous deux aux transports de leur rage!   (971–72)

Scene 3 occupies most of the act. It is significant that, although Antigone, Créon, and Hémon are all present at the interview, only Jocaste and the two brothers speak. The attempt is still Jocaste's, and she returns (to a degree) to the dominant position that she had originally held in the action of the play. Her first effort is to bring the brothers to a civil greeting. This fails; they mean to be uncivil, to repeat only their pretensions to the throne. Jocaste then makes a sentimental appeal, attached to this palace and the scenes of their childhood; but they will not listen. Next, she talks to Polynice alone, proposing a series of alternatives: renounce the throne; take the crown offered him by the king of Argos; conquer a kingdom for himself. All these alternatives are unacceptable to Polynice; he declares that he has come with only one purpose, to challenge Étéocle to a single combat with him, in which he hopes to kill Étéocle and thus regain the throne. Étéocle accepts, expressing similar hopes. Jocaste now realizes the extent of her failure, and sees death for herself as the only solution:

> Allez donc, j'y consens, allez perdre la vie.
> A ce cruel combat tous deux je vous convie.
> Puisque tous mes efforts ne sauraient vous changer ...
>
> . . . .
>
> Je n'ai plus pour mon sang ni pitié ni tendresse.
> Votre exemple m'apprend à ne le plus chérir;
> Et moi je vais, cruels, vous apprendre à mourir.   (1179–90)

In the final scene the brothers leave, Antigone and Hémon recognize their obduracy, Antigone begs Hémon to prevent the single combat. The fifth and final attempt is thus arranged.

If the events of Act IV seem merely to repeat the pattern of "attempt and failure" already established and exploited, the emotional effect seems also to be a repetition. Nothing happens to our feelings about Étéocle, I think, when in scene 1 he reaffirms (perhaps more vigorously than before) his hatred for his brother. When he calls this hatred a

> Triste et fatal effet d'un sang incestueux!   (921)

something of the fatalism that Jocaste had attached to her present sorrows also informs his situation and his emotions. I am not sure that this makes them more striking and more vigorous; the opposite may be the case. Again, no change occurs in our attitude toward Créon when, preparing Étéocle for the interview, he displays his ambition, his duplicity, and his exultation at seeing his hopes about to be realized; we hate him neither more nor less.

The same may be said about the emotions expressed—and aroused—by Jocaste, Étéocle, and Polynice in scene 3. In her first speech, Jocaste displays a certain maternal optimism about the meeting; but the wishful thinking is transparent and is soon dissipated. Having found it useless, she tries again by calling upon the brothers' childhood memories. But she—and we—know what they were, and we see the emptiness of such lines as these:

> C'est ici que tous deux vous reçûtes le jour;
> Tout ne vous parle ici que de paix et d'amour.   (1025–26)

For we have known, from the beginning, that

> Ils ne connaissent plus la voix de la nature.   (1032)

Jocaste's arguments on a purely political ground, meant to turn Polynice toward other goals, are equally ill conceived; they may show her imagination and her skill at argument, but they move us no more than they persuade Polynice. One feels, in all her speeches in this scene, that she has been over the same terrain before, that her shocked maternity and her sorrow have been fully manifested long since and move forward not a whit. Only her final despair and her resolution to die (both of which had been repeatedly expressed since the beginning) seem to give a very slight lift to the emotional monotony of the act.

On the whole, Act IV suffers from the weaknesses of structure that had begun to appear in the previous acts. The sense of pattern becomes stronger as the fourth attempt follows upon the other three and since there is no reason why the fourth should be any more successful than the others—indeed, good reasons are given why it should fail utterly—there is no suspense about its outcome. At the same time, the passions involved come to a standstill, as the personages themselves do no more than re-manifest or re-express passions already ascribed to them previously.

Act V. The final act, if it is to conclude the play properly, must bring to a denouement all the various lines of action previously set in motion. Act V of *La Thébaïde* does so, but there are some doubts about how successful is the denouement that it furnishes. The first line of action we distinguished (and it remained a constant one through the tragedy) was that of the "attempts" to separate the brothers and achieve peace: a fifth attempt takes place here in Hémon's intervention in the single combat. The second line was the prediction of the oracle; after the suicide of Ménecée in Act III had disproved one of the interpretations, the other is shown to be correct when, after the deaths of Jocaste, Hémon, Étéocle, Polynice, and Antigone, Créon (now "last" of the royal blood in point of time) also dies. Of the secondary lines of action, the love of Antigone and Hémon is negated by their deaths, as are Créon's ambition and his love for Antigone; the struggle for the throne ends in the dual killing; and Jocaste's suicide puts an end to her sorrows and her despair.

Each one of these endings presents difficulties. Jocaste's suicide, reported in Antigone's *stances* of scene 1, is fitting to her hopelessness, and indeed she had spoken of it on many occasions. But basically it is only incidental to the working-out of the main action. Jocaste cannot be considered a protagonist who, if she does not accomplish what she sets out to accomplish, must die; her death is not one of the conditions of failure in her attempts to bring peace between her sons. It fulfills, in part, the oracle; but we must ask shortly, and very seriously, whether the fulfillment of an oracle (in this as in the other cases) provides the right kind of structural justification for dramatic events.

Another reported death occupies scene 2; it is that of Étéocle in the single combat, related by Olympe on the basis of partial information. A fuller report, corrected and substantiated by complete information, will be made in the next scene, and one wonders what might be the dramatic usefulness of Olympe's account. In several of his later plays, Racine will use the device of the false report; but it will always be in order to lead one or more of the personages to statements or actions that could not otherwise be elicited (the false report of Thésée's death in *Phèdre* is an example). In the present case all that results is a further estimate, by Antigone, of the characters of Hémon and the two brothers, an estimate that in no wise differs from earlier ones.

Scene 3 contains most of the substance of the act. Créon relates the deaths of the two brothers, which at once put an end to the brothers' ambitions and to the possibility of reconciling them. He also tells of Hémon's "attempt" at stopping the battle, ending in his own death at Étéocle's hands. Since Créon is now king, he proposes that Antigone share the throne with him; she leaves without answering. It is clear that all these events have been prepared by earlier statements in the play and that at least one of them is related to the main line of action. But Hémon's intervention, coming after Jocaste's suicide, is related to it only in a secondary way; since the protagonist (if indeed she be that) has disappeared, we can see in this attempt only another application of the pattern rather than a proper development of the action.

Hémon's death makes Antigone's life useless to her, and we know from her *stances* that she would not wish to survive him. Hence Créon's proposal of marriage (much as she may hate him) is not needed to precipitate her suicide. And Créon's death, once his sword has been taken away from him, must be regarded as an act of the gods—who collaborate in this way in the fulfillment of their own oracle.

Scene 4, in which Créon restates his ambitions and reaffirms his lack of any paternal feeling, leads nowhere; its only usefulness is to provide time for Antigone's suicide, narrated briefly by Olympe in scene 5. The final scene brings death, the gods willing, to the final remaining member of the royal family, thus completing the oracle's prediction and necessarily concluding the action of the play. The artificial character of this conclusion is immediately obvious.

While all these many things are happening in Act V, very little is happening to the audience's emotions. I doubt that there is any sense of a climaxing, of a clarification, of an ultimate relief with respect to these emotions. Antigone's expression (in her *stances* in scene 1) of her despair at her mother's death and of her concern for her brothers' lives, along with her love for Hémon, is no different from what it had been since the very beginning; it may even be less effective through a kind of intellectualization that comes from the neat balancing of passion against passion:

> Un amant me retient, une mère m'appelle ...
> Ce que veut la raison, l'amour me le défend ...
>   Mais, hélas! qu'on tient à la vie,
>   Quand on tient si fort à l'amour!
>
>   .   .   .   .
>
>   Je ne vivrais pas pour moi-même,
>   Et je veux bien vivre pour toi.   (1216–32)

Upon the news of Étéocle's death, in scene 2, she again speaks of her admiration for Hémon, of her brothers' unnatural strife:

Princes dénaturés, vous voilà satisfaits:
La mort seule entre vous pouvait mettre la paix.
Le trône pour vous deux avait trop peu de place;
Il fallait entre vous mettre un plus grand espace,
Et que le ciel vous mît, pour finir vos discords,
L'un parmi les vivants, l'autre parmi les morts.   (1251–56)

But this neither convinces nor moves, any more than does her sudden (and unneeded) declaration at the end of the scene that she now tends to prefer Étéocle to Polynice:

Devenant malheureux, il m'est devenu cher.   (1272)

The play upon the emotions in scene 3 is somewhat more subtle. Starting from the assumption that only Étéocle has died in the combat, we are urged to hate Créon more than before (but is that possible?) for his responsibility:

N'imputez qu'à vous seul la mort du roi mon frère,
Et n'en accusez point la céleste colère.
A ce combat fatal vous seul l'avez conduit:
Il a cru vos conseils; sa mort en est le fruit.   (1285–88)

In a way this is a false start, since it centers our emotion upon Créon. So does Créon's appeal for sympathy as a bereaved father:

... et les destins contraires
Me font pleurer deux fils, si vous pleurez deux frères.
                                            (1297–98)

Yet when the full account of the combat is given by Créon, our feelings once again return, as they should, to the two brothers and to Hémon; they are mixed feelings, since we condemn the two brothers (and especially Étéocle) while we admire Hémon's courage and self-sacrifice. A further mixture and confusion of our feelings comes with Antigone's sorrow and despair (now very similar to her mother's) and with Créon's proposal of marriage to her. At no point in the scene is it possible for one of these emotions to reach a high point of intensity; it is always being expelled by another, concomitant with a new event.

This impression of the dissipation of emotional impact remains and grows through the last three scenes of the tragedy, especially since some of the individual passions introduced fail to convince us. We are ready to accept Créon's joy at acceding to the throne, even his heartlessness toward the death of his sons:

> Le nom de père, Attale, est un titre vulgaire:
> C'est un don que le ciel ne nous refuse guère.
> Un bonheur si commun n'a pour moi rien de doux:
> Ce n'est pas un bonheur, s'il ne fait des jaloux.   (1441–44)

But we are loath to believe that his desire to marry Antigone, which has seemed to be merely a political passion, is a real lover's love:

> Ne me parle donc plus que de sujets de joie,
> Souffre qu'à mes transports je m'abandonne en proie.

> (1453–54)

After the interruption in which Olympe tells of Antigone's death, Créon continues his expressions of love:

> Vous fermez pour jamais ces beaux yeux que j'adore.

> (1481)

> Et toujours mes soupirs vous rediront ma peine.   (1490)

Now this passion is inappropriate, at this point, on two scores; first, because it is difficult for us to see it as sincere in Créon, whose emotions hitherto were all of another order; second, because it is discordant with any tragic feeling that might have been associated with the main personages and the main line of action. It seems to tag along after the others, and while it may be needed to prepare (in a vague way) Créon's heaven-sent death, it represents still another centrifugal movement of our feelings.

Our general judgment on Act V must therefore be that, even if it brings to conclusion all the lines of action set going through the play, it does so in a wooden sort of way, too rapidly and too mechanically; and that it works unsuccessfully upon our feelings because it leaves them in a state of confusion, of attenuation, of indifference.

If now we look back at the total structure of the action in *La Thébaïde,* we can, I think, discover some of the bases of its weakness. First and foremost, it is apparent from the study we have made that there is no clear and unambiguous central action in the play. Having chosen, from among the traditional materials, those parts relevant to the final combat and deaths of the two brothers, Racine then sought to organize those parts into an action. His first hypothesis was that he could make an action by raising obstacles to the combat (and hence delaying it) in the form of a concerted effort to reconcile the brothers. Jocaste and Antigone were to be the prime movers in this effort—above all, Jocaste— and Hémon was to add the special strength of his position as an ally of Polynice to their advantages as mother and sister. Therefore the play begins with Jocaste as apparent protagonist—as the person whose initiatives will determine the direction of the action —and with every indication that there will be a series of attempts and failures, resulting finally in the combat and deaths. But it soon becomes clear to the spectator (as it must have to Racine) that this basis cannot give rise to a sufficient number of episodes, to a sufficient magnitude of action, for a full-length tragedy. Racine therefore invents a kind of counteraction in the form of the prediction of the oracle: whereas Jocaste and the others will try to bring about reconciliation and peace, the gods will that the "last" of the royal blood should be shed before peace may be achieved. This makes it necessary to provide devices and episodes to insure the death of Ménecée ("last" in the sense of youngest) and then of all the others (Créon will be "last" when all the rest have died). It also necessitates the invention of certain auxiliary actions, such as the love of Antigone and Hémon and Créon's proposal to Antigone, as instrumental devices for the accomplishment of the counteraction.

What happens, therefore, is that there ceases to be any single and direct line of action. Instead, there are several lines, pursued simultaneously and ending simultaneously in the holocaust of the last act. While all the episodes of the play may be related (although sometimes tenuously) to one another and to a central subject or theme, they do not combine to constitute an action. I mean by this that there is no original conflict which, as it generates episodes that in turn generate other episodes, leads necessarily to a resolution of the conflict. Instead, the original line of action degenerates into a pattern; rather than a plot, which would have within itself a dynamic principle of development, we have a series of repetitions of the same episode—attempt and failure—with no essential difference between one episode and the next. The organization is static. As for the counteraction, here again a plot structure is lacking. This is a consequence of the kind of basis for action provided by the oracle.

The oracle's prediction that, before peace may be restored, the last of the royal blood must be shed, sets up a group of expectations that are external to the action rather than internal. They are in the audience, not in the plot. We know that one or all must die; but only one of the actors acts in accordance with the prediction, and he is Ménecée. His suicide is a deliberate attempt to fulfill the oracle and to re-establish peace. For none of the others is this the case; each dies as the result of acts that spring from other volitions or motivations; none dies because the oracle had said that he would or because we had expected him to die. Racine was of course aware of this difficulty and tried to invent internal justifications for each of the deaths. In some cases, as with Étéocle, Polynice, and Hémon, he was successful to the degree to which he was able to base these acts in character—in hatred or courage, in love or inhumanity. In others he was less successful. Jocaste's various prior statements to the effect that she could not live if peace were not restored do not suffice to make her die when she does. We could more readily accept her suicide after the deaths of all her children; but that would have made the last act even more bloody. Antigone's suicide, in spite of the protestations in her *stances,* seems merely to be a repetition of her mother's. The most unconvincing death of all is Créon's, not only because it comes about through direct intervention of the gods ("La foudre va tomber, la terre est entr'ouverte" [1514]), but because it is unrelated to previous events or statements in the play. It is neither necessary nor probable.

True plot structure is therefore replaced in *La Thébaïde* on the one hand by a pattern of repetition, on the other by external expectations that cannot properly be made into bases of action. Racine's first attempt at constructing a dramatic plot failed. If we wish to reduce this failure to terms of dramatic technique, we may say that whereas he controlled already, at the beginning of his career, the means for establishing necessity, he had not yet mastered the devices of probability. I use "necessity" in the sense of that foundation for action in character which makes it "necessary" that any personage should always act in a given kind of way; the assumption is that the poet provides him with traits of character in order that he may be disposed to act in certain ways. I use "probability" in the sense of those other bases for action—in circumstances, in past events or actions, in thoughts and arguments, in specific feelings—which, in a particular case, make it more "probable" that a personage will act in one specific way rather than in its alternative. Necessity, founded in character, determines a general line of action; probability, founded in contingent factors, serves to specify this general line in the direction of the particular action.

Now the difficulty with the pattern of "attempt and failure" of which I have spoken is that it provides good necessity but poor probability. Each attempt is rendered necessary by the character of Jocaste (or of one of her allies); her love for her sons, her maternal sense, make it necessary that she should try to prevent the combat and the deaths of Étéocle and Polynice. Étéocle and Polynice are of such character, they are so compounded of hatred, of unnatural ambition, of perfidy, that they must respond negatively to each of the attempts; each must end in failure. More-over, for the first attempt, at least, a fair probability seems to be established. After six months of strife—

> Mes yeux depuis six mois étaient ouverts aux larmes—   (3)

the moment of crisis has arrived:

> Je les ai vus déjà tous rangés en bataille;
> J'ai vu déjà le fer briller de toutes parts.   (8–9)

Jocaste now determines to take decisive action:

> Il faut courir, Olympe, après ces inhumains;
> Il les faut séparer, ou mourir par leurs mains.   (17–18)

It is to be noted that one of these probabilities, "courir après ces inhumains," is exhausted immediately when Étéocle arrives, mak-ing it unnecessary to go out after him; but the attempt to "sep-arate" them will be made. Jocaste recognizes at the outset that it is likely to fail:

> Ni prières ni pleurs ne m'ont de rien servi,   (21)

and that if it does, blood will be shed:

> Ou s'ils oseront bien, dans leur noire fureur,
> Répandre notre sang pour attaquer le leur.   (41–42)

Étéocle also indicates in advance the likelihood of failure:

> Et si quelque bonheur nos armes accompagne,
> L'insolent Polynice et ses fiers alliés
> Laisseront Thèbes libre, ou mourront à mes pieds.   (68–70)

The arguments that he offers in his long speech (91–110), based on past events and on his estimate of the present situation, are of a nature to make his yielding to Jocaste increasingly improbable.

Once these probabilities have been realized in the first attempt and failure, there remains little in the way of probabilities for the additional attempts. Racine occupies himself with organizing the occasions for these attempts—the appearance of Polynice, the ap-

pearance of the two brothers together, Hémon's departure for
the field of battle—but he can do nothing about inventing new
arguments for peace that might be more persuasive or new dispositions on the part of the brothers that might lead them to acceptance. In a sense, all the probabilities on both sides have been
used up in the first attempt and failure; the poet will have to use
them again in subsequent episodes. But it is of the nature of
poetic probabilities that once they have been realized or exhausted,
they are no longer available for reuse. If they are reused, the resulting actions depend upon necessity rather than upon probability, and the effect is one of repetition and of monotony.
Necessity provides a kind of constant, unchanging, static basis
for action; if the dynamics of probability—one probability leading
to another—are not added, the poem will stand still. That is what
happens as a result of Racine's use of the pattern in *La Thébaïde*.

Nor is the device of the oracle used for the counteraction any
better. It may even be worse. For here there is a lack both of
necessity and probability. Créon's death is the best case in point,
although Ménecée's suicide furnishes another excellent example.
Before that event, Ménecée had been mentioned only twice, once
by Étéocle who characterized him in these terms:

> Laissez, pour recevoir et pour donner ses lois,
> Votre fils Ménecée, et j'en ai fait le choix.
> Comme il a de l'honneur autant que de courage,
> Ce choix aux ennemis ôtera tout ombrage,
> Et sa vertu suffit pour les rendre assurés.   (177–81)

Honor, courage, and virtue. The same qualities reappear in the
second mention, the report that Ménecée has left the city:

> Je ne sais quel dessein animait son courage;
> Une héroïque ardeur brillait sur son visage.   (583–84)

These are summary indications of character, supplying a minimal
necessity for the one action that Ménecée has to perform. But
since no probabilities are established for it (except in his speech

preceding the act), the suicide comes as a surprise—as an obvious artistic subterfuge to give and apply quickly one of the possible interpretations of the oracle.

We can now see with greater precision how *La Thébaïde* is constructed. Lacking in the dynamics of probability that would make for a plot moving poetically from the beginning through the middle to the end, the play supplants them by a static structure that is really dual: the pattern and the fulfillment of the oracle. This makes for a division of the line of action—or development —into two, and this in turn leads to the loss of any sense of a protagonist. Jocaste occupies that position only for a very short time; afterward, we can fix neither upon Antigone nor upon Créon nor upon the two brothers as the center of the action. Since there is no single action, there is no single center. At best we see the existence of two separate and opposed camps: Jocaste, Antigone, and Hémon on one side (we are "for" these), the brothers and Créon on the other (we are "against" these). Ménecée exists apart, although in a way his patriotic sacrifice might be considered an "attempt." He says:

«Recevez donc ce sang que ma main va répandre,
Et recevez la paix où vous n'osiez prétendre.»   (647–48)

As a result of this kind of over-all arrangement we find that, instead of being moved through an action by our attachment to a protagonist, we are spectators of an opposition that is as static as it is constant and whose outcome, obvious from the beginning, generates very little suspense.

With the above description of the structure of *La Thébaïde* in mind, we may relate the practice of Racine to that of his predecessors and explain his partial failure by his adherence to their tradition. This is, in a word, the formula of Corneille. In tragedies like *Le Cid, Horace, Cinna,* Corneille falls short of the production of plot; in this respect he is like such Renaissance writers as Jodelle, Grévin, and Montchrestien. The making of plot—surely the most difficult task of the dramatic poet—remained a mystery during the first century of tragic writing in France, and Corneille made few advances upon his forerunners. He tended to think in terms of a theme rather than a plot, of an opposition of persons rather than a protagonist, of a static set of necessities. The general movement of his plays was determined by external devices (history or a pattern or some rhetorical alternation between pro and con), not by probabilities of an internal nature. For the most part there was no protagonist; or there were two or more principal personages who vied, simultaneously or alternatively, for that role. Sometimes a play was built upon a mere opposition of ideas. The familiar struggle between "love" and "duty," "honor" and "affection," extended beyond the limits of the single verse or the individual speech and provided the very basis for the organization of the play.

Racine, in his first tragedy, found himself faced with the same problem: how to make a plot out of a body of historical or legendary material. In *La Thébaïde* we have the impression that he got off to a good start with his conception of a mother engaging in successive actions to prevent the combat and the deaths of her sons. But as he worked with this conception, he discovered that it had certain inherent weaknesses and above all that it would not carry the whole weight of his tragic structure. As, then, he added other lines of action, other necessities, and other ends to it, he not only spoiled the clarity and the directness of his original plan; he also fell into the habits of construction of his illustrious model—with all their pitfalls. The tradition won out, as it is apt to do with any young poet.

This young poet, however, had great gifts, and his first tragedy shows positive merits that will persist and develop in his later plays. First of these, I suppose, is his capacity to imagine characters for his personages that are, in their diversity, their subtlety, and their richness, far more sophisticated than the somewhat wooden and *simpliste* characters that Corneille gives to his heroes. Let us take, as a case in point, the character of Antigone. Her first statements (I, 2) are anodyne; it is not until I, 5, in the dispute with Créon, that we begin to see some of her traits. There she shows her capacity to hide her feelings under objective arguments (247–51), to be temperate in argument (269–70), to penetrate into the feelings of others (274), to be firm and forthright when the occasion demands it:

> Je la sais; mais, Créon, j'en abhorre le cours,
> Et vous ferez bien mieux de la cacher toujours.   (281–82)

Her love for Hémon, indicated briefly at the end of I, 6, receives full expression in Act II; it is mixed, however, with her affection for her mother, with concern over her brothers, with patriotic sentiments, and with anxiety over her lover's faithfulness:

> Et, si mes sentiments se doivent découvrir,
> Je souhaitais, Hémon, qu'elle vous fît souffrir,
> Et qu'étant loin de moi, quelque ombre d'amertume
> Vous fît trouver les jours plus longs que de coutume.
>
> (341–44)

She suffers from the conflict within her (a kind of Cornelian conflict) between love for Hémon and love for her family:

> Chaque assaut à mon cœur livrait mille combats,
> Et mille fois le jour je souffrais le trépas.   (353–54)

She shows special tenderness for Polynice, and some disappointment that he has not lived up to her expectations (363–72); she recognizes the hardness of both brothers. After the announcement of the oracle, she expresses her resignation to die (she is daughter to Oedipus and of the race of Laius) and her preoccupation with Hémon's fate (404–14). In her appeal to Polynice (II, 3), she mixes irony with bitterness, anger with a highly political playing of one brother against the other. Moved by the spectacle of Ménecée's suicide, she recounts it (III, 3) vividly and with passion, deriving from it a hope in the goodness of the gods. Her *stances* in Act V (in spite of the Cornelian oppositions of ideas) display the deepness of her feeling and the primacy of her love over filial piety. After Olympe's account of the death of Étéocle, she expresses her sense of pity—

> Devenant malheureux, il m'est devenu cher—   (1272)

and her contempt for Créon. The latter feeling grows throughout V, 3, reaching a climax in her refusal of Créon's proposal; coupled with her despair over the deaths of all members of her family and of Hémon, it leads to her resolution to die.

It would thus be difficult to summarize in any simple formula all the traits of Antigone's character; they are too numerous, too diversified. Yet out of this richness comes a sense of a single personality, of a woman whose feelings and dispositions, mixed though they might be, combine to make a single moral attitude that we may call her character. Racine has achieved, already, some of the excellence in the creation of character that will mark his later works.

That excellence is accompanied, sometimes if not always, by skill in the establishment of probabilities for action. Although the general dynamics of La Thébaïde suffer, as I have pointed out, from a failure to base enough of the action in probability, there are places where Racine demonstrates that he understands the principles of this part of his art—even though his conception of the total action prevents him from applying them. His handling of Hémon's death may serve as an illustration. In addition to Hémon's love for Antigone and his subservience to her wishes (traits of character already touched upon), many particular motivations had to be provided if the event was to be accomplished. Starting at a considerable distance, we find Jocaste eliciting the assistance of Antigone in separating the brothers (37-42). Still in Act I, we learn from Antigone that Hémon is in the service of Polynice, that he serves him with ardor and valor (251, 257); besides, Jocaste's order in I, 6—

> Appelons promptement Hémon et votre frère—   (296)

prepares the meeting of the lovers at the beginning of Act II. In that meeting, we learn that in the past Hémon has followed Antigone's orders (355–56), making it likely that he will do so again in the future; also, that he himself would hope that the brothers might be reunited (379–80). He might go so far as to expose his own life in order to bring about that peace, especially if Antigone were to wish it (339–46). Hémon intervenes for a first time, with words if not with arms, during the appeal to Polynice (555–63), thereby making probable a later intervention. As Hémon and Polynice leave, Jocaste asks Antigone to use Hémon as an instrument of reconciliation:

> Chère Antigone, allez, courez à ce barbare:
> Du moins, allez prier Hémon qu'il les sépare.   (575–76)

It is important to note that, although he does not speak, Hémon is present throughout the long scene (IV, 3) between Jocaste and the two brothers. He thus hears Polynice (whose partisan he has been) challenge Étéocle to a single combat, hears the sharp words of both brothers and their determination to kill each other if possible, hears the last desperate arguments of Jocaste before she goes off to her own death. He is thus able to conclude:

> Rien ne peut ébranler leur constance farouche.   (1192)

> Madame, il n'est plus rien qui les puisse arrêter.   (1198)

Antigone's conclusion is almost the same; but she still believes that Hémon's interference might be efficacious, and she begs him to follow them:

> Ah! généreux Hémon, c'est vous seul que j'implore.
> Si la vertu vous plaît, si vous m'aimez encore,
> Et qu'on puisse arrêter leurs parricides mains,
> Hélas! pour me sauver, sauvez ces inhumains.   (1199–1202)

This is an appeal—to love and to virtue—that he cannot resist, and he goes to the field of battle. A first report from the field, premature and inaccurate, is given by Olympe, who has heard of Hémon's attempt:

> On parle aussi d'Hémon: l'on dit que son courage
> S'est efforcé longtemps de suspendre leur rage,
> Mais que tous ses efforts ont été superflus. (1241–43)

This report leads Antigone to estimate, on her own, the probabilities of the situation:

> Ah! je n'en doute pas, Hémon est magnanime;
> Son grand cœur eut toujours trop d'horreur pour le crime.
> Je l'avais conjuré d'empêcher ce forfait;
> Et s'il l'avait pu faire, Olympe, il l'aurait fait. (1245–48)

When, finally, Créon gives the correct report, Antigone's assumptions are confirmed in Hémon's words:

> «Je meurs, dit-il tout bas,
> Trop heureux d'expirer pour ma belle princesse.» (1340–41)

Racine thus prepared the probabilities for this event with great care, sowed them progressively throughout the tragedy, brought them into contact with the traits of character that they complemented. His success with this episode displays his awareness of the general problem of creating probability and his ability to solve it.

Allied to the matter of probability is the production of arguments that may influence the action of another personage, the writing of the persuasive *tirade*. Here Racine mastered the technique immediately, undoubtedly profiting from the example of Corneille. He was able to organize the long speech in a way to make it fit both the character of the person speaking and the circumstances, to adapt it to the character of the person addressed, to exploit fully the rhetorical quality of philosophical generalizations. There are many such *tirades* in *La Thébaïde;* we may look briefly at Jocaste's opening speech to her sons in IV, 3. The first six lines (973–78) do not express a real feeling of optimism or joy on the part of Jocaste, for she knows from recent experience that she has no reason for either. They are calculated rather to win the brothers to sympathetic listening through an appeal to sentiment ("Vous revoyez un frère, après deux ans d'absence, / Dans ce même palais où vous prîtes naissance" [975–76]), by feigned happiness ("Et moi, par un bonheur où je n'osais penser" [977]), by the assumption that what she wishes to accomplish has already been accomplished ("Puisque déjà le ciel vous rassemble tous deux" [974]). In the next six lines, pursuing the same argument, she calls upon their feelings as brothers and as sons ("mes fils, son frère, votre frère"), upon the ties of blood ("Surtout que le sang parle et fasse son office" [983]), upon her own interest in the reconciliation ("cette union si chère" [979]). She uses a tone of cajoling and endearment:

> Approchez, Étéocle; avancez, Polynice ...   (984)

The argument fails, the brothers remain distant, a new attack becomes necessary. This time Jocaste feigns innocence ("D'où vient ce sombre accueil et ces regards fâcheux?" [986]) and attempts to find a reason (which she knows is not the real reason) for their coldness (987–90). At this point, also, she states her argument in the abstract, in the form of impersonal generalizations:

> Étrange ambition qui n'aspire qu'au crime,
> Où le plus furieux passe pour magnanime!
> Le vainqueur doit rougir en ce combat honteux;
> Et les premiers vaincus sont les plus généreux.   (991–94)

The device is rhetorically sound; it avoids putting the blame directly upon either of the brothers, and it even seems to avoid reference to the actual, very touchy situation. Jocaste does make the direct reference, however, in the next two lines, where she converts compliance with her suggestion into a positive virtue:

> Voyons donc qui des deux aura plus de courage,
> Qui voudra le premier triompher de sa rage ...   (995–96)

Again the argument fails ("Quoi? vous n'en faites rien?" [997])
and Jocaste is finally forced to appeal directly to one of the
brothers; she chooses Polynice, seeking a cogent reason ("venant
de si loin, vous devez commencer" [998]) and deliberately calling
again upon his fraternal affection ("embrassez votre frère" [999]).
The argument fails, but rather because of the character of the
brothers than because of weaknesses in her argument.

Speeches such as this, if we imagine them on the stage, have a
highly dramatic quality. They are not mere collections of *lieux
communs,* they are not purely rhetorical exercises in opposition,
augmentation, diminution, and so forth. In this respect they are
unlike the display *tirades* of Renaissance tragedy, unlike the
formal and artificial speeches given to Corneille's heroes. They
have already some of that intimate relationship to persons and
situations, some of that swift adaptation to the exigencies of the
drama, that were to characterize the speeches in Racine's best
plays.

One more advance of Racine over his predecessors should be
noted. We might call it the diversification or the particularization
of character. In a play such as *La Thébaïde,* where the personages
fall into two distinct and opposed camps, there is the danger that
the persons in each group may come to be very much like one
another. Since the opposed groups may clash on an idea or a
principle, it is easy for the persons in one group to "represent"
that idea or principle, to become abstractions or idealizations,
while those in the other group represent the other idea. Similarly,
a basis for differentiation among the actors in each group may be
difficult to find. That is what happens frequently in Corneille; it
is hard to distinguish between Chimène and Rodrigue with
respect to the conflict, in each, between love and honor. Racine,
however, immediately sensed the necessity of making such distinctions. Although we have in *La Thébaïde* two opposed groups,
the members of each are characterized as individuals; even the
"frères ennemis" are differentiated clearly. Both brothers, as we
have seen, will be "inhumains, parricides, cruels, méchants,

monstres," and so forth. But to these traits each will add elements peculiar to himself. Étéocle appears from the outset as solicitous of his mother (45), capable of some moderation and reason (48–54), endowed with a sense of responsibility to his people (59–64), patriotic (97–104), ready to push an argument to its absurd limits (123–29). He judges well the virtues of others (177–81); but he insists upon his own "gloire" (737) and refuses to submit to another (783). His hate for Polynice is constant (910) and he would not hesitate to kill him (1076). Polynice's character, except for the basic similarities already noted, is not by any means comparable. Étéocle early describes him as insolent and proud (69), as unpatriotic and willing to ally himself with an enemy (95–104). Hémon speaks of him as hating the war in which he is engaged (375–78), and Antigone indicates a greater tenderness for him than for Étéocle (365). But as soon as he appears, we note the differences. Whereas Étéocle's first words had been:

> Madame, qu'avez-vous? et quel trouble ...,   (45)

Polynice's are:

> Madame, au nom des dieux, cessez de m'arrêter.   (449)

His sharpness and irritation continue, directed not only against his mother but against the people of Thebes, for whom he has nothing but contempt (456–66). It is on this point, indeed, that he differs most markedly from his brother—and that we are meant to give Étéocle the preference. Polynice is irate, intransigent (488–98); Antigone perceives in him a considerable change from his former self—the one she loved (506–18); mother and sister call him "inexorable" (525) and "inflexible" (551). Although his request for an interview seems to contradict what Créon calls his "violent ambition" (792), he soon makes it clear that the only purpose of the interview is to challenge his brother to the single combat (1064–70). All these qualities are manifested in his responses to his mother's last arguments.

If we were to add to these characterizations that of Créon, also in the same camp, we should see again notable differences. Racine was quick to realize that if his characters were to come alive, if he was to give to his actors the traits that would be dramatically useful in his tragedy, he must differentiate and particularize as much as possible. He must avoid the single-minded hero, the monolithic person who stood for something instead of being somebody. Even his first trial, unsuccessful in so many ways, was successful in this respect.

Success or failure, *La Thébaïde* already contains within itself many of the features that will later distinguish Racinian or "neo-classical" tragedy. We may summarize them briefly:

1. It tends to select, from among the available source materials, an episode or episodes fairly close to the end of the story, so that the events depicted may be concentrated in the time preceding a natural denouement. The Renaissance tragedians had already begun to seek this kind of subject.

2. Because of the Renaissance prejudice against the representation of violent actions upon the stage, it makes these actions happen at a distance and has them narrated on the stage. This has several consequences: "Action" is rarely visible, and the spectator has to acquire the habit of imagining events that he does not actually see; the *récit* becomes the principal device for helping him to do so. He must also learn to recognize the existence of another kind of "action," the drama of events within the minds or the hearts or the souls of the actors, succeeding upon or related to actual happenings.

3. As a result, the emotional effect upon the audience does not depend upon the spectacle of material and external actions, but rather upon an evolution or development of the passions attributed to a hero or heroine.

4. As a further consequence, if this effect is to be clear and vigorous, the line of that emotional development must be perspicuous and the protagonist in whom it is seated must be unambiguous. The main difficulty with *La Thébaïde* is that neither of these conditions is met.

5. In drama of this kind, the poet concentrates his attention upon the the inner workings of his personages, to a greater extent than he would in a drama which contained more external action. He is apt therefore to produce character that is more subtle and varied, a revelation of the emotions that is more intimate and complete, and dialogue that follows more closely the complex workings of the spirit. The main virtue of *La Thébaïde* is that these things sometimes happen.

II

Alexandre le Grand

In 1665, somewhat less than two years after *La Thébaïde,* Racine wrote and produced his second tragedy, *Alexandre le Grand;* he published it in the following year. The materials on which it was based were drawn from several ancient historians.

We may suppose that it was some discontent with the multiplicity of external events in *La Thébaïde*—deaths, suicides, battles, and combats—that led Racine to invent, in his next play, an entirely different kind of action. Perhaps the extent of the reduction of external events may best be seen by summarizing, for each of the major persons, what he does throughout the course of the play.

Alexandre. Having conquered the Persians, Alexandre is now approaching the camp of Taxile, one of the princes of India. Before the action begins, he has asked Cléofile, whom he loves, to persuade her brother Taxile to surrender. He has also sent Éphestion as ambassador to the two princes, Taxile and Porus, with the same message. Later, when Porus has apparently been defeated, he orders him spared; he rewards Taxile for his aid and offers his love to Cléofile. He also tries to persuade Axiane to accept Taxile now that her other suitor, Porus, is presumably dead. When he finally does defeat Porus, he pardons both him and Axiane and restores their crowns to them.

Porus. The action of Porus centers about his resistance to Alexandre. Even before the arrival of Éphestion, he tries to arouse Taxile to action against Alexandre; he of course turns down Éphestion's proposal, after having declared his love for and his

39

solidarity with Axiane. When Taxile defects, he decides to resist Alexandre alone, meets him in battle, is apparently defeated, and flees. But he rallies his troops, kills Taxile in single combat, reports the event to Alexandre when he is led to him as a prisoner. He accepts Alexandre's pardon.

Taxile. Taxile's action, on the other hand, centers upon his surrender to Alexandre. He heeds Cléofile's arguments, resists those of Porus, presents counterarguments to him. Hence he offers his submission to Éphestion, abstains from the battle, and holds Axiane prisoner within his camp. It is he who announces the defeat and flight of Porus; when Porus' renewed resistance is discovered, he decides to oppose him directly, since Porus threatens his love for Axiane. He is killed by Porus.

Axiane. Queen of part of the Indies, Axiane remains throughout on the side of Porus and resistance. She offers to persuade Taxile to resist and, if that fails, to arouse his camp against him; she declares her love for Porus and rejects Taxile's. If Porus dies, she will die also. She reproaches Alexandre for his invasion of India, refuses his suggestion that she accept Taxile's love.

Cléofile. Cléofile's role is secondary; she acts as intermediary for Alexandre, persuading Taxile to surrender to him. She assures him (via Éphestion) of her love and accepts his. It is she who announces to Taxile that Porus has not been defeated and is still alive; after Taxile's death, she urges Alexandre to punish Porus. In grief over her brother's death, she postpones her marriage to Alexandre.

Now if we compare this action to that of *La Thébaïde,* we note several important differences. The "events" of a material or external nature are very few: the battle between the armies of Alexandre and Porus (Taxile abstains while he holds Axiane prisoner), the defeat and flight of Porus, Porus' rallying his troops with the consequent resumption of hostilities, his killing Taxile, the final victory of Alexandre's troops. All these events, of course, take place at a distance and are merely reported on the stage, just as similar events had been in *La Thébaïde.* On the contrary, most of the "events" in the action are of another kind: they are "internal" in the sense that they have to do with decisions of one kind or another by the various personages involved. People are persuaded or they persuade, they accept or reject suggestions, they declare their love, they accept or refuse the declarations of others, they produce arguments or rebuttals, they praise or blame. I hesitate to call these "psychological" actions, since for the modern reader that term would imply a complexity of spiritual activity, a depth of introspection, a sense of conflict, completely absent in these decisions. They are, as we shall see later, for the most part straightforward manifestations of character, constant and unchanging through the play, demanding very little in the way of conflict or hesitation. Perhaps we might call them "rhetorical" events, since to so large an extent they are concerned with argument and decision.

Racine had, of course, developed this kind of event in *La Thébaïde;* each of the "attempts" by Jocaste and Antigone consisted in the presentation of arguments with the hope of persuading; each of the "failures" consisted in a decision by Étéocle or Polynice. But in *Alexandre le Grand* the proportion of events of this kind to "external" events is much greater and thus a larger part of the total action resides in them. In a peculiar way, they make up that action.

That is, they make up the action if it is possible to speak of a single and central action in this tragedy. I think that we need merely to look again at the activities of each of the persons in it to realize that none of the "actions" is dominant in the sense that all the others are subordinated to it and determined by it. Alexandre wins a battle, intercedes for his allies, and pardons his enemies. He really has no decisions to make, having determined his line of action long in advance and having done little else than display the *générosité* or magnanimity of his character. The actions of all the others are related to his but do not depend upon them; and this is an extremely important distinction to make when we talk about the structure of an action. Porus remains firm in his determination to oppose Alexandre, opposes him in battle, loses, and is pardoned; it would not be possible to say, though, that any other person does what he does because of Porus' actions—and that is the vital consideration. Taxile is persuaded to submit to Alexandre, remains inactive during the battle (except for the imprisonment of Axiane), finally is moved to activity through jealousy, and loses his life. Axiane follows the same patriotic impulses as Porus, resists her enemies with forceful arguments and reproaches, benefits from the same amnesty as Porus. Cléofile acts as an auxiliary and an intermediary to the actions of the others. The question is: Can we see any one of these actions as providing the focus for the others? Do all the others converge in one, causing it to develop and evolve as they bring in new elements or change the situation? Does the relationship of any one of the persons to his circumstances, and his consequent action, change materially because of the actions of others? I think not.

I think not because, while there may be interrelationship and intertwining of the actions, there is no interdependency. This amounts to saying that there is little or no basis in probability for the succession of the events. Let us suppose that Racine created a basic situation: Alexandre is about to attack three rulers of India —Porus, Taxile, and Axiane. That Alexandre will win is a foregone denouement, given his invincibility. The problem then remains one for the others: Will they resist, and in what way, and what will be the consequences for them? Two will resist, lose, and be pardoned; one will submit, fight against his compatriots, and be killed. (The loves of all five personages will be of only instrumental importance in this development.) Now each one of these lines of action will be a "necessary" outcome of the characters assigned to the personages. Separate out any one of the careers; ask why the person does what he does; and you will find in almost every case that it is because he is the kind of man he is, because of his character.

This does not mean that there is no forward motion, no

chronology, no sense of a development toward a conclusion. Racine uses a number of devices to create the impression of movement. There is a chronology: an ambassador is announced, he arrives and does his embassy, the battle fought is of a special kind because of it; a false report holds that the enemy is defeated, perhaps killed; a true report that he is alive leads to an intervention of another ruler, to his death, to the defeat and pardoning of the first enemy. All these events are successive to one another, and their order could not be changed. But, in the first place, these events do not in themselves seem to constitute the main action of the tragedy, and, in the second place, their order is a natural one rather than a poetic one. I mean by this that the plan of events as outlined has both the kind of totality and the kind of consecutiveness that we might find in reality or in history; in that sense it is "natural." We can see it as a general scheme that the poet contrived in order to arrange, from the outside, the events of his play. Since, however, it is rarely "because" of what precedes that any event is as it is, since we have sequence or succession but not causality, the order here never becomes a "poetic" one.

As a matter of fact, any poetic structure or contrivance is to a degree "external"; the poet adopts a plan, conceives a plot, makes an order in advance of his work of composition. He may use this plan as a skeleton onto which he hangs the various events or episodes of his action; or he may use it as an organizing principle which helps him integrate them into a whole. In *Alexandre le Grand,* Racine used his scheme as a skeleton. No organism results.

I think that we can see this most clearly if we consider the position of Alexandre himself in the whole play. The play is named for him and I have said that most of the action was "related" to him even though he could not properly be considered its protagonist. If related to him, how? Perhaps the simplest answer is to suggest that Racine thought of both the "internal" and the "external" events of his play as providing the occasion to glorify Alexandre. (In his First Preface, replying to those critics who had

blamed him for entitling it *Alexandre,* he says, "... quoique Alexandre en fasse la principale action, et que le véritable sujet de la
pièce ne soit autre chose que la générosité de ce conquérant.") If
générosité is the quality to be extolled or exemplified, then the
external events must provide the occasion for the hero to demonstrate that he possesses it; and the internal events must be of
such character that they either make the external events seem
necessary and probable or that, in themselves, they constitute acts
of praise. In Alexandre, *générosité* is analyzed into a group of
component virtues: military prowess to the point of invincibility,
intelligent and liberal treatment of his conquered enemies, boundless ambition for great deeds, a capacity for love and for faithfulness in love even when the woman is a captive, gratitude toward his friends, recognition of the virtues of his enemies.

Cléofile's opening speech in the play begins the praise of
Alexandre:

> Quoi? vous allez combattre un roi dont la puissance
> Semble forcer le ciel à prendre sa défense,
> Sous qui toute l'Asie a vu tomber ses rois,
> Et qui tient la fortune attachée à ses lois?
> Mon frère, ouvrez les yeux pour connaître Alexandre;
> Voyez de toutes parts les trônes mis en cendre,
> Les peuples asservis, et les rois enchaînés.   (1–7)

It continues a little later:

> Son amitié n'est point le partage des lâches;
> Quoiqu'il brûle de voir tout l'univers soumis,
> On ne voit point d'esclave au rang de ses amis.   (42–44)

It is taken up by his enemy, Porus, after a strong statement of
condemnation:

> Loin de le mépriser, j'admire son courage;
> Je rends à sa valeur un légitime hommage.   (153–54)

Porus sees in him above all a worthy opponent:

> Du bruit de ses exploits mon âme importunée
> Attend depuis longtemps cette heureuse journée.   (237–38)

In the conversation (II, 1) between Cléofile and Éphestion, both interlocutors of course extol Alexandre, first as a lover:

> Vous sauriez que l'amour précipitant ses pas,
> Il ne cherchait que vous en courant aux combats.
> C'est pour vous qu'on l'a vu, vainqueur de tant de princes,
> D'un cours impétueux traverser vos provinces,
> Et briser en passant, sous l'effort de ses coups,
> Tout ce qui l'empêchait de s'approcher de vous.　(375–80)

Éphestion emphasizes the delicacy of Alexandre's feelings (411–20). To Porus and Taxile, in the next scene, he lauds first Alexandre's power and generosity, then his ambition and his capacity to pardon:

> Et du plus ferme empire ébranlant les colonnes,
> Attaquer, conquérir, et donner les couronnes;
> Et puisque votre orgueil ose lui disputer
> La gloire du pardon qu'il vous fait présenter,
> Vos yeux, dès aujourd'hui témoins de sa victoire,
> Verront de quelle ardeur il combat pour la gloire.　(589–94)

These might, of course, merely be the official statements of a subordinate; but they are confirmed in the later developments of the play.

A very special role in this praise of Alexandre is assigned to the traitor Taxile. He must justify, as he can, his treachery, and one way is to express a boundless admiration for the man to whom he has turned. His arguments are in part historical:

> Alexandre sait mieux ce qu'on doit à des reines.
> Souffrez que sa douceur vous oblige à garder
> Un trône que Porus devait moins hasarder.　(774–76)

> Des reines et des rois vaincus par sa valeur
> Ont laissé par ses soins adoucir leur malheur.
> Voyez de Darius et la femme et la mère:
> L'une le traite en fils, l'autre le traite en frère.　(783–86)

Again, this is an action that will be repeated at the end of the play. For the most part, it is Taxile's direct impression of

Alexandre that contributes to our own feeling; a long speech in
III, 3, is devoted to that purpose, and it is followed immediately
by Alexandre's first appearance on the stage.

Alexandre, of course, is his own best spokesman. His opening
words confirm one of the qualities previously ascribed to him:

> Allez, Éphestion. Que l'on cherche Porus;
> Qu'on épargne sa vie, et le sang des vaincus.   (835–36)

Next, in short order, he demonstrates his gratitude to Taxile:

> Mais ne le craignez point: son empire est à vous.   (839)

The next scene permits him to tell Cléofile of his love—and incidentally to speak of other virtues:

> Les sceptres devant vous ou rendus ou donnés,
> De mes propres lauriers mes amis couronnés,
> Les biens que j'ai conquis répandus sur leurs têtes,
> Font voir que je soupire après d'autres conquêtes.   (851–54)

At the same time, Cléofile may declare her recognition of these
merits (867–73) along with her fear that Alexandre's ambition
may cause him soon to desert her (913–924). By way of anticipating his last great gesture, Alexandre reveals his opinion of Porus:

> Porus était sans doute un rival magnanime:
> Jamais tant de valeur n'attira mon estime.
> Dans l'ardeur du combat je l'ai vu, je l'ai joint;
> Et je puis dire encor qu'il ne m'évitait point:
> Nous nous cherchions l'un l'autre. Une fierté si belle
> Allait entre nous deux finir notre querelle.   (937–42)

He expands on this opinion in the conversation with Axiane,
calling Porus "un prince magnanime" (1010) and speaking of
"L'éclat de sa vertu" (1014). As the same conversation continues,
he shows his sensitivity to Axiane's sorrow, his moderation of
temper, and he makes good his promise to intercede for Taxile.

Both the statements by others and his own representation of
himself prepare for Alexandre's noble act at the end of the play;

this is probably what Racine meant when he referred to the "principale action" (rather than the whole of the action in the play). The first scenes of Act V, although they begin with a statement of Alexandre's desire for revenge upon Porus, expose him to arguments by Cléofile and Axiane. It is Axiane who exclaims upon his magnanimity:

> Vos soins s'étendraient jusqu'à lui?
> Le bras qui l'accablait deviendrait son appui?
> J'attendrais son salut de la main d'Alexandre?
> Mais quel miracle enfin n'en dois-je point attendre?
> Je m'en souviens, Seigneur, vous me l'avez promis,
> Qu'Alexandre vainqueur n'avait plus d'ennemis.   (1371–76)

The report of Taxile's death removes the danger that Porus' enemy and rival might participate in deciding his fate, and thus Alexandre alone—as needs must be for the purposes of this play —is responsible for the final great decision:

> Hé bien! c'est donc en roi qu'il faut que je vous traite.
> Je ne laisserai point ma victoire imparfaite.
> Vous l'avez souhaité, vous ne vous plaindrez pas.
> Régnez toujours, Porus; je vous rends vos États.
> Avec mon amitié recevez Axiane:
> A des liens si doux tous deux je vous condamne.
> Vivez, régnez tous deux; et seuls de tant de rois
> Jusques aux bords du Gange allez donner vos lois.   (1501–8)

The "principale action" is accomplished in this way.

I think it not impossible that Racine may have thought of solving his dramatic problem by the following means: With the purpose of "glorifying" Alexandre, to select those traits of character, those virtues and merits that will be the proper subjects of praise. (Traits historically or traditionally associated with the hero would be useful here in part but would not provide the whole answer to the problem.) Next, to invent (or select) such actions or episodes as will bring out the hero's potential for action contained in these qualities. Then, somewhere along the line, to create other personages who may provide the occasions for these actions, or who may engage in direct praise either because of their knowledge of the hero's past or because of their present relationship with him or because of their anticipation of the future. To organize the play in such a way that preliminary statements about the hero's character, introduction of the personages and situations, and an initial impulse to the movement will constitute its "beginning"; that its "middle" will augment the praise, move the action along toward the hero's greatest display of virtue; that its "end" will not only consist of this display but will also exact from the other persons involved a full recognition of the hero's glory. In *Alexandre le Grand,* the hero's qualities are the ones I have already described: they are all proper subjects of praise. To permit their manifestation, we will have the "principale action," the show of generosity in the final pardon of Porus and Axiane; the gratitude toward Taxile, witnessed by the intercession with Axiane and by the final intention to erect a "tombeau superbe"; the love displayed at various points for Cléofile. The personages mentioned do not merely provide the occasions for Alexandre's virtuous action. They all make speeches of praise, to one another or to him. Some of them are in such a position (Porus, Axiane) that praise from them has a special quality; others (Taxile) of such situation that Alexandre's action is of extraordinary magnanimity; Cléofile is the occasion for the manifestation of love both directly and indirectly.

As for the organization of the play, it is clear that its ending is rather a culmination than a denouement; this is perfectly proper in a poem of praise. The greatest show of *générosité* must come at the end. Love, gratitude, valor, and magnanimity are all displayed at once. The middle makes this possible: the reported defeat and death of Porus prepare the way both for Alexandre's proposal to Axiane that she accept Taxile and for Taxile's angry jealousy, leading to his active opposition to Porus; Axiane's conversation with Alexandre gives him a proper notion of her character; Cléofile finds the occasion to test his love and to establish her place among his various ambitions. The beginning lays the foundation for all this in preliminary statements about characters and situations.

All this looks very much like a proper poetic and a proper dramatic organization of a play. But I think that it is not. We do have a hero, something that looks like an action, a movement from beginning through middle to end, auxiliary and secondary personages who contribute to that movement. But, in a very real sense, the organization of the play is the very opposite of a poetic organization. I think that we may make the distinction very simply on the basis of the relationship between character and action: Had Racine been constructing his work according to proper poetic principles (toward which he was already slowly working), he would have begun with a conception of action—plot, *intrigue, fable* as he might have called it—and fitted the character of his hero, and the rest, to that conception; in *Alexandre le Grand,* he begins with a conception of a character and fits the rest, including the structure of the action, to it. This means that the action, being subordinate, does not have its own dynamics, but has instead that general shape and form dictated by the need to glorify a hero of a particular character. As compared with *La Thébaïde,* another "external" device has been adopted as a means of organizing the action of the play: instead of a pattern or the accomplishment of a predicted end, *Alexandre* uses the device of the display and glorification of character.

Perhaps I should modify my statement about the use, here, of "proper poetic principles." For there are indeed completely "poetic" genres that are based, much in the same way, upon a principle of character rather than upon a principle of action. The picaresque novel is one of these: if it is not concerned with the "glorification" of a "hero," it is devoted to the "display" or manifestation of the character of its principal personage. It begins, as does *Alexandre,* with a notion of the various traits to be attributed to a man, proceeds to the multiplication of episodes that put character into action, follows some geographical or social or bio-

graphical plan of organization. It may or may not end with a
culminating event that shows all elements of character in their
best expression. Such a structure is sufficient for what it sets out
to do. It makes it possible to establish a relationship—albeit a
loose one—among a smaller or a larger number of episodes by
relating them to a central figure, to whom are related also the
various secondary actors. It is susceptible of a variety of effects,
depending upon the kind of man the central figure is and the
kinds of events in which he is made to participate. But the effects,
as sequential and detached, are not cumulative and they ordinarily
do not reach the degree of intensity attained by more highly organized poetic forms.

Now it is clear from what he did in *Alexandre le Grand* that
Racine was seeking a more highly organized form than the
picaresque novel or the *roman d'aventures* and a more rapid and
concentrated effect. He was, in a word, writing a drama. We may
deduce this from the way in which he went about intertwining
his various actions, relating them to a hero through a small number of personages themselves intimately connected with him. We
may also see it in the sense of climaxing or culmination that he
tried to give to his denouement. For purposes of the drama,
however, the device that he chose was insufficient, improper. It
did not contain the potential for integration of the parts and for
dramatic effect that he needed. (I shall discuss later the kind of
effect that he does achieve.) While it could produce intertwining,
it could not produce interdependency; for all the internal relationships that it achieved were relationships of necessity (from character), not of probability (from the conditions of a developing
plot). And the external pattern imposed upon the events gave
merely a semblance of a real dramatic action.

Perhaps what results from this kind of structure may best be
described as "rhetorical drama." In *Alexandre* we get the praise
of character through statements and speeches of praise and
through acts that demonstrate the component virtues of character. Character dominates, action is incidental. The type is not a

rare one in the Renaissance; indeed, just as it seems to have been one of the steps on the way to Racine's discovery of tragedy, so it was one of the intermediate forms in the development of modern European tragedy. It may be what we have in Shakespeare's "historical tragedies"; it is almost certainly present in such a play as Jacques Grévin's *César,* and possibly in many of Corneille's plays. Why it should have appeared when it did is fairly evident. The dramatic poet, from Jodelle on, was faced with the problem of organizing into dramatic form materials that came to him in essentially non-dramatic form. Or, sometimes, of reorganizing the dramas of antiquity into forms that corresponded more fully with the principles and the prejudices of his contemporaries. One of the solutions was to bring together a large number of actions or episodes, to found the play upon complication of external action. This was Racine's solution in *La Thébaïde.* Another was, by moving in the opposite direction, to minimize external action by concentrating upon character—by building around character as Racine did in *Alexandre le Grand.* When such building was accompanied by the clear effort to praise or to blame, "rhetorical drama" was the result.

I suppose that Racine's chief advance in his second play as compared with his first was in this passage from the dispersed to the concentrated structure. *Alexandre* still falls short of a successful dramatic form; but in so far as it reduces the number of violent physical events, it moves closer to Racine's ideal of internal drama. Moreover, while it does not achieve in Alexandre himself an unambiguous protagonist, it does succeed in focusing attention upon one of the several dominant figures. This is a "rhetorical" rather than a "poetic" concentration; yet it is superior to the kind of multivalence that marked the personages of *La Thébaïde.* The mere decision to make of "la générosité de ce conquérant" the main subject of the play and to assign to him the "principale action" enabled Racine to avoid some of the weaknesses of his first tragedy. He could avoid the awkwardness of a dual movement toward the denouement; especially, he could avoid the scattering of effect that accompanied the scattered sympathies and antipathies of its audience.

What he achieved in the way of effect in *Alexandre le Grand* is fairly curious. I have characterized the work as "rhetorical drama"; I think it not unfair to characterize the effect as a rhetorical one. That is to say, instead of becoming involved with the hero, instead of developing the antipathies or sympathies that lead to a passionate participation in the affairs of the personages, the spectator remains distant and detached and develops reactions of the judgment rather than of the feelings. What I say here is only partially accurate, since some "poetic" feelings will be generated by the poetic devices employed. We will like or dislike the individual actors, be concerned with their fates, feel some suspense over their successes and failures. But the great emotions, the overpowering conviction—and they were present in part in *La Thébaïde*—will be lacking. I think that if we look in detail at the chronology of presentation of the materials, we shall be able to see how this mixed effect is brought about.

Act I. Scene 1 has much to do by way of exposing the initial situation. The feelings that it arouses are varied: an original admiration for Taxile because he resists the suggestion of treachery and expresses patriotic motives, diminished somewhat by the hint that jealousy and love may be stronger than patriotism; a dislike for Cléofile, who proposes the treachery and uses jealousy as an argument; a preliminary disposition in favor of Porus and Axiane, merely because they are placed in opposition to Cléofile and Taxile; above all, the beginnings of our admiration for Alexandre. It is important to note that the first speech of the play is a speech in praise of Alexandre (1–7). We are left with a total impression of Alexandre's greatness, commingled with a respect for those who would be great enough to oppose him and a disdain for those who, for private ends, would sacrifice the public good to him. It is this commingling that is important, since it sets up a kind of "poetic" conflict of feelings and prevents the play from being a monotonous and undramatic *éloge*—from being an unsubtle form of rhetoric.

Some of these sentiments are augmented in scene 2, where Porus' greatness of soul and courage are placed in sharp contrast with Taxile's increased willingness to defect, for selfish and not very admirable motives. If we ask why Alexandre's enemy should be exalted to this extent, I think that the answer is an obvious (and a rhetorical) one: the ultimate pardon of such an enemy is more magnanimous, more to Alexandre's credit, than the pardon of a lesser enemy, just as Alexandre's victory over Porus is in itself more considerable. Were the enemy inconsequential, his defeat and grace would contribute much less to our estimate of Alexandre. Similarly, the growing distastefulness for Taxile, whose motives are jealousy and self-interest rather than admiration for Alexandre, serves at once to increase our esteem for Porus and (through contrast) to enhance our appreciation for Alexandre's nobility.

The sharp difference between the two Indian princes, apparent to us through their speeches, is clearly summarized by Axiane in scene 3; she calls Taxile "une âme incertaine," speaks of "sa timide valeur," whereas Porus is epitomized as "ce grand cœur." Axiane, in her first appearance, confirms our anticipation of firmness of spirit, intelligence, and love for Porus. The scene continues the development of emotions toward a constantly greater esteem of Alexandre's enemies.

As a result, the whole of the act (although it begins with praise of Alexandre) results in the establishment of feelings other than admiration for the hero: a basic distrust of those who are going to be his allies, a basic trust in those who will be his enemies. The personages seem to be falling, once again, into two camps, with the spectator moved to approve of one and disapprove of the other. A semblance of dramatic conflict is present. What warns us that it may only be apparent is the fact that, so far, it remains an opposition of characters more really than an opposition of situations. Whether or not Alexandre will win is not an issue; whether or not Taxile will surrender is decided; the determination of Porus and Axiane is clear-cut, and we see no likelihood that Éphestion's embassy will change it. This relatively static nature of the situation leads, in our feelings, to a balance, a suspension of favor and disfavor that is at this point itself essentially static.

Act II. As in the preceding act, scene 1 here begins with praise of Alexandre; this time, it is his qualities as a lover that are lauded along with his generosity toward his conquered enemies. A by-product of the conversation between Cléofile and Éphestion is the revelation of her quality as a lover—a quality that disposes us more to like her. We admire her as a woman in love, although we still doubt her as the woman who influenced her brother to surrender. Éphestion's answers to her questions about Alexandre attribute to him qualities as a general which may or may not be real; but if they were, we should respect him even more.

The extraordinary effect of scene 2 is to elevate the reputations of all three male actors, Alexandre, Porus, and Taxile. For even Taxile, in his speech of surrender, states his case nobly and in a way that would seem to impose conditions upon Alexandre:

> Je reçois à ce prix l'amitié d'Alexandre;
> Et je l'attends déjà comme un roi doit attendre
> Un héros dont la gloire accompagne les pas,
> Qui peut tout sur mon cœur, et rien sur mes états.
>
> (501–4)

He pays tribute to Alexandre's greatness, as do Éphestion and Porus himself. But while Éphestion's praise is that of a subject and subordinate, Porus' shows him to be Alexandre's peer. The magnification of Porus' character may even be excessive; for we begin to wonder—since he is so much present and Alexandre has not yet been seen on the stage—whether this might not turn out to be a poem in praise of Porus. We are obliged to give our full admiration to such statements as the following:

Mais nous, qui d'un autre œil jugeons des conquérants,
Nous savons que les dieux ne sont pas des tyrans;
Et de quelque façon qu'un esclave le nomme,
Le fils de Jupiter passe ici pour un homme.
Nous n'allons point de fleurs parfumer son chemin;
Il nous trouve partout les armes à la main;
Il voit à chaque pas arrêter ses conquêtes;
Un seul rocher ici lui coûte plus de têtes,
Plus de soins, plus d'assauts, et presque plus de temps
Que n'en coûte à son bras l'empire des Persans. (571–80)

Once again, in the last scene of the act (scenes 3 and 4 are transitional), Axiane reduces to clear statement certain impressions about character that have been slowly building; especially, she corrects any possible misjudgment in favor of Taxile:

Cette sombre froideur ne m'en dit pourtant rien,
Lâche; et ce n'est point là, pour me le faire croire,
La démarche d'un roi qui court à la victoire.
Il n'en faut plus douter, et nous sommes trahis. (620–23)

There is no longer any doubt, indeed; and we return to our original attitude toward Taxile. This clarifies the alignment of our feelings, and our stand in favor of Porus and Axiane, fortified by what they say in this scene about their love and their patriotism, becomes more vigorous.

To a certain degree, there is a symmetry of pattern in Acts I and II. Both begin with the supporters of Alexandre who sing his praises, both end with his enemies who (while they admit the merits of the hero) really contribute more toward the firming-up of their own positions. This makes for a kind of balancing, almost a seesawing of two rival sets of emotions within the spectator. Admiration for Alexandre on the one hand, admiration for his opponents on the other. The movement back and forth between these two feelings—which are really two expressions of the same feeling—has the kind of static equilibrium that we noted earlier in the organization of the action.

Act III. In the third act, whatever symmetry of pattern there may have been is broken; for now, for the first time, Alexandre is present on the stage and the whole act is built around him. The first scene, however, as it brings together Cléofile and Axiane, permits another contrast of the two loyalties, to Alexandre and to Porus. The general effect is to enhance further our respect for Axiane, to the disparagement of Cléofile. That respect grows in scene 2, when Taxile's report of Porus' defeat leads to a reaffirmation of Axiane's principles and of her love for Porus. The report means a victory for Alexandre—the first real "event" of the play —and a demonstration, thus, of his military qualities. But it is in scene 3, which stands at the center of the play and which precedes the appearance of Alexandre, that we get the most striking praise of Alexandre. It comes from Taxile. In the speech beginning with these lines,

> Oui, ma sœur, j'ai vu votre Alexandre.
> D'abord ce jeune éclat qu'on remarque en ses traits
> M'a semblé démentir le nombre de ses faits, (810–12)

he gives a visual and moral impression of the hero that will soon be corroborated by his entrance. In a way, Taxile becomes here a part of the audience, feels (as he directs) what it will feel.

The remaining scenes of the act are occupied by Alexandre. In scene 4 (two lines long) he shows his quality of mercy; in scene 5 he rewards Taxile munificently and wishes him well in his loves; in scene 6, declaring his love to Cléofile, he offers her the throne of Asia and promises to take her with him on further expeditions; in scene 7 he proposes to support Taxile's love for Axiane. Each of these actions is the actualization of a trait earlier attributed to him; each serves to increase our admiration for him. The total effect of the act is to bring to a climax—which will merely be a subclimax to later ones—the feelings toward Alexandre that had so carefully been implanted since the opening of the play.

Act IV. Axiane, in the long monologue that constitutes scene

1, discovers that it was love for Porus rather than patriotism that had motivated her earlier decisions. Assuming now that Porus is dead, she too wishes to die. The reader wonders about the usefulness of the monologue; for the sentiments expressed are already well known to him, and since Axiane will not ultimately die, her resolution establishes no probability. There is no change in our attitude toward her. Next, the confrontation of Alexandre and Axiane in scene 2 suggests another pattern in the organization of the play, what we might call the "ascending scale" of Alexandre's encounters. Having been absent from Acts I and II, when he does appear in Act III it is to speak with his allies, with those of his camp, Cléofile and Taxile. Now, in Act IV, he will meet Axiane; the climactic meeting with Porus will come in Act V. In this scene some of the movements of that final encounter are already present. Axiane reproaches Alexandre with his excessive and senseless ambition; but this merely gives him the chance to defend himself in a way that improves his credit with the audience. He can show that he does not lose his temper, that he is sensitive to the feelings of others, that he admires greatness in his enemies, that he is faithful to his friends. The scene also contains the first extended *éloge* by one of Alexandre's enemies, in Axiane's speech beginning:

> Ah! Seigneur, puis-je ne les point voir,
> Ces vertus dont l'éclat aigrit mon désespoir? (1107-8)

And it prefigures, in Alexandre's offer to restore Axiane's throne (1135-40), the similar gesture at the end of the play. In a word, in scene 2 he confirms by his presence what we had been led to feel about him in his absence.

Scene 3 is devoted to two hopeless missions: Axiane's attempt to persuade Taxile to return to Porus' side and Taxile's attempt to win Axiane's love. Not only is there little probability that either will succeed, but it is not even probable that the attempts should be made, given what each person knows of the other's character. As a result, we feel that something that has happened before is

happening again, that we are at a standstill, and that no growth
has taken place in our feelings. It is not until later that we discover that the usefulness of the scene was purely instrumental,
to make Taxile decide upon open hostility to Porus. Before he
can make that decision, however, he must be exacerbated by
Cléofile's cutting assertion that anything he might do would only
serve his rival, and by her announcement that that rival has reappeared (scene 4).

Act V. The last act is the only one in which Alexandre is
present throughout—in which, consequently, he comes to look
something like a protagonist. Scene 1 serves rather to rehabilitate
Cléofile than to magnify Alexandre. She does two things that
bring us around to her side; she indicates her true sentiments of
respect for Porus—

> Je vous dirais qu'il fut le plus grand de nos princes,
> Que son bras fut longtemps l'appui de nos provinces,
> Qu'il a voulu peut-être en marchant contre vous
> Qu'on le crût digne au moins de tomber sous vos coups;
> Et qu'un même combat signalant l'un et l'autre,
> Son nom volât partout à la suite du vôtre—   (1293–98)

and (just as Axiane had done) she reproaches Alexandre for
adding conquest to conquest. Alexandre's replies are what they
must be to maintain our sentiments toward him. So they are,
also, in scene 2, where, in his second meeting with Axiane, he
can once again affirm his tendency toward clemency to Porus:

> Non, Madame, mes soins ont assuré sa vie.
> Son retour va bientôt contenter votre envie.   (1369–70)

In turn, this leads Axiane to wonder at Alexandre's magnanimity
(1371–80) in a speech which makes Porus worthy of clemency at
the same time that it makes Alexandre more capable of granting
it. Hence it is with some disappointment that we see the hero
proposing to allow Taxile to decide Porus' fate (1386)—this
violates all our feelings about all personages in the play—and we
are pleased to see Axiane flare up against him (1389–1400). Per-

haps this exchange was calculated to make even more striking Alexandre's action in the final scene; but we may doubt that it really has that effect.

A similar disappointment attends upon Alexandre's proposal, in scene 3, that Porus accept his pardon conditional upon his renunciation of Axiane to Taxile; it reminds one of the king's trick on Chimène and produces the same kind of revulsion. Fortunately, Porus is sufficiently unafraid to show his contempt for the proposal; in vigorous words (and in his first meeting with Alexandre he adopts a condescending *tutoiement*) he chides Alexandre and announces Taxile's death. We are all for Porus. Speech by speech, now, the play concludes its various emotional lines. Éphestion's account of the battle and of Taxile's death satisfies our antipathetic feelings toward Taxile and our need for sympathizing with Porus. When, therefore, in the next speech Cléofile asks for revenge upon Porus, we reject it (as we would reject Chimène's appeal for revenge upon Rodrigue) and consider it an idle gesture. Contrariwise, Axiane's ironical and bitter speech is immediately acceptable to us; and when, next, Porus makes his noble statement—

> Voyons comme tu sais user de la victoire—　　　(1494)

we return fully to the side that we had originally favored. Alexandre is thus in a difficult position, as far as our feelings are concerned, and must either justify himself in some remarkable way or lose out completely. The next exchange with Porus assures Alexandre's moral victory: first, as he proposes that Porus be his own judge—

> Comment prétendez-vous que je vous traite?—　　　(1500)

next, as Porus replies, "En roi" (a speech that recalls Corneille's flair for the strikingly dramatic phrase), finally, as Alexandre "perfects his victory" by restoring their kingdoms to Porus and Axiane and approving their marriage, and (after begging her acquiescence) offers to marry Cléofile. This last long speech of

Alexandre's (1501–24) restores him to the place that he is supposed to occupy in the play—the principal object of praise—and
removes any hesitations that we might have had about him.

Now that the reconciliation of enemies has been made, we can
participate in the final words of praise for Alexandre that come
from Axiane and Porus, Axiane when she says "J'admire le grand
cœur d'un héros qui vous aime" (1526), Porus when he admits:

> Je me rends; je vous cède une pleine victoire.
> Vos vertus, je l'avoue, égalent votre gloire.   (1533–34)

Even Cléofile, who in a way had been in the wrong ever since
the beginning, redeems herself through her acceptance of Alexandre's "principale action" and through her plea for time to
manifest (and ultimately to erase) her sorrows. Alexandre con-
sents; his final speech, promising the moral and material monu-
ment to Taxile, completes his own self-praise. We have now
reached the point, therefore, where we can regard with almost
equal favor Alexandre, Porus, and Axiane (giving a slight edge
to Alexandre because of his last actions), where we can extend
some tolerance to Cléofile, and where we can feel that Taxile has
been sufficiently punished through his death—and will be sufficiently rewarded in the memory of his allies. Act V has resolved
any conflict of feelings within us, even though it may have done
so through rather extraordinary devices.

A restrospective view of this development of the emotions
through the play may bring into relief certain of its features and
certain of the devices that Racine chose to employ. One of the
first things that strikes us is that, if indeed Racine wished to
celebrate Alexandre and create a general feeling of admiration
for him, he realized that that could not be done in any unilinear
way. That is, the accumulation of speeches in praise of him and
of praiseworthy actions done by him would be as boring as ineffective. It would be, moreover, completely undramatic. For how
convert into stageable and actable form a series of that kind without risking the production of pure "rhetoric" with no "drama"?

The Renaissance tragedians had tried it and failed. Racine's solution was to invent other lines of emotion and to develop them concurrently or alternatively with the central line of admiration. Some of these he constituted by taking individual traits or qualities of the hero and turning them into passions. Alexandre is capable of love: the woman whom he will love (Cléofile) must be provided, the circumstances that will give to his love the proper quality, the events that will allow it to result in praiseworthy acts. Alexandre is capable of gratitude: somebody (Taxile) must render him a great service that will permit Alexandre to express his gratitude in at least three different ways. And so forth. Each of these person-situation complexes will do two things: it will arouse emotions in the spectator relevant to the additional person, and it will modify the total feeling toward Alexandre.

Second, Racine worked through the creation of counteremotions. These are of two kinds. On the one hand, he devises personages and situations that might tend to detract from Alexandre's stature and that might make us admire him less. His use of Cléofile as an intermediary, the treachery of Taxile, Alexandre's appeals to Axiane to favor Taxile, the decision to allow Taxile to determine Porus' fate, are examples of this type. On the other hand, he assigns to certain of his personages the very opposite of admiration for Alexandre, hatred. These are his natural enemies, Porus and Axiane. With both types, however, the same end result must be achieved; everything must be turned in such a way that admiration for Alexandre will ensue. Each of the persons and situations that had raised doubts about Alexandre must therefore evolve toward its opposite. The way that he treats his conquered enemies, demonstrating the real reasons underlying his conquests, makes Taxile's treachery less reprehensible and Cléofile's intermediation less suspicious. His relationships with Taxile and Axiane, an ally and an enemy, are tempered by the fact that, for a time at least, he had not known of Axiane's preference for Porus (Racine is careful to leave this in doubt as far as others are concerned, although Porus knows the truth and

Cléofile suspects it); besides, the promises springing from gratitude must be fulfilled if that particular virtue is to be established.
In keeping with this necessity, both Axiane and Porus begin by
admitting Alexandre's merits, proceed to less stinting recognition,
end up by being completely won over.

This kind of arrangement of the materials has some resemblance to the division, in *La Thébaïde,* of the main personages
into two camps. But the resemblance is only superficial. For in
the first play the division was made in order to render possible a
certain kind of dramatic action, whereas in the second it leads
only to a certain kind of rhetorical opposition. More specifically,
in *Alexandre le Grand* the development of the various emotional
lines, subordinate to the principal one of admiration for Alexandre, is an end in itself. Personages and situations are invented
to serve this end, and external events are introduced at useful
points in order to further the development. This is what makes
of it what I have called "rhetorical drama." Perhaps a theoretical
distinction would be helpful here: All drama, as all poetic forms,
ultimately seeks the arousal, the augmentation, and the final
resolution of an emotion proper to the particular work. All rhetorical forms use emotions aroused in the audience as one of the
sources of persuasion. But while in rhetoric the appeal to the
listener is made directly and exploits factors of character and
circumstance peculiar to himself, in poetic forms the emotional
effect is an indirect by-product of formal elements that have
nothing to do with the particular nature of the audience. In the
narrative and dramatic forms, at their best, the effect is the result
of an action; it is aroused as the initial elements of the action are
placed into juxtaposition, it progresses as the action develops, it is
brought to some kind of a state of tranquillity or satisfaction as
the action concludes. (We have seen that there are also narrative
and dramatic forms that are built around character and derive
their effect from it, and we might discover, in another context,
that lyric forms are sometimes based on the direct expression of
passion or argument.)

Alexandre le Grand, as our analysis has shown, is a bastard form. It tries in part to develop a direct emotional appeal through the kinds of eulogistic speeches and exemplary actions of which I have spoken. To this extent it is "rhetorical." But it also tries to simulate an action, to create personages in situations and carry them through to a resolution of the initial conflict, and by so doing to arouse the kinds of emotions that accompany poetic structures. To this extent it is "drama." Its difficulties come, I believe, from the imperfect realization of either one of the possibilities. The attempt to provide secondary lines of emotion and even counteremotions reduces the efficacy of the central emotion of admiration—this on a purely rhetorical level. The wish to make the action a servant to the rhetorical goal, and hence the production of an action that does not develop internally but is, instead, externally directed, leads to a lack of poetic conviction and a failure in the emotional effect—this on a purely dramatic level.

If there is any one source of poetic failure, it is probably in the fact that the play has no protagonist. Alexandre, for all his importance as the subject of praise and as the doer of praiseworthy actions, is not the center of the action. The action relates to him, but is done neither by him nor to him; he is neither an active nor a passive focal point of an action. Obviously, Racine was eager to improve upon *La Thébaïde* by concentrating the action of his next play about a central personage, by creating a real protagonist. But the way in which he sought to do this introduced into his play two personages who are more constantly present, more alive and real, possibly even more sympathetic than the would-be protagonist; I mean, of course, Porus and Axiane. The "counteremotions" become precisely that. For these two personages come to be rivals, in the balance of the spectator's emotions, to Alexandre himself. This happens in part because they appear on the stage long before he does, have the opportunity of obtaining the audience's attention and sympathy at a time when, because of the impressions created by Cléofile and Taxile, it is already predisposed to be harsh upon the "camp" of Alexandre. This early favor for the enemy camp is never completely eradicated; there are even strong recrudescences when Porus and Axiane demonstrate their great qualities or when Alexandre appears as less than perfect. Consequently, the audience is never firmly attached to any one central personage and maintains an ambivalence with respect to the two groups.

Moreover, the nature of the spectator's emotions relative to the three main personages raises the question of the general nature of the tragic emotion and of whether *Alexandre le Grand* might in any way be considered a tragedy. Racine spoke of it as "ma tragédie" (First Preface) and obviously considered it to be such. But that does not necessarily mean that it is. All that we can conclude from his designation of it is that he did not consider a "tragic ending" (e.g., the death or mutilation or exile of the protagonist or of the main personages) an essential condition of tragedy. The ending of *Alexandre* is not tragic in this sense. Whether he thought of it as tragedy because of the rank or the moral excellence of his hero is unimportant to us. We must resolve the doubt for ourselves on the basis of our own theoretical distinctions, and I think that the most useful one here is the presence, in the right form and to the proper degree, of the tragic emotion. If we assume that this is pity, and that pity results when a person of moral excellence finds himself in circumstances of undeserved misfortune, then we can immediately eliminate Alexandre himself as a candidate for a tragic hero. At no time are his circumstances those of "undeserved misfortune"; it is even difficult to see the presence of any misfortune. Axiane and Porus, however, would both fit the description, through their moral excellence, through their misfortune (in the unprovoked attack by Alexandre), which they do not deserve.

Here, again, there are difficulties. For in this undeserved misfortune Axiane and Porus have no responsibility. We can hardly admit that their refusal to surrender to Alexandre constitutes a decision on their part that brings on their plight; indeed, were they not to make this decision they would lose their moral excellence (as Taxile does). Consequently they become to a degree innocent victims, and the quality of the emotion attaching to them is a pity of a less-than-tragic kind. In addition, since they are not the protagonists, we have the curious situation of a play in which the emotion attaching to the main personage, Alexandre, is admiration—a "rhetorical" emotion—while the nearest thing to a proper poetic emotion attaches to two secondary personages. Once again the mixture of forms, the hesitation between rhetoric and drama, leads to a strange dichotomy of development within the poem: the main line, the whole effort to invent devices that will contribute to the glorification of Alexandre, is constructed along rhetorical principles, while the secondary line, the attempt to introduce conflicts and variety and an action, is constructed along poetic principles. The fusion is badly made, and the resulting emotion (or set of emotions) is indecisive and unsatisfactory.

For we are bound to conclude that Racine's trial at a formula for tragedy different from the one used in *La Thébaïde* was no more successful than the first one; it may even have been less successful. He succeeded in reducing the claimants to the central attention of the audience—but to three rather than to one. Even so, this marks a progress. But he chose for his hero a character, a situation, and an action that could not be productive of the tragic emotion of pity; hence he had to arouse for him another feeling, admiration, that could most aptly be cultivated by the use of rhetorical rather than of poetic devices. Seeing this difficulty, he worked with properly poetic devices and with a proper tragic emotion in handling two of his secondary personages. He tried to give to the whole an air of concentration and of unity by relating everything and everybody to his hero; but because the relationships so established were largely those of character (hence of necessity) and because the only distinguishable movements in the action were externally generated (hence without probability), he failed to construct a convincing and a moving dramatic action. The characters themselves are well differentiated from one another, well filled out, convincing; Racine's early superiority in this aspect of his work continues to be manifest. The speeches that the persons make are at times highly effective as revelations of character and as statements of intentions; their rhetorical excellence is rarely in doubt. It is in the most poetic of all aspects of his work, in the construction of the action, that Racine is still groping, that he has not yet found his solutions.

III

Andromaque

THE THIRD OF Racine's dramatic pieces, *Andromaque*, was produced toward the end of 1667 and was published early in 1668. In both prefaces, Racine indicated that his source was the *Aeneid*, with some borrowings from later treatments of the Andromache theme.

In the two years that had intervened since the writing of *Alexandre le Grand*, Racine must have pondered constantly and seriously the problem of the structure of a tragic action. For in his new play he adopted a new formula, not only different from the ones used previously, but essentially better. He solved, with this formula, two difficulties: that of the protagonist and that of the "probable" interrelationship of episodes. His solution was not complete and perfect, for certain weaknesses and hesitations still persisted; but at least one could now point to a single personage as the central one in an action, and to a better causality than had previously been achieved to link the parts of that action.

Basically, the new formula is a simple one; one single device accounts for both the achievements that I have mentioned. It consists in making of the protagonist what we might call a "pivotal" personage. Pivotal in the sense that any decision on the part of that personage, any change in her situation (for it is, of course, Andromaque), brings about an immediate change in the situations of all the other actors. If this is to happen, the initial circumstances must be such that all the persons are linked together and that the links, in each case, are indeterminate to the degree that either of two opposing actions might result. Here

again Racine simplified, reducing all the links to the single passion of love and creating a general situation in which no person
was loved by the one he loved. Oreste loves Hermione, but is not
loved by her; Hermione loves Pyrrhus, but is not loved by him;
and so on down the line. This takes care only of the individual
pairs; the general linking comes about through the device of
making each loved one love somebody from the "adjacent" pair.
Thus:

> Oreste loves Hermione.
> Hermione loves Pyrrhus.
> Pyrrhus loves Andromaque.
> Andromaque loves . . .

Andromaque loves an ideal and a memory, the ideal of Troy as
represented by Priam, Hector, and Astyanax, the memory of her
husband, Hector.

This is, as I have stated it so far, a static situation involving a
relationship exclusively on the basis of the passions; indeed,
statements early in the tragedy indicate that the relationship has
prevailed for some time—upward of a year in several cases. There
is another set of static circumstances, of some duration, that has
resulted from past events in the lives of the various persons. Thus:

> Hermione has refused Oreste.
> Hermione has been betrothed to Pyrrhus.
> Pyrrhus has taken Andromaque and Astyanax captive.

Passions and circumstances will remain in this state (in this *stasis*)
of uneasy equilibrium until some new element is introduced to
upset it; and any such new element will immediately produce
changes in each of the relationships. Racine destroys the balance
by having Hermione, through jealousy of Andromaque, arouse
the Greeks to the dangers present in the existence of Astyanax:

> J'ai déjà sur le fils attiré leur colère.   (445)

(This has happened before the beginning of the action of this
play.) The Greeks send Oreste to Pyrrhus to demand that he

hand over the boy to them. And now the series of choices or decisions may begin: Pyrrhus may decide to grant or to deny the request. Which he will do will depend upon the effect of his decision on Andromaque, for he will use the son as an instrument to influence the mother; if Andromaque will consent to marry him, he will refuse the request; if she will not, he will grant it. Andromaque must thus decide: she may refuse the bargain, or accept it, or temporize by seeming to accept it. In any case, her action will have repercussions upon Hermione. If Andromaque marries Pyrrhus, Hermione will be abandoned; if Andromaque refuses, Pyrrhus may possibly marry Hermione. In his turn, Oreste will be affected; for if Hermione is jilted by Pyrrhus, she may turn to Oreste; if she marries Pyrrhus, Oreste will be hopelessly excluded.

We thus come to a kind of reverse formulation of the effects of these decisions:

Andromaque's decision affects Pyrrhus.

Pyrrhus' decision affects Hermione.

Hermione's decision affects Oreste.

Perhaps "decision" is not the right word for Hermione; "plight" might be better. But in any event, the causal chain works "backward" from Andromaque, whereas the chain of passions works "forward" from Oreste. Neither is reversible. It is in this sense that the formula is "pivotal" and that the whole action comes to hang upon Andromaque's situation and choices.

By adopting this formula, Racine was able to achieve a structure that was superior in both necessity and probability to what he had done before. I spoke, in connection with *Alexandre le Grand,* of an interrelationship of persons that was not an interdependency, of Alexandre as a focal or central personage. All other persons there are related to him, and all of them directly: Porus and Axiane as his enemies, together and separately; Taxile as his ally; Cléofile as his beloved. There are of course other relationships among these same persons: Cléofile and Taxile are sister and brother; Porus and Taxile are lovers of Axiane, one successful, one not. But these relationships affect only indirectly, if at all, the basic connection with Alexandre. If one were to diagram the relationships, one would put Alexandre at the center of radial lines leading to the other personages, with occasional lines connecting pairs of them. In *Andromaque,* the diagram would rather be a straight line, leading from Oreste to Andromaque (and back), or a stair-step figure with a new riser for each person (in the same order). For the people in *Andromaque* are interdependent as well as interrelated; what one does affects all the others, changes the total situation. And this is because the fundamental passion attributed to each, the basic necessity for action inherent in his character, involves a relationship to the person "next in line" in the chain.

Similarly, because of the way in which the initial situation is established, no external events need be supplied—at useful points —to bring about changes in the situation or new decisions. Once Oreste arrives and makes his request, everything else follows: Pyrrhus says "no" because of his love for Andromaque; when he asks, as recompense, that Andromaque marry him, she says "no" because of her devotion to Hector; when Pyrrhus says that he must therefore deliver Astyanax to the Greeks, she asks for time for meditation. The rest of the events in the tragedy follow from one another in the same probable, causal sequence. We have what I have called a "self-generating" series of episodes, ones that do not need outside stimuli (after the first) to bring them about through a change in the material situation. *Andromaque* is Racine's first play to enjoy this kind of structure. In both *La Thébaïde* and *Alexandre le Grand* it had been necessary to invent external (and usually distant) events to provide the occasion for each forward movement in the action—a combat, a battle, a reported flight or death—and these events had themselves been arranged in an order determined by some arbitrary or independent schematism. As a result, the impression had been one of a fairly static arrangement, artificially set and kept in motion.

Andromaque has its own dynamics, based upon the probabilities inherent in the original circumstances, and its order comes from within rather than from without.

Such a formula or device as I have described does not of course make a play. At best it may serve as an organizing principle; Racine needed to do much in order to transform it into an effective tragedy. He needed to enrich the characters so that adequate necessity would be provided for the complex decisions and actions, he needed to multiply and refine the circumstances so that adequate probabilities would ensue, he needed to establish a dramatic order. In connection with character, Racine once again hit upon an extremely useful expedient. The passion of love that he had attributed to each of his main personages established a basic, static relationship with the "next" person in the forward movement of the chain; as long as the status quo maintained, each would continue to love his beloved. (Love, as we shall see later, had a particular quality in each case.) But what if something should happen—and it inevitably did—that would cause the "next" person to refuse the proffered love? On what basis would he act and react? Racine invented for each actor in *Andromaque* a companion passion, a complementary talent or disposition that might account for actions not attributable to his love but necessary when his love was frustrated.

Andromaque's love was one that could have no return. In so far as she remained faithful to the memory of Hector, and through him to Troy and all those who represented Troy, she could expect only the joys of fidelity and honor. Her love for Astyanax, as a part of this memory, was equally selfless. But if she was to preserve this faithfulness to Hector, not only must any other suitor be rejected, but she must be given the talent to find a satisfactory alternative solution. She must refuse Pyrrhus' proposal, but she must also save Astyanax' life so that the line of Troy may be continued. Racine therefore endows her with the wiliness or ruse that will make her last decision possible. It is associated with her the first time she is mentioned in the play:

J'apprends que pour ravir son enfance au supplice
Andromaque trompa l'ingénieux Ulysse.   (73–74)

Oreste speaks of it again in his embassy to Pyrrhus:

> Seigneur, vous savez trop avec quel artifice
> Un faux Astyanax fut offert au supplice.   (221–22)

Andromaque herself refers to it in a phrase which, spoken by
another, might merely be a conventional formula:

> O ma chère Céphise,
> Ce n'est point avec toi que mon cœur se déguise.   (1073–74)

She calls her decision, to marry Pyrrhus and then die, an "innocent stratagème"; innocent or not, the stratagem, the "artifice,"
would not be possible without this trait in Andromaque's character.

But this is not enough. For long before the stratagem was devised, Andromaque had given a categorical "no" to Pyrrhus (I,
4), and she had stuck by this even after "consultation" with her
son; she remains firm even after an ultimatum from Pyrrhus:

> Quoi? je lui donnerais Pyrrhus pour successeur?   (984)

The play might well have been over after the first decision, since
it springs from Andromaque's unfailing fidelity to Hector. In
order to make hesitation and re-examination possible, it was necessary to impress upon Andromaque the consequences of her
decision, and this Racine does by endowing her with what the
modern psychologist would call the "visual imagination." If we
look at I, 4, where her first decision is made, we discover that her
arguments and her own conception of the situation are completely "non-visual"; she thinks of herself and of her sorrow, of
Hector and of Troy, almost in terms of ideals and abstractions.
Everything is rationalized and intellectualized, and Andromaque
is thus able to say of Astyanax:

> Hélas! il mourra donc. Il n'a pour sa défense
> Que les pleurs de sa mère, et que son innocence.   (373–74)

In the second interview with Pyrrhus, reported by him, she again sees in Astyanax only his father:

> «C'est Hector, disait-elle, en l'embrassant toujours;
> Voilà ses yeux, sa bouche, et déjà son audace;
> C'est lui-même, c'est toi, cher époux, que j'embrasse.»
>
> (652–54)

Yet it is a simple statement of Céphise's, evoking an image, that changes Andromaque's mind:

> Hé bien! allons donc voir expirer votre fils.   (1012)

If this is possible, it is because Racine has begun long before to emphasize the power of visual images over Andromaque. In her conversation with Hermione (III, 4) she had said:

> Par une main cruelle, hélas! j'ai vu percer
> Le seul où mes regards prétendaient s'adresser.   (863–64)

When she speaks again with Pyrrhus (III, 6), she insists:

> J'ai vu mon père mort, et nos murs embrasés;
> J'ai vu trancher les jours de ma famille entière,
> Et mon époux sanglant traîné sur la poussière.   (928–30)

Her description of the same events to Céphise goes into more precise detail:

> Dois-je oublier Hector privé de funérailles,
> Et traîné sans honneur autour de nos murailles?
> Dois-je oublier son père à mes pieds renversé,
> Ensanglantant l'autel qu'il tenait embrassé?
> Songe, songe, Céphise, à cette nuit cruelle
> Qui fut pour tout un peuple une nuit éternelle.
> Figure-toi Pyrrhus, les yeux étincelants,
> Entrant à la lueur de nos palais brûlants,
> Sur tous mes frères morts se faisant un passage,
> Et de sang tout couvert échauffant le carnage.
> Songe aux cris des vainqueurs, songe aux cris des mourants,
> Dans la flamme étouffés, sous le fer expirants.
> Peins-toi dans ces horreurs Andromaque éperdue:
> Voilà comme Pyrrhus vint s'offrir à ma vue.   (993–1006)

In this mood of visual retrospection, she is suddenly affected in a very special way by Céphise's "voir expirer votre fils," and after other similar recollections (relating now to Astyanax) she asks herself:

> Et je puis voir répandre un sang si précieux?   (1027)

She readily finds her own answer, and the definite change of heart is found in the line:

> Non, tu ne mourras point: je ne le puis souffrir.   (1036)

In all this development, Racine works slowly and carefully on the factor needed to effect the change of heart, on the kind of turn of mind in Andromaque that must supplement love, fidelity, and wiliness. The emphasis upon "voir" and all its cognates is not a matter of diction (nothing in good poetry is ever a mere matter of diction); it is integral to the creation and completion of a character and to its capacity to respond to a situation.

If from Andromaque we work back to Pyrrhus, who will (in the "chain of regression") be the one most directly affected by her decisions, we find that he too has been given the complementary passion needed for him to act in the event that his love is unrequited. This is the instability, the anger, the rage that Racine builds into his character from the very beginning of the play. Pylade characterizes Pyrrhus in I, 1:

> Hermione elle-même a vu plus de cent fois
> Cet amant irrité revenir sous ses lois,
> Et de ses vœux troublés lui rapportant l'hommage,
> Soupirer à ses pieds moins d'amour que de rage.
> Ainsi n'attendez pas que l'on puisse aujourd'hui
> Vous répondre d'un cœur si peu maître de lui:
> Il peut, Seigneur, il peut, dans ce désordre extrême,
> Épouser ce qu'il hait, et punir ce qu'il aime.   (115–22)

But he recognizes the basic constancy of Pyrrhus' love for Andromaque:

Leur haine ne fera qu'irriter sa tendresse.
Plus on les veut brouiller, plus on va les unir.
Pressez, demandez tout, pour ne rien obtenir.   (138–40)

As was the case with Andromaque, Pyrrhus' first decisions will
derive from his major passion; first in the parley with Oreste,
then in the long conversation with Andromaque, he indicates
that he means to be guided by this love. Yet he recognizes already
his capacity for counteraction:

Songez-y bien: il faut désormais que mon cœur,
S'il n'aime avec transport, haïsse avec fureur.
Je n'épargnerai rien dans ma juste colère.   (367–69)

The counteraction comes in II, 4, where (as a result of Andromaque's refusal) he announces to Oreste that he means to
marry Hermione; but the reasons for his so doing, along with
his instability, are revealed to Phœnix in the following scene:

Ma colère à ses yeux n'a paru qu'à demi;
Elle ignore à quel point je suis son ennemi.
Retournons-y. Je veux la braver à sa vue,
Et donner à ma haine une libre étendue.   (675–78)

A few minutes later he passes to an ecstasy of revenge:

Non, non, je l'ai juré, ma vengeance est certaine;
Il faut bien une fois justifier sa haine.
J'abandonne son fils. Que de pleurs vont couler!
De quel nom sa douleur me va-t-elle appeler!
Quel spectacle pour elle aujourd'hui se dispose!
Elle en mourra, Phœnix, et j'en serai la cause.
C'est lui mettre moi-même un poignard dans le sein.
(693–99)

In his last interview with Andromaque, he confesses the ambivalence of his intentions:

Et là vous me verrez, soumis ou furieux,
Vous couronner, Madame, ou le perdre à vos yeux.
(975–76)

The complementary passion in Pyrrhus is thus relatively simple; and this is because it does not need to be any more complex. It will operate at a point relatively early in the tragedy—at that point where he must promise marriage to Hermione out of a spirit of revengefulness—and will be responsible for an episode that affects the denouement only indirectly. Racine gives it as much extension as it requires.

Such is not the case with the "reverse" passion attributed to Hermione; for this is the one that makes the denouement possible. Racine wished to arrive at a solution that would assure Astyanax' safety and Andromaque's life. To do this, it was necessary to have Pyrrhus killed, but only after he had married Andromaque and guaranteed Astyanax' future. To achieve this, Oreste (the assassin) had to be impelled to commit the murder, and he could be impelled only by Hermione. Only by an Hermione, that is, who would have—in addition to her overpowering love for Pyrrhus—such other passions as would lead her to insist upon his murder. Racine was fully aware of the difficulty of making such an assortment of passions dramatically convincing, and he prepared and advanced with great care the complexities of Hermione's character. Oreste's earliest epithet for her, "une inhumaine" (26), might be taken at face value as designating only a woman who refused his love; but it is also applicable to all her future actions in the play. Hermione herself, however, best displays the range and the violence of her passions. Her pride, with the sensitivity and the shame that accompany any infringement upon it:

> C'est cet amour payé de trop d'ingratitude
> Qui me rend en ces lieux sa présence si rude.
> Quelle honte pour moi, quel triomphe pour lui,
> De voir mon infortune égaler son ennui!
> Est-ce là, dira-t-il, cette fière Hermione?
> Elle me dédaignait; un autre l'abandonne.
> L'ingrate, qui mettait son cœur à si haut prix,
> Apprend donc à son tour à souffrir des mépris?   (393–400)

And again her pride:

> Si je le hais, Cléone! il y va de ma gloire. (413)

Her readiness to anger, her "fureur," which will be the dominant motive for much of her later action:

> Ah! laisse à ma fureur le temps de croître encore! (418)

Her hope against hope that Pyrrhus will return to her, which, when it seems to be realized, will lead her to extremes of elation; and when it is disappointed, to extremes of fury:

> Mais si l'ingrat rentrait dans son devoir!
> Si la foi dans son cœur retrouvait quelque place!
> S'il venait à mes pieds me demander sa grâce!
> Si sous mes lois, Amour, tu pouvais l'engager ... (436–39)

Her vindictiveness, her wish (in a sentiment that Racine will later find useful for Ériphile in *Iphigénie*) to destroy the happiness of others:

> Demeurons toutefois pour troubler leur fortune;
> Prenons quelque plaisir à leur être importune;
>
> .   .   .   .
>
> Rendons-lui les tourments qu'elle me fait souffrir:
> Qu'elle le perde, ou bien qu'il la fasse périr. (441–48)

Of all these dispositions, the most important is undoubtedly Hermione's "fureur"; for from it will come her mad determination to have Pyrrhus killed, and subsequently her condemnation of Oreste for following her orders. Pylade quite properly calls her "une furie" (753) and foresees her future behavior. Only Oreste, because of his blindness, fails to realize what is happening, and hence Hermione has every right to reproach him, after the deed is done, with his failure to understand her:

> Ah! fallait-il en croire une amante insensée?
> Ne devais-tu pas lire au fond de ma pensée?
> Et ne voyais-tu pas, dans mes emportements,
> Que mon cœur démentait ma bouche à tous moments? (1545–48)

Other traits, such as the basic cruelty which she displays to
Andromaque and to Oreste, the readiness to believe in her own
good fortune, are secondary. All in all, Racine enriches her
character beyond those of the other personages, and he does so
because of the multitude of things that she has to do and the
extremeness, the illogicality, of some of them. Perhaps some of
this is due to her place in the general schematism: the farther one
goes back from the pivotal personage, the more the action depends
upon reaction to reaction, the greater must be the complexity of
motives and hence of character.

The farthest from Andromaque in the regressive chain is
Oreste. His character is not the most complex (Hermione has that
distinction), but it is the most extreme. That is, it is he who
will be called upon to perform the actions most improper to his
official position and, in a sense, to the basic goodness of his character. He must therefore possess, in addition to his great love for
Hermione and the fidelity that accompanies it, a potential for
violent, irrational, and essentially wicked action. This is found in
his latent madness, in a kind of "fureur" that is not the same as
Hermione's (which is rage, cholera, viciousness) but that consists rather in a complete loss of rational control; it is real folly.
Once again, Racine saw the necessity of building this potential
solidly into the structure of his tragedy, and he worked at it in
the earliest lines. Pylade gives us the first intimations:

> Surtout je redoutais cette mélancolie
> Où j'ai vu si longtemps votre âme ensevelie.
> Je craignais que le ciel, par un cruel secours,
> Ne vous offrît la mort que vous cherchiez toujours. (17–20)

When we meet Oreste, then, he is already at the point of desperation, he seeks death, he is a victim of melancholy. He is "un
malheureux qui cherche le trépas" (24), a man who thinks in
terms of fate and destiny (5, 25, 27)—and of these forces as allied
against him—and who speaks of "mon désespoir ... mes ennuis

... cet état funeste" (43–45). He sees the uncertainty of his will and reason, identifies his "fureur" (47) and his excesses:

> Je pris tous mes transports pour des transports de haine. (54)

He perceives clearly the alternating moods and emotions of his life:

> En ce calme trompeur j'arrivai dans la Grèce;
> . . . .
> Que, mes sens reprenant leur première vigueur,
> L'amour achèverait de sortir de mon cœur. (58–64)

Above all, he realizes that he is no longer in control of himself:

> Je me livre en aveugle au destin qui m'entraîne. (98)

Knowing himself as he does, he can foresee alternative possibilities for his future actions:

> Heureux si je pouvais, dans l'ardeur qui me presse,
> Au lieu d'Astyanax, lui ravir ma princesse! (93–94)

> J'aime: je viens chercher Hermione en ces lieux,
> La fléchir, l'enlever, ou mourir à ses yeux. (99–100)

Some of these probabilities will result in actions later in the play.

In order to bring about Oreste's striking act in the denouement, it was not sufficient to give him the traits of character that I have listed. Racine needed, in addition, to augment the depth and the force of each one; by so doing, he would increase probability within the tragedy and credibility for the audience. Many subsequent speeches and scenes serve this purpose. In II, 2, Oreste refers again to his "aveuglement funeste" and to "le destin d'Oreste" (481–82), to "la fureur de mes derniers adieux" (488), emphasizing his desire to die and the extent to which his life depended upon Hermione. In III, 1, after Pyrrhus has decided to marry Hermione, Pylade and Oreste engage in this exchange:

PYLADE

Modérez donc, Seigneur, cette fureur extrême.
Je ne vous connais plus; vous n'êtes plus vous-même.
Souffrez ...

ORESTE

Non, tes conseils ne sont plus de saison,
Pylade; je suis las d'écouter la raison.   (709–12)

The whole scene indicates the extent of Oreste's despair, his readiness to take extreme action, and he expresses it at length toward the end:

... Mais, s'il faut ne te rien déguiser,
Mon innocence enfin commence à me peser.
Je ne sais de tout temps quelle injuste puissance
Laisse le crime en paix et poursuit l'innocence.
De quelque part sur moi que je tourne les yeux,
Je ne vois que malheurs qui condamnent les dieux.
Méritons leur courroux, justifions leur haine,
Et que le fruit du crime en précède la peine.   (771–78)

He is thus completely disposed, in the fourth act, to allow Hermione's urgings to overcome his own reason; and in the fifth, when his reason has been taxed beyond bearing, to lose that reason.

Having thus invented the central formula for his tragedy, and through it having achieved both a protagonist and the possibility of a dynamic action, Racine exploited the two potentialities for character inherent in his schematism of personages. For each personage he developed a particular passion of love that would link him to the "next" person in the forward chain of relationships; and for each he also developed one or more passions (or talents or dispositions) that would make possible an alternative line of action if his love were not successful. Consequently, he established a firmer basis for "necessity"—for the kinds of actions that his people would do—than he had achieved in the two preceding plays. Each of his persons was now less limited in his potentialities than the earlier ones had been, and each had the passions that would link him properly to the other persons in the play and to the general situation.

The formula for *Andromaque,* as I have already pointed out, also obviated the necessity of seeking, as causes for the major episodes, actions or events outside the play itself; that is, it gave to the structure its own system of "probabilities" as well as its own set of "necessities." To a degree, Racine included in his statements of character a certain number of specific indications of what particular actions—within the kinds—might take place. Some of these have already been touched upon. Oreste, for example, is the kind of man whose frustrations in love will lead to violent and irrational actions. Which ones, specifically? He runs through the list himself: actions that would affect Hermione and himself, "La fléchir, l'enlever, ou mourir à ses yeux" (100), actions that would affect Pyrrhus, "Ah! plutôt cette main dans le sang du barbare" (733). These are specific actions, and the mere fact that Oreste conceives of them as such, that he includes them among the alternatives for his future activity, makes them more "probable" than other solutions. In some cases he develops very elaborately one of these intentions. For example, the determination to kidnap Hermione (which, ultimately, does not come off) is first expressed as a general wish:

> Heureux si je pouvais, dans l'ardeur qui me presse,
> Au lieu d'Astyanax, lui ravir ma princesse! (93–94)

Then (II, 2) he proposes to Hermione that she leave with him, and obtains a tentative acquiescence (590), which he interprets as an assurance:

> Oui, oui, vous me suivrez, n'en doutez nullement. (591)

When, after Pyrrhus' announcement that he will marry Hermione, that kind of willing departure becomes impossible, he turns to kidnapping as an alternative:

> Il faut que je l'enlève, ou bien que je périsse. (714)

Already he misinterprets completely the situation, imagines that Hermione has begun to love him and that Pyrrhus' decision is merely an act of spite against him; he turns a deaf ear to the arguments of Pylade, who calls him "Oreste ravisseur" (766), and finally obtains Pylade's complicity. It should be noted that this kind of intention on the part of Oreste, to act in violation of his official mission, increases the probability of another such act, his final murder of Pyrrhus; indeed, this whole development with respect to the kidnapping of Hermione is merely auxiliary to the motivations for the denouement. In the scene (IV, 3) in which Hermione orders him to kill Pyrrhus, Oreste first proposes that they leave together (1163), and her final argument is her consent to do so:

> Allez. De votre sort laissez-moi la conduite,
> Et que tous vos vaisseaux soient prêts pour notre fuite.
>
> (1253–54)

We should not overlook the fact that Oreste makes this final decision only with the greatest difficulty and after long hesitation; he argues vigorously against Hermione, calling upon his own virtue, and might possibly have refused had she not held out the prospect of flight with him. Hence the importance of the departure-kidnapping-flight in the total elaboration of Oreste's role. Even so, there are other hesitations later, described by Cléone:

> Oreste vous adore.
> Mais de mille remords son esprit combattu
> Croit tantôt son amour et tantôt sa vertu.
> Il respecte en Pyrrhus l'honneur du diadème;
> Il respecte en Pyrrhus Achille et Pyrrhus même;
> Il craint la Grèce, il craint l'univers en courroux;
> Mais il se craint, dit-il, soi-même plus que tous.
> Il voudrait en vainqueur vous apporter sa tête;
> Le seul nom d'assassin l'épouvante et l'arrête.
> Enfin il est entré sans savoir dans son cœur
> S'il en devait sortir coupable ou spectateur.   (1462–72)

And, as the event finally develops, Oreste himself strikes no blow at Pyrrhus (1516); his guilt is limited to his having participated in the organization and accomplishment of the plot. Racine apparently worked out these details of the denouement for two reasons: by decreasing Oreste's guilt, to render less justified Hermione's calling him a "monstre" (1564) and more probable his madness; and, through the same device, to retain and perhaps even to augment the sympathy of the audience for Oreste. But I shall want to inquire, shortly, whether this attention upon Oreste, this care to create a special effect with respect to him, might not constitute one of the weaknesses in the total structure of the tragedy.

In any case, Racine's painstaking concentration upon the kinds of probability relating to character (and thus, to a degree, independent of circumstance) demonstrates the advantages of the kind of general schematism that he had adopted, at the same time as it shows the progress he had made, since the beginning of his career, in the tightening-up of his dramatic structures. The more he was able to make his plays self-integrating and his actions self-generating, the more he was able to refine his techniques of preparing for the crucial events to be presented. Another refinement in technique, exemplified by *Andromaque*, comes in the handling of that other kind of probability, the probability of circumstances. We may take as an example another aspect of the scene in which Pyrrhus is murdered. Among all the conditions that must be present in order that the murder may be accomplished, not the least is the fact that Pyrrhus must be unguarded. Racine begins very early to make the necessary preparations. The presence of an enemy mission threatening the safety of Astyanax and Pyrrhus' resolution (through love for Andromaque) to protect him are background conditions of a general nature. The condition is still general when, in his conversation about Astyanax with Andromaque, Pyrrhus declares:

Je défendrai sa vie aux dépens de mes jours,   (288)

and when, conditional upon Andromaque's acceptance, he offers:

> Je vous rends votre fils, et je lui sers de père.   (326)

One of the more particular details is introduced when Pylade mentions the guards:

> Ces gardes, cette cour, l'air qui vous environne,
> Tout dépend de Pyrrhus, et surtout Hermione.   (721–22)

When Andromaque does consent, Pyrrhus "exposes" himself by assigning the guard to Astyanax:

> Déjà contre les Grecs plein d'un noble courroux,
> Le soin de votre fils le touche autant que vous.
> Il prévient leur fureur, il lui laisse sa garde;
> Pour ne pas l'exposer, lui-même, il se hasarde.   (1059–62)

Hermione is quick to take advantage of this fact as she plans the assault:

> Enfin qu'attendez-vous? Il vous offre sa tête:
> Sans gardes, sans défense, il marche à cette fête;
> Autour du fils d'Hector il les fait tous ranger;
> Il s'abandonne au bras qui me voudra venger.   (1217–20)

Cléone confirms it as she describes the scene at the altar:

> Autour du fils d'Hector il a rangé sa garde,
> Et croit que c'est lui seul que le péril regarde.   (1453–54)

As a result, Pyrrhus is unprotected and vulnerable when the Greeks interrupt the ceremony and attack him. The minor detail —minor but essential—has been prepared long in advance, and the probabilities for it have been carefully established. Racine's control of his dramatic technique is becoming surer in many areas, and especially in those where the general conception of the total structure of his play allows him to make improvements and refinements.

One such refinement in *Andromaque* that is really not dependent upon general conception, but that shows nevertheless the progress being made in artistry and execution, is Racine's handling of the subtle relationship between the play and its audience. This leads in turn to the achievement of effects that would not have been possible in the earlier dramas. If I might generalize boldly, I should say that in Racine's first two plays (as in most of Corneille's) the audience is presumed to be in a direct relationship with the personages and the actions on the stage; it is meant to feel exactly what each of the actors feels, to respond immediately to arguments, to take situations and actions at their face value as far as an emotional response is concerned. Thus I was able to say, at each point in the discussion of those plays, "We feel such-and-such"; for feeling such-and-such merely meant that the personage himself felt that way, or that he said or did things that normally or naturally would elicit such a feeling. The audience itself needed to add nothing except its inherent capacity to understand and sympathize. All this was the result of the fairly simple relationships within the plays themselves between persons and persons and between persons and situations. There was already, however, that kind of complication of feelings that comes when one passion is held in suspension (a kind of *sostenuto* effect) while another is being exploited. In II, 2, of *Alexandre le Grand,* for example, Taxile's speech to Éphestion is made against a background of the audience's remembrance (1) of Cléofile's effort to persuade Taxile, (2) of Porus' conversation with Taxile, (3) of Axiane's indication of her attitudes toward both Taxile and Porus. The audience thus realizes that what Taxile says is much less than what he means, and it feels a resentment against Taxile that is far greater than his present words would justify.

In *Andromaque,* Racine manipulates this device with superior effectiveness. We might take as an example Pyrrhus' first speech (I, 2, 173–220), his reply to Oreste's demand that he hand over Astyanax to the Greeks. The audience knows, from scene 1, that Oreste (to whom the speech is addressed) has long been in love with Hermione, that Hermione has been affianced by her father,

Ménélas, to Pyrrhus and is here in Buthrote awaiting her marriage, that Pyrrhus has spurned Hermione because of his love for
Andromaque. It knows, therefore, that if Pyrrhus refuses the
demand, he will do so out of love for Andromaque; that consequently Hermione will be rejected and Oreste may stand a better
chance of taking Hermione back with him. As a result of this
knowledge, the audience feels in certain ways: it has a basic
sympathy for Oreste, for his problems and his future; it is unfavorably disposed toward Hermione because of her treatment
of Oreste; it has some doubts about Pyrrhus because of the uncertainty of his own conduct; and it has, I suppose because he is
a child, some concern for the safety of Astyanax. Oreste's demand,
at the beginning of I, 2, is made in purely official terms; he
presents the arguments of the Greeks without allusion to any of
the personal factors that affect himself, Pyrrhus, and Astyanax.
Yet the audience takes these into account. When Oreste praises
Pyrrhus, it knows that he is praising a hated rival; when he
makes the demand in completely objective terms, it knows that
he is thinking of the repercussions on his own life of Pyrrhus'
decision. Hence it has to a degree taken Oreste's side in the debate, and when Pyrrhus begins to speak, it will hear him with
Oreste's ears and with all the overtones of feeling that that identification involves.

Pyrrhus' speech is carefully composed in view of a complex reaction from the audience. Its first lines are full of ironic disdain
for Oreste and his mission:

> La Grèce en ma faveur est trop inquiétée.
> De soins plus importants je l'ai crue agitée,
> Seigneur, et sur le nom de son ambassadeur,
> J'avais dans ses projets conçu plus de grandeur.
> Qui croirait en effet qu'une telle entreprise
> Du fils d'Agamemnon méritât l'entremise;
> Qu'un peuple tout entier, tant de fois triomphant,
> N'eût daigné conspirer que la mort d'un enfant?   (173-80)

We know immediately that the demand will be rejected by Pyrrhus; we know why; but we know that the real reasons will be suppressed in favor of good reasons. Because we hear through Oreste's ears, we are offended by Pyrrhus' mocking tone, we begin to resent his character, we espouse more definitely the cause of Greece and of Oreste. These feelings are augmented by Pyrrhus' haughtiness in the next lines, where we feel that, although his legal case may be good, his way of putting it is unacceptable:

> Mais à qui prétend-on que je le sacrifie?
> La Grèce a-t-elle encor quelque droit sur sa vie?
> Et, seul de tous les Grecs, ne m'est-il pas permis
> D'ordonner d'un captif que le sort m'a soumis?
> Oui, Seigneur, lorsqu'au pied des murs fumants de Troie
> Les vainqueurs tout sanglants partagèrent leur proie,
> Le sort, dont les arrêts furent alors suivis,
> Fit tomber en mes mains Andromaque et son fils.
> Hécube près d'Ulysse acheva sa misère;
> Cassandre dans Argos a suivi votre père:
> Sur eux, sur leurs captifs, ai-je étendu mes droits?
> Ai-je enfin disposé du fruit de leurs exploits?   (181–92)

In these lines, moreover, we realize that he is really talking about Andromaque rather than about Astyanax—he uses the ambiguous "un captif" and the other examples he cites are of women—and that he is making, indirectly, his case for marrying her in defiance of Hermione, Ménélas, and the Greeks. The following lines continue the note of sarcasm; they insult Oreste and the Greeks. At the same time, through the image they present of Troy destroyed, they at once prepare us for Andromaque's rejection of Pyrrhus and they arouse our sympathy for her. We are thus moved simultaneously to sentiments relevant to three of the four main personages in the play:

> On craint qu'avec Hector Troie un jour ne renaisse;
> Son fils peut me ravir le jour que je lui laisse.
> Seigneur, tant de prudence entraîne trop de soin:

Je ne sais point prévoir les malheurs de si loin.
Je songe quelle était autrefois cette ville,
Si superbe en remparts, en héros si fertile,
Maîtresse de l'Asie; et je regarde enfin
Quel fut le sort de Troie, et quel est son destin.
Je ne vois que des tours que la cendre a couvertes,
Un fleuve teint de sang, des campagnes désertes,
Un enfant dans les fers; et je ne puis songer
Que Troie en cet état aspire à se venger.   (193–204)

The next argument seems to be more dispassionate, to introduce
considerations of history and of timing. Still, it contains a justification of Pyrrhus' actions then and of his attitude now, and it is
once again merely an indirect assertion of the negative and a plea
for understanding:

Ah! si du fils d'Hector la perte était jurée,
Pourquoi d'un an entier l'avons-nous différée?
Dans le sein de Priam n'a-t-on pu l'immoler?
Sous tant de morts, sous Troie, il fallait l'accabler.
Tout était juste alors: la vieillesse et l'enfance
En vain sur leur faiblesse appuyaient leur défense;
La victoire et la nuit, plus cruelles que nous,
Nous excitaient au meurtre, et confondaient nos coups.
Mon courroux aux vaincus ne fut que trop sévère.
Mais que ma cruauté survive à ma colère?
Que malgré la pitié dont je me sens saisir,
Dans le sang d'un enfant je me baigne à loisir?   (205–16)

I am not sure but that the plea is successful, at least for the audience. The arguments seem good, Pyrrhus' claim to pity (and
disclaimer of cruelty) seems sincere, the wish to spare a child is
attractive to us. Indeed, some tempering of our attitude toward
Pyrrhus is necessary at this point. He must not in any sense be
a black villain; and if we are to sympathize with Andromaque
rather than with him, we must nevertheless moderate our feelings
if the whole of the plot against him and his ultimate murder are
to produce their proper effect. Thus his final flourish—this is

the direct negative—is more to his credit than not; and although we judge, with Oreste, that important factors are being hidden, we applaud (as Oreste could not) his decision not to immolate Astyanax:

> Non, Seigneur. Que les Grecs cherchent quelque autre proie;
> Qu'ils poursuivent ailleurs ce qui reste de Troie:
> De mes inimitiés le cours est achevé;
> L'Épire sauvera ce que Troie a sauvé.   (217-20)

As the speech develops, then, our feelings are played upon in very complex ways—not directly and in a one-to-one relationship as they would be by a piece of rhetoric designed to move us, but in a complex and subtle fashion. The poetic or the dramatic dimension makes us at once participants and observers of the emotions; several planes or levels of feeling, related to the situation and to the persons both present and absent, develop simultaneously. It is of course extremely difficult to say what each of these passions is like and impossible to describe the combined effect. The only sure road for the critic is to distinguish, as finely as possible, the elements in the work capable of producing the effect.

Not all the effects are as surely and as deftly achieved in *Andromaque* as is this one. Indeed, we might say that while in certain scenes or passages Racine mastered the art of building into his work the right potentials for emotional effect, with respect to the whole work he remained uncertain and groping. His major difficulty lay in establishing the primacy, in our feelings, of his protagonist. He had been somewhat more successful in this in *La Thébaïde*, where Jocaste (if indeed she be the protagonist) for a time at least enlists and holds our sympathy; somewhat less successful in *Alexandre le Grand*, where all kinds of rival emotions are given the chance of taking hold before our admiration for Alexandre begins to develop. To a degree, the same thing occurs in *Andromaque*. I suppose that Andromaque is the protagonist; at least her position as "pivotal" personage in the action would seem to accord her that role. Yet the total impact of her action upon our feelings is spasmodic and fragmentary, and at times is completely obscured by more powerful reactions to other personages.

Act I. Andromaque does not appear until the last scene of the act; when she does, it is as a personage whose situation has been fully described and for whom a basic sympathy has already been engendered. Much earlier in the act, the situations and the plights of other persons have been presented, and the spectator has had a chance to develop, with respect to them, much stronger and much clearer emotions. First of these is Oreste. Regardless of what expository materials may be included in scene 1, of what sensitivities may be awakened toward other persons, the net effect of the scene is to create a strong identification with Oreste. This arises from our approval of his capacity for faithful friendship (the meeting with Pylade, 1–8), from our awareness of Pylade's devotion to him (9–20), from our sense that he is a man pursued by fate and by it driven to despair and melancholy (2–3, 17–24), from our discovery of his unhappy love for Hermione (26, 31–36). These are all intensified by Oreste's long *récit* (37–104), which also initiates, in passing, a number of responses to Hermione, to Pyrrhus, to Andromaque and Astyanax. Pylade's role at the end of the scene, besides clarifying the situation and directing our feelings relevant to the other persons, is to reassure Oreste with regard to his prospects—and in so doing to raise our own hopes for his success. We are, at this point, Oreste's audience.

Anything that comes about in scene 2 regarding our feelings for Andromaque comes about, again, indirectly. As I have indicated, Oreste's speech (the speech of official demand) serves to augment our conviction of the rightness of Oreste's position and of his character, while Pyrrhus' speech (the speech of official refusal) proceeds from a relatively negative impression of Pyrrhus to one that is less completely damning. Again, some slight addition is made to Andromaque's figure, as it is in what Oreste says immediately afterward. Pyrrhus' last speech, with its evasiveness about Hermione, its definiteness about Astyanax (hence about Andromaque), and its offer to bring Hermione and Oreste together, states clearly his relationships to all these persons; I think that, in spite of its haughtiness, it once more helps to redeem Pyrrhus. The brief third scene removes any doubt. Pyrrhus wishes that Hermione might leave ("Qu'elle m'épargnerait de contrainte et d'ennui!" [256]), he shows his subjugation to Andromaque ("Andromaque paraît" [258]). We might note, also, that the probability for a successful flight of Hermione and Oreste is established in the line:

> Tous nos ports sont ouverts et pour elle et pour lui.   (255)

Racine is attentive to matters of situation and future action at the same time that he characterizes his personages.

In scene 4, Andromaque finally comes onto the stage. (This is much earlier, incidentally, than the initial appearance of Alexandre.) Her traits emerge rapidly—and they are all traits that we can admire. Her noble dignity, her meek acceptance of captivity and suffering, her complete devotion to her son, are all contained in her first lines:

> Je passais jusqu'aux lieux où l'on garde mon fils.
> Puisqu'une fois le jour vous souffrez que je voie
> Le seul bien qui me reste et d'Hector et de Troie,
> J'allais, Seigneur, pleurer un moment avec lui:
> Je ne l'ai point encore embrassé d'aujourd'hui.   (260–64)

These will be the traits that will dominate the rest of the discussion with Pyrrhus. When he tells her how her son is threatened, she is incredulous of the demand and of the possibility of his granting it; when he asks for her love, she points out, calmly, how unbecoming would be the marriage for him and how impossible for her. She describes her own state:

> Captive, toujours triste, importune à moi-même.   (301)

She is unmoved by his promise of future glory for her son, asks only to be exiled with him. When Pyrrhus threatens to deliver

Astyanax to the Greeks, she accepts the thought of losing her son
with resignation, almost content that it will provide an excuse
for her own death. In all these reactions, we are impressed by her
serenity, her dignity, and her unfaltering devotion to her son,
that is, to Hector and to the tradition of Troy. We are convinced
that her cause is the right one and, by retrospection, we blame
the Greeks for having demanded the child and Pyrrhus for
having imposed the conditions that he did for saving him.

Had the first act contained only its last scene, we should have
had a proper introduction to a tragedy in which Andromaque
was to be the heroine and protagonist. We should have had the
correct feelings with respect to her and to the other persons involved in her fate. Our sympathy for her would have been dominant and undivided. As it is, other feelings of a more vigorous
nature are allowed to assert and ensconce themselves beforehand;
they cannot be erased; and what we feel about Andromaque is
by no means clean-cut and exclusive. Oreste and then Pyrrhus
are rivals for our attention, one for our commiseration and the
other for our mitigated disapproval. The basis has been laid for
a play in which a delicate balance of the passions will have to be
maintained with great subtlety.

Act II. Against this background of two strong sympathies—
taking the form of two very different kinds of pity—Hermione
is presented to us in the first scene of the next act. We are
predisposed against her, merely because we are disposed in favor
of Oreste. But our feelings toward her, as the scene progresses,
will be quite mixed. We are meant to continue to dislike her. Her
condescension toward Oreste ("Je lui veux bien encore accorder
cette joie" [386]), her emphasis upon pride hurt and honor
violated (rather than upon the quality of her own love), her
declaration of hatred for Pyrrhus, her revelation that it was she
who set the Greeks against Astyanax (through jealousy of Andromaque), all these contribute to this feeling. Most especially,
we are disturbed by her fury and her unpredictability—

> Ah! laisse à ma fureur le temps de croître encore!
> Contre mon ennemi laisse-moi m'assurer;
> Cléone, avec horreur je m'en veux séparer— (418-20)

by her spirit of revenge against Pyrrhus and her misjudgment of Andromaque, by her willingness to sacrifice a child to her hatred. Her statement of impatience with Oreste—

> Ah! je ne croyais pas qu'il fût si près d'ici— (476)

is distasteful to us, and we compare it unfavorably with Pyrrhus' "Andromaque vient" of the preceding act. If we have any pity at all for Hermione, it is merely through her general position as a woman who has been wronged, who has been promised a marriage that apparently will not now take place, and who has loved in vain. The most important part of our reaction, I think, is the fact that we feel now that the balance of the passions has again been disturbed, and that a very strong one (our feelings about Hermione are vigorous) has for the time being wiped out the ones that had been so carefully developed in Act I.

Scene 2 brings together Oreste and Hermione. Our fresh impressions of Hermione are fortified by her basic dishonesty throughout the conversation (contrasted with Oreste's basic honesty), by her high-handed treatment of Oreste and her obvious intention to use him for her own purposes (regardless of the effect upon him), by her egotism and her unwillingness to face the fact of Pyrrhus' desertion. More and more, we disapprove of her character and her conduct. Contrariwise, the sympathy for Oreste that we had felt long since is enhanced by Hermione's presence and behavior. We see him as essentially upright and forthright; we recognize that his fate—his "destin"—resides in no supernatural power but merely in the will and the caprice of Hermione; we are sorry for his incapability to free himself from a "cruel" and "inhuman" woman. We begin to wonder whether he might not be the real captive, the real victim in the tragedy. His present sufferings ("Je sais que vos regards vont rouvrir mes blessures" [485]) are added to his past sufferings ("J'ai mendié la mort chez des peuples cruels" [491]), and we are sure that his future sufferings will be even greater as a result of his involvement in the present situation with Hermione. If there be any development of pity for a personage's present state and of concern for his future, it relates at this point rather to Oreste than to Andromaque.

For the spectator, the brief monologue of scene 3 has a curious effect. He discounts Oreste's optimism (knowing Hermione); the "heureux destin" proclaimed—for once!—by Oreste can have only bitter overtones. He both feels "with" Oreste and is detached from him when, shortly, Pyrrhus arrives and makes his startling announcement. Scene 4, for all its brevity, is full of events and implications. Pyrrhus' first speech is recognized as a calm expression of a violent state in the speaker, and simultaneously it has repercussions on Andromaque's situation and on our feelings for her. Oreste's mild reply covers his agitation over the reversal of his "heureux destin" and points again toward Andromaque. On the other hand, Pyrrhus' second speech is directed at Oreste, contains the most devastating news possible for him, and by implication represents Hermione's triumph. The spectator turns more definitely against Pyrrhus, appreciates all the passion of despair in Oreste's "Ah! dieux!" At the same time, he is prepared for the beginning—if not for the whole—of the following scene, in which Pyrrhus' true state of soul becomes apparent.

In a way, Pyrrhus' announcement had been as startling to the spectator as it was catastrophic for Oreste. When last seen, Pyrrhus had sent Andromaque to "consult her son," to decide whether to accept or reject his proposal of marriage; he had promised:

> Pour savoir nos destins, j'irai vous retrouver.   (383)

The audience can only infer, now, that Andromaque has refused; but Pyrrhus' tone in the announcement is too objective to be taken as representing his real state of feeling, and the audience awaits with some impatience a revelation or an explanation. This impatience grows as, early in scene 5, Pyrrhus continues his pose of contentment and placidity. As Phœnix joins in congratulating him on a return to reason and on a victory of patriotism, we know that we have as yet no reasons to forgive him for a return to Hermione—and every reason to condemn him for his action against Andromaque. His true motives soon emerge, however: first, in the almost involuntary "un regard m'eût tout fait oublier" (640), then in the speech beginning, "Tu l'as vu comme elle m'a traité" (644). As he re-creates for us the interview with Andromaque (paying no attention to Phœnix' interruptions), we pass more definitely to applause for Andromaque (whose cause is still the right one) while we condemn Pyrrhus for being cruel, hasty, "infirm of purpose"; and this condemnation grows as, toward the end of the scene, he displays his revengeful sentiments in an almost masochistic form. The scene closes, hence the act, with the weak and indefinite "Faisons tout ce que j'ai promis" (708), leaving us with the judgment that he will not do what he has promised, that Andromaque still remains in jeopardy, and that Oreste's affairs—for the moment at least—are in a sorry pass. Our passions and involvements are still sufficiently distinctly on the side of Andromaque and Oreste so that we feel anxiety over their future; as for the others, we are concerned only with their roles as counteragents. It is important to remark that we still give Andromaque no great preference, if any, over Oreste.

Act III. In the total structure of the action, the third act presents the reactions to the first of the possible alternative decisions. Andromaque has refused Pyrrhus; Pyrrhus has announced his intention to marry Hermione. What, then, will be the further consequences of these decisions? We are, if you wish, working backward down the chain of relationships linking the various personages, and the "reverse" or counterpassions of certain actors will be called into play. But in the same act, the groundwork must be laid for possible reversals of this movement; in the eventuality that Andromaque might change her mind, preparations must be made for a shift in each person's intentions. Act III develops both strains simultaneously, and as a result the audience's feelings must be quite complex.

The person most affected—or perhaps I should say most adversely affected—by Pyrrhus' decision is Oreste; it is sufficient to start him toward desperation and madness. The first scene of Act III is devoted to presenting, for Oreste, both reaction and the possibilities for action. Reaction is summarized in Pylade's formula, "fureur extrême," the possibilities for action in Oreste's "Mon innocence enfin commence à me peser" (772). As the scene opens, Oreste states three possibilities for his future action:

Il faut que je l'enlève, ou bien que je périsse.   (714)

Ah! plutôt cette main dans le sang du barbare ...   (733)

The spectator disapproves of all three; he is interested in Oreste's well-being, wishes to see him alive and happy, knows that neither kidnapping Hermione nor killing Pyrrhus will provide a satisfactory solution for him. He takes, in a word, the position that Pylade represents in the scene, that of reason, of Oreste's legal responsibilities, of non-violence. We fear for Oreste at this point, realizing that he is no longer master of himself, that reason no longer operates in him ("Du coup dont ma raison vient d'être confondue" [730]); yet, because of our sympathy with his plight, we understand why he should reject Pylade's sensible arguments. We are pleased when Pylade capitulates and promises to help in the kidnapping; we are even more pleased when Oreste promises to "dissimulate" ("je réponds de moi" [804]), since we know that this will alleviate the immediate danger.

Oreste does dissimulate in scene 2, and except for the momentary "Ah! que vous saviez bien, cruelle ..." (825) he discharges his duty as messenger in a completely contained fashion. We wonder and we are concerned, however, because we know what he feels and that he is, for the nonce, playing a game (the exclamation of line 825, incidentally, is there to remind us of the fact); how long will he be able to keep up the show? As for Hermione, we know that she is duping herself when she believes that Pyrrhus is marrying her out of love and we are sensitive to the insincerity and the cruelty of her efforts to placate Oreste; we like her none the better for it. Cléone's first statement in scene 3, clairvoyant about Oreste's real state, reawakens our fears for him. On the other hand, Hermione's long expression of her joy, full of self-delusion, is also full of foreboding about what she might do and say if, suddenly, her joy should be brought to an end. Cléone's "Dissimulez" (855), parallel to Pylade's "Dissimulez, Seigneur" of the first scene, sets the stage for another hiding of the "counterpassion" that accompanies these events, hence for a further complication of the emotions expressed by the actors and felt by the audience.

When Andromaque appears in scene 4, "en pleurs," we are suddenly reminded that the really important reaction to Pyrrhus' announcement is hers; for the fate of Astyanax is now clearly decided, and with it the fate of her love. Moreover, by a kind of compensatory movement, our negative feelings about Hermione in the preceding scene have led to a more positive disposition toward Andromaque. Both feelings grow when Andromaque humiliates herself before Hermione—so much less worthy than she in every way—and asks her to intercede for Astyanax. Andromaque uses the same arguments, the arguments of a mother, as she had previously used; when Hermione coldly and insultingly turns them aside, she merits Andromaque's "la cruelle" (887) and our own disapproval. In the brief fifth scene, Céphise predicts the probability of a change in Pyrrhus' mind. Her words, "Un regard confondrait Hermione et la Grèce" (889), recalling Pyrrhus' "un regard m'eût tout fait oublier" (640), remind us that the situation is still unstable and that it still depends upon Andromaque. We will therefore observe with greater anxiety Andromaque's behavior in the last three scenes of the act.

For a few minutes, at the beginning of scene 6, the two pairs of interlocutors are at opposite sides of the stage, pretending not to see each other but speaking loudly enough to be overheard. These are minutes of great tenseness for the audience, for upon them depends Andromaque's fate: if she and Pyrrhus speak, a reconsideration on both parts may be possible; if not, not. They do speak, but only after Pyrrhus has threatened to carry through on his decision: "Allons aux Grecs livrer le fils d'Hector" (900). They do speak, but it is only to remain firm in their positions: Pyrrhus will give up Astyanax, Andromaque will make no concessions. As they do, the audience feels some division in its feelings toward Andromaque; it wishes her both to remain constant to Hector and to save Astyanax. It applauds her long appeal to Pyrrhus to maintain the status quo, an appeal in which she calls upon his goodness, his honor, his magnanimity. In Pyrrhus' speech of reply (scene 7) he gives Andromaque a final chance to change her mind, a final choice between alternatives—"ou périr, ou régner" (968), "Vous couronner, Madame, ou le perdre à vos yeux" (976)—and he does so in a way and with a tone that is all to his credit. At this point, the audience is ready to resolve its hesitations with respect to Andromaque: it wishes her to save Astyanax.

Céphise takes the same position in scene 8, with arguments that seem as reasonable as were Pylade's to Oreste:

> Madame, à votre époux c'est être assez fidèle:
> Trop de vertu pourrait vous rendre criminelle.
> Lui-même il porterait votre âme à la douceur.   (981–83)

Yet Andromaque's rebuttal, made up of a visual reconstitution of the destruction of Troy and of her family, is equally moving and convincing. The audience is torn, put in concern and suspense over the decision that will be made. Both alternatives are undesirable. We participate in Andromaque's anguish of indecision, epitomized in her words:

> O cendres d'un époux! ô Troyens! ô mon père!
> O mon fils, que tes jours coûtent cher à ta mère! (1045–46)

And we are left in this state as the act ends.

The second half of Act III has thus concentrated our attention, for a long period of time, upon Andromaque, and has left us with an essential concern for her fate. For the first time in the play, we are not distracted by our interest in Oreste or by our feelings about Pyrrhus or Hermione. Racine has succeeded, as the act comes to a close, in focusing our feelings upon his central personage. For another thing, we should note that whereas the other persons have all had the opportunity to manifest what I have called their "counterpassions," those capacities for action in the event that their main passions were frustrated, and whereas they have done so in one way or another, Andromaque has not yet seized upon this opportunity. She has called, so far, only upon her single-minded love for Troy-Hector-Astyanax; she has made no use of that talent for deceit, that wiliness that was from the beginning a part of her character. If we ourselves are wary and attentive, we should expect it to be manifested in some way in the decision that she will make.

Act IV. The link with Andromaque is maintained in the first scene of Act IV; as a matter of fact, it is very carefully made through the diction of lines 1048 ("consulter mon époux") and 1049 ("c'est votre époux"). Our feelings will still be concentrated on Andromaque, first as we learn that she has promised to marry Pyrrhus, next as we discover that the promise is merely a subterfuge to save Astyanax, since she means to die immediately after the ceremony. By this decision, both of our feelings with respect to Andromaque are satisfied: we wanted her to save Astyanax, and she will; we wanted her to remain faithful to Hector, and she will. Only our wish that she might continue to live will be frustrated, and herein will lie the tragic emotion of the play. The scene is carefully constructed to pass from one of these emotions to another. Céphise (like Pylade, an expression of the audience's attitudes) tells of Andromaque's decision and of Pyrrhus' actions consequent upon it; she also expresses her joy in the saving of

Astyanax. Andromaque reveals her intentions and, in her final speeches, expresses her hopes for Astyanax' future with the same calm dignity that had characterized her throughout.

This is Andromaque's last appearance in the play and these are her last words; her ultimate fate will be recounted in the *récit* of the ceremony, but it will be in the context of an entirely different set of emotions. As far as she is concerned, our feelings here reach their fullest and their final form. After all, she has now done all that the situation and her character had prepared her to do: she has refused Pyrrhus, she has then accepted Pyrrhus and determined to die. All the necessities and the probabilities—with respect to her alone—have been exhausted. If they are exhausted so early in the play, if her part has been played by the beginning of Act IV, it is because the general schematism gave her only a limited function to perform. Racine succeeded in making of her a protagonist, a "pivotal" personage; but he did not succeed in making of his protagonist a person whose action would dominate the whole of the play. What the consequences of this failure are for the total effect of the tragedy will emerge as we continue with our study of the effects.

Beginning with scene 2, it is Hermione who occupies the center of the stage almost to the very end of the act. Scene 2 is merely preparatory; it describes to us, through Cléone's words, and then it shows us, Hermione's outward reaction to Pyrrhus' announcement, "un calme si funeste" (1141). We thus know that her "counterpassion" has not yet manifested itself, and we expect that it will as soon as Oreste appears. He appears in scene 3. The effect of his initial hopeful statement is to make us feel more keenly the cruelty of Hermione's demand, "Vengez-moi" (1157); and Oreste's hopeful misinterpretation (that she wishes to flee with him) makes more damnable her real desire, "Il faut immoler ... Pyrrhus" (1172). Andromaque is forgotten, our sympathies have shifted to Oreste and our antipathies to Hermione. Both of these are more colorful and more vivid persons, both have a greater capacity for diverse actions, and in both cases their plight is so far unresolved. We respond quickly and positively to Oreste's resistance, to his arguments that spring from the basic goodness of his character and from his sense of his official responsibilities; quickly and negatively to Hermione's rabid vengefulness, to her conceit, to her own awareness of her unpredictability ("Ah! courez, et craignez que je ne vous rappelle" [1174]). Oreste is all reason, Hermione all fury. When finally he succumbs to her persuasion—and she uses every instrument, from the carefully laid plan to the taunts about his courage and his constancy—we realize that he has made the wrong decision, but one that he could not help making. His love, his impatience with his own innocence, his prior meditation of the same deed (733), his madness, all force him to it. We understand, but we deplore the decision; we know that it can bring no good to Oreste. We foresee the possibility that Hermione may ultimately again turn against him:

> Et mes sanglantes mains, sur moi-même tournées,
> Aussitôt, malgré lui, joindront nos destinées;
> Et, tout ingrat qu'il est, il me sera plus doux
> De mourir avec lui que de vivre avec vous. (1245–49)

And we recognize sadly with Oreste that she may never fulfill her promise:

> Et vous reconnaîtrez mes soins, si vous voulez. (1252)

The net result of the scene is to raise our feelings toward Hermione to a pitch of resentment and condemnation.

These feelings are not improved by Hermione's words in scene 4, since they display on the one hand her bloodthirsty wish for revenge and on the other hand her readiness to reverse her commands. During the whole of scene 5, others of her traits manifest themselves: her biting sarcasm as she replies to Pyrrhus, her wilful misinterpretations and misstatements, her contempt for both Pyrrhus and Andromaque and her wrath against them, all are completely understandable in terms of what we know about her character—and perfectly distasteful to the audience at the present moment. There is perhaps something admirable in the vigor with which she defends herself and in the general positiveness of her personality; but they are insufficient to redeem her in our eyes. On the contrary, everything that Pyrrhus says in the scene increases his credit with us. He makes a frank admission of his failings toward Hermione, avoids both rhetoric and sophistry (Andromaque had characterized him as "violent, mais sincère" [1085]), tries to explain if not to justify. Even though he may, to a degree, be in the wrong—after all, he has jilted Hermione —we tend rather to praise than to blame him for what he now says, especially as it contrasts with Hermione's violent responses. In a way he comes to be worthy of Andromaque (he rises to her level of quiet dignity) and, what is more important, unworthy of death at the hands of a vixen. Hermione's final threat, "Va, cours. Mais crains encor d'y trouver Hermione" (1386), fills us with alarm for his safety, and this is augmented by his refusal, in scene 6, to take any precautions. His final words (and they will be his last words on the stage) demonstrate his devotion to Andromaque and his intention to keep his promise:

> Andromaque m'attend. Phœnix, garde son fils.   (1392)

They leave us with an admiration for the man that has completely wiped out our initial disfavor, especially since his promises here will fulfill Andromaque's wishes.

Act V. Just as she had dominated most of Act IV, so Hermione will be the most striking and persistent figure in Act V. Andromaque disappeared from the stage at the beginning of the preceding act, Pyrrhus at the end. Only Hermione and Oreste, of the leading personages, will be present in the last act—and, in dramatic poetry, presence on the stage is of the utmost importance in the directing of the audience's emotions. Hermione's monologue in scene 1 is made up of her vacillation between her love and the hatred that, from the start, has been the other side of her love; jealousy and spite also enter into it. We realize that the

only effect of Pyrrhus' visit to her has been to make her desist
from stopping Oreste:

> Non, ne révoquons point l'arrêt de mon courroux.   (1407)

> Non, non, encore un coup, laissons agir Oreste.   (1418)

Both her "transport" and her "chagrin" displease us, and they
are not even mitigated by her realization that she has ordered a
monstrous and unmerited crime. All these doubts of Hermione's
are dissipated in scene 2, where Cléone's *récit* informs her of the
progress of the ceremony; she realizes that Pyrrhus has no re-
grets and determines that she will have none. The effect of this
scene is a curious one, and one that Racine has learned to use
with increasing skill through the writing of his first three plays.
It is a multiple effect and hence a rich one: we are given a description, in visual terms, of something that has happened far from the
stage, involving persons with whose destinies we are concerned;
it is told by somebody on the stage who gives to the description
his own color and interpretation; and it is told to somebody on
the stage who is deeply involved with both event and persons. In
a sense, this is the most dramatic way possible of presenting an
event, and much more so than the raw representation of the action
on the stage; for it permits the addition, to that action, of several
distinct levels of emotional response. In V, 2, the events themselves
are the approach of Andromaque and Pyrrhus to the altar, the
entrance of the Greeks into the temple, and Oreste's hesitation
to commit the crime; these add up to the likely consummation of
Pyrrhus' promise and of Andromaque's stratagem, and to the
possible—but not fully probable—carrying-out of Hermione's
order. One layer of our emotion attaches to these events themselves, since we do or do not wish them to take place. A second
(and related) layer of emotion attaches to Pyrrhus and Andromaque; we have reached the point, I think, where we share both
the joy of the first and the sorrow of the second. We are perhaps
even more concerned, at this point, with Oreste's fate, and his

hesitation is full of suspense for us. Third, since the story is told
by Cléone, who had previously tried to calm her mistress but who
had always been devoted to her interests, we feel that the account
she gives is accurate, not slanted in order to arouse Hermione, not
understated in order to deceive her. This gives us, especially with
respect to Oreste's thoughts, a sense of sympathetic penetration
into his own emotional crisis. Lastly, Hermione is present; she
reacts in her usual violent fashion to the successive parts of the
account. Moreover, through her questions ("Que fait Pyrrhus?"
[1431]; "que t'a dit Oreste?" [1458]) affecting the two men—one
of them involving her main passion, the other her "counterpassion"—she directs the order of the account at the same time
as she points it all toward herself. Her reactions, in the spate of
questions about Pyrrhus (1441–48) and in the unfair condemnation of Oreste (1473–92), dominate the emotions of the scene and
place themselves at the top of our own feelings.

Scene 3 brings, in many ways, the emotional climax of the play.
As Oreste reports the murder of Pyrrhus and his own success and
failure in it, we are horrified that he should have carried out
Hermione's orders; but we are pleased that he himself did not
commit the murder; and, incidentally, we rejoice both in Pyrrhus'
self-justification through the keeping of his promise and in Andromaque's ultimate victory. Again, a very mixed response to a
récit, somewhat more vivid through the fact that the teller is
also one of the actors. All these emotions, however, are reduced
to a secondary status by what Hermione says: her disclaimer of
responsibility, her accusations of Oreste, the epithets she applies
to him, her own recognition of her inconstancy, all these are
stated so vigorously that we flare up in a passion of wrath against
Hermione. All our carefully developed sympathies for Oreste and
antipathies for Hermione come to a sudden maximum. We apply
to Hermione her own last words:

> ... et c'est assez pour moi,
> Traître, qu'elle ait produit un monstre comme toi.
>
> (1563–64)

I might point out again, in passing, that this crisis of our feelings does not relate to the major or "pivotal" personage, but to some who are near or at the end of the chain of relationships.

In the two remaining scenes of the tragedy, Oreste will suffer two blows to his sanity; both will elicit our sympathy, and the whole of our feeling as the play ends will be concentrated upon Oreste. In scene 4, his monologue expresses his incredulity, his incapacity to believe that Hermione should have turned upon him in this way. He understands the futility of having sacrificed his virtue, his principles, his reason ("j'étouffe en mon cœur la raison qui m'éclaire" [1569]) and that he has become, in fact, a monster. We blame Hermione; we have infinite pity for Oreste, and this grows constantly during the last scene. Other feelings are secondary: our pleasure in the continued triumph of Andromaque, who has saved both Astyanax and herself, our satisfaction that Hermione, through her suicide, should have punished herself in the only fitting way. Oreste remains the only sufferer. All his latent tendency to melancholy, to transport, to furor, now suddenly becomes realized; reason and reality are submerged, and he is left with visions and fantasies that represent the ruin of his whole life along with the loss of his mind. Hermione's death has finished what her intolerable treatment of him had started.

In the general nature of its emotional effect we may discern the principal weakness of *Andromaque* as a drama. This is a weakness of dispersion or distribution, where we should wish instead for concentration; it is also a weakness in proportion. While Racine found, more successfully than in his first two plays, a general plan that would give him a central or pivotal personage —and while he discovered the devices that made it possible to derive a self-generating action from that plan—he did not succeed in making of his central personage the dominant focus of his audience's emotions. A part of the difficulty arose from the plan itself; the situation and the relationships among the persons were such that the "pivotal" personage had the least to do. Andromaque needs to make only two important but fairly simple

decisions, and her character does not have to be very complex to
provide those decisions. But as we work "backward" down the
chain of personages, both actions and traits of character have to
be more numerous and more complicated; Hermione and Oreste,
as we regress, become more vivid, more real, more interesting
than either Pyrrhus or Andromaque. As a result, the feelings that
they arouse are more violent, and thus have a greater hold upon
us. In any case, they compete with our feelings for the heroine
herself.

A second difficulty comes from the order of representation or
the "economy" of the play. As I have pointed out, Andromaque
appears only after strong feelings have been associated with
Oreste and Pyrrhus, and she disappears long before even stronger
feelings will continue to be attached to Oreste and Hermione. If
any personage dominates the play by his continued presence, it
is Oreste; if any one dominates by the striking quality of her
personality, it is Hermione, especially in the later parts of the play
after Andromaque has ceased to be present before us. Racine
must have been aware of this fact, since in the original version
of the play he included, as V, 3, a scene in which Andromaque
reappeared (see the variants in the editions of 1668 and 1673);
but what Andromaque had to say was ineffective and unconvincing, and Racine dropped the scene in favor of the present text.
By so doing, he allowed Hermione and Oreste to remain in
control of our passions to the end of the play. At both the beginning and the end, then, other persons hold our attention;
Andromaque, much as we feel with her while she is present on
the stage, is reduced almost to the role of a secondary personage.
The order of representation here is all-important. Had Andromaque elicited our sympathy from the very beginning, had she
continued to do so in a mounting progression throughout the
play to the end, the total effect would have been different—and
it would have been Andromaque's. But that would be a different
play.

The same conclusions impose themselves if we ask which of

the personages is "tragic" through his character and his situation. The answer is again multiple; almost all the leading persons qualify. Andromaque surely: the qualities that we have discerned in her all constitute moral greatness and her situation—the necessity of choosing between two impossible alternatives—is certainly one of "unmerited misfortune." But also Oreste, whose basic character is admirable and whose circumstances, through Hermione's actions, become increasingly pitiable. And possibly even Pyrrhus, who demonstrates increasingly as the play progresses his positive virtues and who dies in the situation of an innocent victim. Only Hermione is disqualified, on the score both of certain defects in her character and of the nature of her circumstances; we cannot but admit that—except for her initial abandonment by Pyrrhus—the misfortunes that she suffers are fully deserved. The fact that two or three of the main personages might well be tragic heroes means, once again, that we develop strong interests in their fates and strong feelings toward them. What is more, in so far as pity is involved for all three of them, there is a similarity among these feelings that puts them into competition with one another. We can make no clear preference for one over the other (above all in the cases of Andromaque and Oreste), we can develop for neither one a constant and overriding emotion. Rather, about the action of the play we have a general "tragic sense," which moves from one to another of the leading personages. The rights of the protagonist are infringed upon; equality or near-equality prevails where a marked inequality would better produce the emotional effect proper to the play.

IV

Britannicus

Two YEARS elapsed between the production of *Andro-maque* and that of *Britannicus,* the first performance of which came at the end of 1669, the publication early in 1670. For his fourth play, Racine chose a subject from Roman history rather than one from Greek poetry or legend.

Andromaque had brought striking advances over its predecessors. Not only was the conception of its general structure more proper to a dramatic poem, but all kinds of refinements appeared in the execution of the form. Principal among these were the greater individualization of the characters, the subtlety in the handling of representation, the multilevel nature of the effect, certain happy solutions in the diction that resulted from all these other improvements. The play still had marked weaknesses, both in the general structure and in details; some of these were corrected in later versions, some persisted because they were integral to the total plan and their correction would have involved a complete rewriting. We do not know whether, in the writing of *Britannicus,* Racine sought to overcome specifically some of these difficulties; but we do know that he set about organizing his poem in an essentially different way.

Racine named his new play for the personage he regarded as its protagonist, its hero; in his First Preface, he replied to those who had attacked him because "j'eusse choisi un homme aussi jeune que Britannicus pour le héros d'une tragédie." Besides, he considered him not merely as the hero of a tragedy but also, through his capacity to arouse pity, as a tragic hero: "un jeune prince de dix-sept ans qui a beaucoup de cœur, beaucoup d'amour, beaucoup de franchise et beaucoup de crédulité, qualités ordinaires d'un jeune homme, m'a semblé très capable d'exciter la compassion. Je n'en veux pas davantage." (It is interesting to note that for Racine the qualities of character are sufficient to constitute a tragic hero, without reference to his circumstances or his progress through the action of the play.) From this restricted point of view, Britannicus may indeed be a tragic hero; but an analysis of his role in *Britannicus* raises many doubts about the propriety of considering him its protagonist.

Britannicus appears late in the first act, after the seizing of Junie and after Agrippine's complaints about Néron's insubordination; when he does appear, it is in order to bewail the seizure and to express to Narcisse the wish to react against Néron's persecution of him. He appears briefly in the second act, in the trap set by Néron, to express his love for Junie and to wonder at her coldness; once again, he speaks of a plot against Néron. In the third act his intervention is more considerable. First he expresses to Agrippine his hopes that an action against Néron might be organized; then he learns from Junie that Néron had heard and watched their previous interview; finally he openly challenges the authority and the activity of Néron and is placed under arrest by him. Britannicus is absent from the fourth act. In the fifth, he shares the first scene with Junie, to whom he expresses his joy at the apparent reconciliation with Néron and his confidence in the future; he refuses to heed Junie's fears. We hear of his murder by Néron later in the act.

This is not, however, the full extent of Britannicus' presence in the play. I mean by this that, even when he is absent from the stage, he is frequently spoken of by other persons; they discuss his character, allude to the effect upon him of other actions, plot against him or for him, praise or blame him. But even this kind of secondary presence is not very important, and is far from making of him the dominant personage of the drama. Indeed, his total participation in the action is that of a secondary actor;

or rather, his role is that of one who reacts more than he acts.
Most of his appearances follow upon and respond to things that
Néron has done. He himself does very little in the way of positive
action: he declares his love to Junie, speaks vaguely of a plot
against Néron that never materializes, enters just once into open
hostility with Néron. These acts hardly constitute a connected
and integrated action, and surely they do not make up the dominant action of *Britannicus*. Rather, the name-personage everywhere follows in the wake of Néron's action and depends upon
it. He is a victim, much in the same way as Andromaque and
Oreste were victims; but he has less to do than they did, is less
vital to the development of the plot, makes less of a total contribution to the dramatic structure. He is passive to Néron's
activity.

In his Second Preface to the play (1676), Racine says this of
Agrippine: "C'est elle que je me suis surtout efforcé de bien
exprimer, et ma tragédie n'est pas moins la disgrâce d'Agrippine
que la mort de Britannicus." Even if we do not interpret this statement as an admission of Britannicus' weakness as hero of a
tragedy or as tragic hero, we may see in it an awareness, on
Racine's part, of the fact that another figure in the play was at
least as important as Britannicus (the "surtout" and the "n'est
pas moins" are clear indications of this). We thus have every
right to ask whether, instead of Britannicus, Agrippine might not
be the protagonist of the play. Surely her past actions are more
fully expounded, her character is more vigorously delineated, and
her interventions in the action are more numerous.

Agrippine's recitation of past deeds, both recent and remote, is
one of her principal arguments in her attempt to retain the devotion and the subservience of Néron; her great point is that she
alone was responsible for his position as emperor, and that he
should be constant in his gratitude to her (IV, 2). She even admits certain misdeeds, suggests that she may have committed
certain crimes in order to further his career. The crimes and the

misdeeds are occasionally alluded to by others, rather in condemnation than in defense. So Britannicus:

> N'est-ce pas cette même Agrippine
> Que mon père épousa jadis pour ma ruine,
> Et qui, si je t'en crois, a de ses derniers jours,
> Trop lents pour ses desseins, précipité le cours?   (307–10)

At the same time, the account of Agrippine's past is the most expeditious device for revealing her character; combined with direct
characterization by herself and by others, it provides a complete
insight into her traits. She herself refers to the pride that marks
all members of her family:

> Il mêle avec l'orgueil qu'il a pris dans leur sang
> La fierté des Nérons qu'il puisa dans mon flanc.   (37–38)

She hints at the lack of scruple that permits her to play Britannicus against Néron for her own purposes (68–72), describes in
full her overriding ambition to dominate (88–114). This is perhaps the central mark of her character, and it is accompanied by
extreme egotism and haughtiness:

> Moi, fille, femme, sœur et mère de vos maîtres!   (156)

It means that she exacts absolute obedience from all (even from
the emperor), that she will stand for no diminution of her authority, that she expects all to act in accordance with her wishes.
Néron refers to her as "l'implacable Agrippine" (483) and confesses his inability to escape from her influence:

> Mon génie étonné tremble devant le sien.   (506)

Burrhus speaks of her "transports" (765), recognizes that she is
"toujours redoutable" (768)—alluding to the influence she still
exerts over the Romans, warns her that her "menaces" and "cris"
(831) might not be the best instruments for persuading Néron.

From all these witnesses (and others) there emerges a strong
delineation of Agrippine's character; all its most remarkable

features are manifested in the long harangue with which she tries to recapture Néron's obedience. She is, from the start, domineering and matriarchal:

> Approchez-vous, Néron, et prenez votre place. (1115)

As she retails the "crimes" that she has committed in his behalf, she tries to make him believe that it was ambition for him—and not for herself—that underlay her actions:

> Je souhaitai son lit, dans la seule pensée
> De vous laisser au trône où je serais placée. (1127–28)

Yet her mere insistence on her role (a conceited "Je" introduces most of the sentences) raises doubts about the extent of her self-sacrifice; and the last part of the *tirade,* in which she accumulates such words as "reconnaissant, respect, soupçons, infidélité, confiance, mépris, injures, affronts," reveals clearly that it is her own position, not Néron's, that preoccupies her now as it had from the beginning. Later in the scene, the conditions that she wishes to impose upon Néron would represent, if they were met, a complete submission of everybody's will to her own.

It is because, from the beginning of the action, certain things have been done that go counter to her will that Agrippine finds herself in a state of "transport"; she summarizes these in the same long speech to Néron:

> Aujourd'hui je promets Junie à votre frère;
> Ils se flattent tous deux du choix de votre mère:
> Que faites-vous? Junie, enlevée à la cour,
> Devient en une nuit l'objet de votre amour;
> Je vois de votre cœur Octavie effacée,
> Prête à sortir du lit où je l'avais placée;
> Je vois Pallas banni, votre frère arrêté;
> Vous attentez enfin jusqu'à ma liberté:
> Burrhus ose sur moi porter ses mains hardies. (1211–19)

For her (given her character) such a state of affairs is intolerable; something must be done about it; stability must be brought out of instability. This motive accounts for all Agrippine's actions in the play. The report that Junie has been seized brings her, at dawn, to Néron's door (I, 1); she accuses Burrhus of having helped him (I, 2); she invites Britannicus to meet with her and Pallas for possible retaliation (I, 3). By the time Agrippine next appears, in Act III, Pallas has been banished and Néron has announced his intention to divorce Octavie and marry Junie. Enraged, she threatens to reveal all the crimes that led to Néron's accession (III, 3), promises to foment dissatisfaction among his enemies (III, 5). She takes positive action in the fourth act when, after accusing Néron of disobedience, she states the conditions of his return to grace (IV, 2). In the last act (where she is present throughout except for the first scene) Agrippine, believing that she has won her case, urges Britannicus to join Néron and celebrates her victory to Junie. After Britannicus is killed, she reprimands and then curses Néron for his action, exculpates Burrhus and expresses to him the hope that Néron may soon again return to proper principles of conduct.

As is the case with Britannicus, Agrippine contributes to the total structure of the play reaction rather than action. Whatever she does follows upon an action by Néron, responds to it, displays disapproval or approval of it. Even so, she actually does very little; she may scold and rant, she may accuse and complain, but nothing that she says is of any consequence in the subsequent action of the play. Her plans for a plot against Néron are never realized, her attempt to persuade Néron to docility (although it apparently succeeds) is counteracted by Narcisse, whose arguments of course are much more acceptable to him. We cannot say that she performs or causes any important action. She is—if we may stretch the meaning of the term and remove from it any sense of pity—a victim; that is, she is acted upon (and always to her disadvantage) by Néron, all of whose actions ultimately result in a deterioration of her position. The summary that she gives of what has happened (IV, 2) is the summary of one who thinks that she is—and of one who is—a victim.

Britannicus and Agrippine both stand, thus, in a similar relationship to Néron: they are acted upon by him, he is responsible for the positive action to which they react. This means that it is he rather than either one of them who occupies the place of protagonist in *Britannicus*. If we look at the other personages in the play, we find that they too exist as means to the accomplishment of an action of which Néron is the agent. That action is dual: it needs to be described in terms of a change that takes place within Néron during the course of the play, and in terms of the outward manifestations of that change. The "internal" action consists in Néron's gradual arrival at the determination to act in accordance with his own will, to liberate himself from all outside domination. The "external" action consists in all those acts of his that spring from that determination.

It should not be thought that the internal "change" in Néron is sudden and unprepared, nor that it consists in a change in character. Racine had sufficient experience with serious drama, by this time, to know that character—as the truly constant and static element in poetry—does not change but is rather revealed or discovered; and he had developed sufficiently his own conceptions of the drama to recognize the usefulness of the "critical point" in dramatic materials—that point which follows upon and brings to climax a long antecedent evolution. Therefore he makes it quite clear in *Britannicus* that what now begins to happen to Néron is merely the realization of a potential that goes back many years. Burrhus traces it back to his years of tutelage over Néron:

> Enfin, Burrhus, Néron découvre son génie.
> Cette férocité que tu croyais fléchir
> De tes faibles liens est prête à s'affranchir.   (800–802)

Agrippine sees it as inherited from both lines of his ancestry:

> Il se déguise en vain: je lis sur son visage
> Des fiers Domitius l'humeur triste et sauvage.

> Il mêle avec l'orgueil qu'il a pris dans leur sang
> La fierté des Nérons qu'il puisa dans mon flanc,   (35–38)

and, continuing, she recognizes his past as merely a "disguise" for an inevitable future:

> Toujours la tyrannie a d'heureuses prémices.   (39)

All the personages pay tribute to Néron's three years as emperor (two years according to later editions), to the public and private virtues he has evinced. Albine makes the first generalizing statement:

> ... toute sa conduite
> Marque dans son devoir une âme trop instruite.
> Depuis trois ans entiers, qu'a-t-il dit, qu'a-t-il fait
> Qui ne promette à Rome un empereur parfait?
> Rome, depuis trois ans, par ses soins gouvernée,
> Au temps de ses consuls croit être retournée;
> Il la gouverne en père. Enfin Néron naissant
> A toutes les vertus d'Auguste vieillissant.   (23–30)

Burrhus (early in the play, when he is still a proponent of Néron) summarizes simply:

> Que dis-je? la vertu semble même renaître.   (203)

Junie, in very extraordinary circumstances to be sure, reflects what may have been Britannicus' judgment:

> Vous-même, vous m'avez avoué mille fois
> Que Rome le louait d'une commune voix;
> Toujours à sa vertu vous rendiez quelque hommage.
>   (725–27)

In his conversation with Burrhus about his reign, Néron speaks about "ma gloire passée" (1332) and Burrhus agrees:

> Vertueux jusqu'ici, vous pouvez toujours l'être:
> Le chemin est tracé, rien ne vous retient plus;
> Vous n'avez qu'à marcher de vertus en vertus.   (1340–42)

He expands, in an eloquent appeal, upon Néron's well-justified credit with his people.

We thus have a situation in which, over a long period, Néron has really had two characters: a "real" character, made up of all the potentials for tyranny and cruelty, which has been known only to his mother and his intimate associates; an "apparent" character, made up of the virtues that lead to good government, which has been responsible for his reputation among the Romans. For it is the apparent character that has been manifested in his action so far. In order for him to pass to the manifestation of his real character (this is what happens in *Britannicus*) we do not need any "change" in character; all we need is that Néron should reach the point where, for internal or external reasons, he wishes to change the direction of his will and act in accordance with his hidden potential. What changes first is his will to act; the change in action follows upon it. Even the change in will is not sudden or unprepared: Agrippine recounts to Albine a previous occasion on which Néron had suddenly shown a tendency to revolt against his customary attitudes. Many ambassadors had come to do honor to Néron:

> Sur son trône avec lui j'allais prendre ma place.
> J'ignore quel conseil prépara ma disgrâce.
> Quoi qu'il en soit, Néron, d'aussi loin qu'il me vit,
> Laissa sur son visage éclater son dépit.
> Mon cœur même en conçut un malheureux augure.
> L'ingrat, d'un faux respect colorant son injure,
> Se leva par avance, et courant m'embrasser,
> Il m'écarta du trône où je m'allais placer.
> Depuis ce coup fatal, le pouvoir d'Agrippine
> Vers sa chute à grands pas chaque jour s'achemine.
>
> (103–12)

But this had been, as far as we know, an isolated occurrence. For the rest, Néron had been held in check by all kinds of considerations; he himself enumerates them in response to Narcisse's query, "qui vous arrête, Seigneur?":

> Tout: Octavie, Agrippine, Burrhus,
> Sénèque, Rome entière, et trois ans de vertus. (461-62)

Of all these, the predominant factor for stability is Néron's fear
of his mother; none of the others exerts nearly so strong a hold
upon him, none will require so violent an effort to overcome it.
Néron himself gives the best estimate of this state of affairs in
a confession to Narcisse:

> Eloigné de ses yeux, j'ordonne, je menace,
> J'écoute vos conseils, j'ose les approuver;
> Je m'excite contre elle, et tâche à la braver.
> Mais (je t'expose ici mon âme toute nue)
> Sitôt que mon malheur me ramène à sa vue,
> Soit que je n'ose encor démentir le pouvoir
> De ces yeux où j'ai lu si longtemps mon devoir;
> Soit qu'à tant de bienfaits ma mémoire fidèle
> Lui soumette en secret tout ce que je tiens d'elle,
> Mais enfin mes efforts ne me servent de rien:
> Mon génie étonné tremble devant le sien.
> Et c'est pour m'affranchir de cette dépendance,
> Que je la fuis partout, que même je l'offense,
> Et que, de temps en temps, j'irrite ses ennuis
> Afin qu'elle m'évite autant que je la fuis. (496-510)

Yet this confession itself proclaims the change that has begun
to take place in Néron. He has begun to revolt inwardly, partly
because of his own pride, partly because of Narcisse's "counsels";
he has even begun to revolt outwardly, and the irritations and of-
fenses to Agrippine have, even before the beginning of the action,
alerted her to the dangers of her situation. The single event—if
indeed there be a single event—that turns Néron toward an assertion of his own will is, I believe, his falling in love with Junie.
For if the kidnapping itself may be regarded as another act of
protest against an absent Agrippine, Néron's first vision of Junie
provides him with a whole new range of emotions that will lead
him to wish for independence: love, accompanied by jealousy,

accompanied by the sadistic joy in the suffering of others that
will characterize so much of his later action:

> J'aimais jusqu'à ses pleurs que je faisais couler.   (402)

Perhaps, also, the challenge of overcoming the resistance of the
first woman who has not willingly offered her love (419–26).
Thus it is that when Junie says to him, speaking of Agrippine,

> Vos désirs sont toujours si conformes aux siens ...,   (561)

he retorts hotly:

> Ma mère a ses desseins, Madame, et j'ai les miens.   (562)

The internal transition from subservience to self-assertion has
been made; and, as through his actions Néron comes to be more
sure of himself, he will in the course of the play eliminate progressively all the inhibiting factors. One part of the plot consists
in this progress toward complete independence of his will.

There remains the manifestation of this will in action. That is a
more difficult and complicated problem, since it involves breaking
open a situation which has been closed and stable for a long time,
and that in turn means destroying a whole set of personal relationships and replacing them by others. For some of the episodes
that comprise this total action, the original motivation will suffice,
for others more special and more vigorous motives—forming a
part of the dynamics of the play—will have to be provided. It is
one of the former kind of episodes, the kidnapping of Junie, that
sets the plot in motion; Agrippine recognizes it as one of the
first signs of a change:

> L'impatient Néron cesse de se contraindre;
> Las de se faire aimer, il veut se faire craindre.   (11–12)

She also recognizes it as a step directed both against herself and
against Britannicus; for not only does Britannicus love Junie,
but Agrippine has openly supported their marriage. Furthermore,
when she ascribes to Néron "le plaisir de leur nuire" (56), she

perceives one of the aspects of his character that is now coming to the fore. Next, Néron sends Burrhus to inform Agrippine of his order—not to apologize for it; is it to this kind of act that he refers when he says "et tâche à la braver" (498)? Third, and again making a move against Britannicus and Agrippine, Néron banishes the freedman Pallas (II, 1), even before he knows that a rendezvous has been arranged among the three. His falling in love with Junie, announced to Narcisse in II, 2, follows upon the kidnapping and in turn furnishes the motive for subsequent actions, first of which is his permission for a meeting of Junie and Britannicus (519) that is merely a trap for Britannicus, second of which is his announcement to Junie that he means to marry her after divorcing Octavie (II, 3). For both of these, more "additional motivation" is provided by the arguments of Narcisse in II, 2. We may consider Néron's next action, the cruel order to Junie to dismiss Britannicus while he watches, as having the same bases.

It is in connection with this last act that Néron once again reveals one of the kinds of feeling that underlie his plans:

> Mais je mettrai ma joie à le désespérer.
> Je me fais de sa peine une image charmante,
> Et je l'ai vu douter du cœur de son amante. (750–52)

It recurs in his order to Narcisse, "va, cours le tourmenter" (754). In a sense, it is a special manifestation of his urge to display his "real" character, irrespective of his liberation from others, and especially if the manifestation will contrast with the virtue that has so long constrained him. His love for Junie, justified to Burrhus in the words "Il faut que j'aime enfin" (778), may be in the same category, for faithfulness to Octavie (presumably without love) would be a kind of virtue. On the other hand, his rejection of Burrhus' advice (III, 1) belongs to his earlier springs of action: Burrhus, along with Agrippine who had made him Néron's tutor (149), now stands among those who would impede his march toward independence. The actions that follow are more

important, constituting major steps in this same march: after
having been taunted by Britannicus for the course he has chosen
to follow ("Ainsi Néron commence à ne se plus forcer" [1053]),
Néron puts Junie under guard, orders the arrest of Britannicus
and then the arrest of Agrippine. These actions come from his
sense of the open opposition on the part of his two principal
opponents.

Sometime before his interview with Agrippine (IV, 2), Néron
has decided upon the death of Britannicus, although the decision
is not revealed until later. His last important "action" will thus
consist not in making that decision but in determining whether
to stick by it or to abandon it; this is the subject of Act IV. There
are three interviews, the first two of which are calculated to lead
Néron to reverse his decision, the third to remain firm. In the
first, Agrippine speaks only in general terms; she does not know
that Britannicus is to die, and the case she presents applies to the
whole of the situation since the beginning of the play. The demands that she finally makes (1288–94) encompass all aspects of
that situation. However, since her principal argument rests on
what she has done for Néron and the extent to which he is indebted to her—the very sentiment against which he most rebels—
it must necessarily fail. Néron's final speech of reconciliation
(1295–1304) is sheer hypocrisy, and Agrippine (who just a few
minutes before had spoken of his "feintes caresses" [1272])
should recognize it as such. But her wish to triumph is so great
that it leads her to believe in her victory. (The audience knows
better, seeing the whole of Néron's thought and being put on its
guard by the excessive character of his concessions.) The second
interview, with Burrhus, seems to shake Néron and ends with an
ambiguous statement of his intentions. Burrhus, taken in at the
beginning, is quickly disabused by Néron:

> J'embrasse mon rival, mais c'est pour l'étouffer.   (1314)

He is thus able to present a direct argument against a precise
project, and he does so by evoking the image of Néron's past

virtue and glory and of the present love of his people for him.
He indicates, moreover, the kind of total change in the direction
of Néron's life that is involved in this decision:

> C'est à vous à choisir, vous êtes encor maître.
> Vertueux jusqu'ici, vous pouvez toujours l'être:
> Le chemin est tracé, rien ne vous retient plus;
> Vous n'avez qu'à marcher de vertus en vertus.
> Mais si de vos flatteurs vous suivez la maxime,
> Il vous faudra, Seigneur, courir de crime en crime,
> Soutenir vos rigueurs par d'autres cruautés,
> Et laver dans le sang vos bras ensanglantés. (1339-46)

If Burrhus is a proper judge, Néron seems to weaken, and his
last words in the scene, "Dans mon appartement qu'il m'attende
avec vous" (1390), might possibly indicate that he has capitulated
and that he will be reconciled with Britannicus; but they might
also mean the summons to the assassination.

The beginning of scene 4 (the third interview, with Narcisse)
tends to confirm the first hypothesis: Néron announces to Narcisse, "on nous réconcilie" (1400). Narcisse is of course the worst
of the flatterers to whom Burrhus had referred, and his whole
role in the action has been to push Néron toward rebellion, vice,
and the manifestation of his "real" character—for his own ends
and not for Néron's (see 757-60). In this way he provides the
additional or fresh motivation that is needed to supplement
Néron's initial impulse toward the inward change and its outward expression. In the present, critical scene Narcisse proves
himself to be a better rhetorician than Burrhus; for instead of
appealing to the good in Néron, he appeals to the evil. His argument is trinitarian—and one: if Néron changes his mind about
Britannicus' death, he will show that he is still subservient to
Agrippine, to the people of Rome, and to Burrhus. The argument cannot fail, especially since he dramatizes each part of it
with a statement that expresses the "enemy" point of view—the
indirect quotation of Agrippine's gloating over her victory, the

direct quotation from the people of Rome (1418–22, 1468–78); the latter also includes Burrhus. If, otherwise, he should remain with his decision, Néron would achieve definitively what he has sought throughout his recent acts—his liberty:

> Vous seriez libre alors, Seigneur; et devant vous
> Ces maîtres orgueilleux fléchiraient comme nous. (1465–66)

Néron is persuaded; his last words, this time, indicate to the wary that he has chosen to ally himself with Narcisse rather than with Burrhus:

> Viens, Narcisse. Allons voir ce que nous devons faire.
> (1480)

Consequently, no further decision, no further "action" is required from Néron to bring the plot to its denouement. The coming of Britannicus to the rendezvous occurs because Néron has not withdrawn his invitation; and when Britannicus says that Néron

> Dans son appartement m'attend pour m'embrasser, (1482)

we know (harking back to line 1314) in what the embrace will consist. After three scenes in which the rendezvous is prepared and the persons assembled to hear its outcome (V, 1–3), the murder is reported in V, 4 and 5, and we know that Néron's original plans have been faithfully carried out by Narcisse. Any doubts raised by the innocence of Britannicus or the self-confidence of Agrippine—doubts opposed by Junie's instinctive fears—are now dispelled. After the murder, we need list only three minor episodes involving Néron; they form a kind of epilogue to his action. First is his reaction to the murder itself, as recounted by Burrhus (1637–40) and then judged by him in words that indicate that the "inward" change has now been completely effected:

> Néron l'a vu mourir sans changer de couleur.
> Ses yeux indifférents ont déjà la constance
> D'un tyran dans le crime endurci dès l'enfance. (1710–12)

(We might note, in passing, that Burrhus here reaffirms his judgment that the change is merely a manifestation of traits that he has recognized in Néron since childhood.) Second is Néron's cynical denial of any responsibility for the assassination (V, 7). Last is the kind of madness brought on by his witnessing of Junie's entrance into the temple of the Vestals; this is the one part of his plan that has not succeeded, and whether it be love or the inability to stand defeat, he is driven to somber despair.

Néron thus does a great number of things in the course of *Britannicus*. Within his own mind or soul, he makes the transition from the state of one who has been dependent upon the direction and the advice of others—and is hence virtuous—to the state of one who follows only his own instincts—and is hence vicious. (We must regard Narcisse and the "flatterers" merely as persons who encourage him to self-assertion.) The transition is accompanied by many external actions, ranging from the kidnapping of Junie, to the banishment of Pallas, to the arrest of Britannicus and then Agrippine, to the murder of Britannicus. Some of these, especially the last, pass through various stages of doubt, hesitation, indecision before the final decision is made; but they are always decided in accordance with the mounting progression toward the ultimate crime—representing the ultimate liberation. What is more, the progression constitutes a real action: beginning from certain necessities formulated in the character of Néron, in a set of circumstances that are incompatible with that character, it moves from an initial act that would tend to change those circumstances, through subsequent acts that spring from new probabilities in the form of events or arguments, to a denouement that consists in the realization of all the antecedent probabilities. This is a true poetic action, since it has within itself all the necessary factors for its initial impulsion and for the immediate and the remote consequences of that impulsion—for its beginning, its middle, and its end. Stated another way, it is an action that has its own, completely independent system of cause-and-effect relationships.

Of this action Néron is the protagonist. If he were the pro- tagonist only of what I have called the "inward" action, the es- sential change in an attitude or an emotional stance, he might well serve as the hero of a modern novel—and that without the help of other personages except in a very secondary way. What I mean to say is that the change is sufficiently great, its bases go deeply enough into his essential character, it comes about through a large enough number of steps and stages so that in itself it might be subjected to the kind of careful study that has been the stuff of so many novels in our century. But such a study would be un- dramatic—not for the conventional stage—and Racine had both enough sense and enough experience of the theater to know that "inward" change had to be transmuted into "outward" action, and it was for this reason that he invented the kind of action for Néron that I have just traced. The existence of the substratum of "inward" change, however, made Néron's action ideal for a "Racinian" play. The inward action, although it could not itself be directly represented on the stage, could be externalized in speeches and gestures; it could be described, discussed, con- demned by others; it could form the topic of debate between the protagonist and other personages. Besides, since the decisions themselves were more important than their accomplishment, the actual events need not happen before the eyes of the spectator. They could happen elsewhere and be described by one of the actors—the perfect situation for a Racinian drama.

The making of the "outward" action—and the manifestation of the "inward" one in a dramatic way—necessitated the creation by Racine of a number of personages in addition to the protago- nist. In *Britannicus* these fall into a few clearly defined groups, each having a specific function with respect to the protagonist. If the change was to involve a change from something, it was away from an attitude of subservience to authority; some of the persons in the play are therefore those to whom Néron had been subservient. Most important of these is Agrippine; she exists as a victim in so far as the throwing-off of her authority by Néron means an end not only to her influence but also to her position in Rome, to her liberty, and to her political career. Pallas and Burrhus are in the same category, Pallas who does not appear but against whom one of the acts of liberation is committed, Burrhus who is rejected in favor of Narcisse when the counsels of virtue are replaced by those of vice. In a way, Octavie also belongs here, although her victimizing is not completed within the play; she too represents a tie with the past that will have to be broken if the new future is to be achieved. The change is also to something, and it is to a line of conduct in which liberty and "self-determination" are expressed through acts of violence against innocent persons. Britannicus and Junie are the two personages in this class; but they are victims of different kinds. For although he is a victim in his own right, as one against whom Néron can direct his basic cruelty and bloodthirstiness, Britannicus is also a kind of secondary victim, one through whom Néron can strike at Agrippine. Junie's role is more complex. Her original kidnapping represents an attack upon Britannicus and Agrippine; but when Néron falls in love with her, her status changes. She may be used to display defiance of Agrippine and Britannicus, to flout Britannicus directly, to serve as an instrument against Octavie, finally to become a victim herself by being forced into an unwanted marriage. The last two actions are prevented by her flight to the temple; but she remains one of Néron's main victims through the death of Britannicus.

Only two personages remain who are not among Néron's victims, Narcisse and Albine. Albine, as confidante to Agrippine, really has no part in the action, largely serving only to provide Agrippine with the occasion to express her feelings. But Narcisse has two important functions: as counselor-flatterer to Néron, he must prevent Néron from weakening in his purpose to free himself, he must provide arguments against those (especially Burrhus) who would keep Néron virtuous. And as false friend to Britannicus, Narcisse must both lead him into an erroneous sense of security (this is made easier by Britannicus' trusting and naïve

nature) and he must be an instrument of the action (as when he
hurries off to tell Néron that Britannicus and Junie have met, at
the end of III, 6). He thus contributes to both parts of Néron's
action.

In this way, the particular nature of Néron's role as protagonist, the specific kind of double action in which he is engaged,
is responsible for the presence and the activity of each of the
other personages. If we ask how he is related to all of them (and
they to him), we find that it is neither as a "central" personage
around whom the others are clustered (as was Alexandre), nor
as a "pivotal" personage standing at the end of a chain of relationships (as was Andromaque), but rather as a true protagonist
whose action—positive and negative, inward and outward—could
not be what it is without them. That is, they are integrated into
the action in such a way that it becomes a whole action in which
each plays a part; and Néron is distinguished from the others as
the center of an action which he very largely accomplishes
through his own volition. Racine has thus succeeded, for the first
time, in building a truly dramatic action around a real protagonist.

There is, however, one difficulty, one failure, and it is a major
one: Néron is not a tragic hero and the action he accomplishes
is not a tragic action. At no time can it be presumed that his
character is such as to elicit our sympathy, let alone our pity. He
has no admirable virtues, no superiority of spirit, no nobility of
soul. Rather, he is characterized by the contraries of all these,
and our impulse at all times is to condemn rather than to approve
what he is. We are interested, we may even be fascinated, but we
are not compassionate. Nor is his situation such, at any point in
the play, as to merit pity: there is no misfortune at the beginning,
and such deterioration in his circumstances as occurs at the end
(in the sequestration of Junie) is amply merited. There is even a
sense in which one might regard his affairs as moving from bad
to good—bad at the beginning, since he lives under the authority
and according to the will of others; good at the end, since his

own will is now dominant. He would thus be an essentially bad man who moves from an unsatisfactory state, as far as he is concerned, to a satisfactory state; and for this kind of movement there can be no pity. Racine thus produced a serious drama with many poetic excellences; but he did not write a tragedy.

Of this he must have been quite conscious, and we can see a result of his awareness in his attempt to give prominence to the affairs of Britannicus and Junie and in his choice of *Britannicus* as the title. Racine wished to write a tragedy; on this point the statements in his prefaces are unequivocal. But according to those same prefaces, it is clear that he saw in Néron anything but a tragic hero. If he wished to create the tragic emotion, he must thus attach it to some other personage, and the one who was most capable of arousing it was undoubtedly Britannicus. The one, that is, among the participants in this particular action: for Racine did not change his fundamental conception of the play in order to emphasize the tragic note. If he had, we should have before us another play. Rather, he singled out, from among the "victims" of Néron, the young Britannicus and sought to build a tragic action around his loss of Junie, his imprisonment by Néron, the end of his political ambitions, and his death. This action involved, in addition to the tragic fate of Junie, the interventions of Agrippine and Narcisse, and, in a more remote way, the banishment of Pallas. Such an action could presumably have been made the central action of a play and Britannicus could have become its hero. But that does not happen in *Britannicus*. Instead, Néron remains the hero, the action is his, and Britannicus is reduced to the status of a secondary personage. There is thus a kind of fundamental dichotomy in the play: Néron is the hero and performs the central action, but such tragic effect as there is—and it is secondary—belongs to a secondary personage.

In addition to the progress in the establishment of the protagonist and the definition of the line of action, we might note in *Britannicus* the success with which Racine organizes the presentation of his materials. Whereas in *Andromaque* we might feel that somehow the emphasis had, at the beginning, been put upon the wrong persons and events, making it impossible ever to transfer it properly to Andromaque herself, in *Britannicus* there is from the start an impression of the rightness of the order. Act I raises the central question with respect to Néron, whether he will continue to be virtuous or whether the abduction of Junie marks a turn toward vice, and presents the reactions of the two main victims, Agrippine and Britannicus, to the new state of affairs. Néron does not appear; but he is present through most of Act II, where he both states clearly what his intentions are and begins to carry them out. In Act III, after the others have responded to Néron's announcement that he will marry Junie, he pushes forward his general plan by ordering the arrests of all three major victims. One of these, Agrippine, attempts in Act IV to influence the course of his action; but neither she nor Burrhus is successful, and Néron yields to Narcisse's urgings to kill Britannicus. This is accomplished in Act V, in spite of some hopes that it might not be, and the consequences for all three remaining personages —Agrippine, Néron, and Junie—are shown. This is a perfectly distinct and perspicuous order. Once the spectator has discovered that it is the "line of Néron" rather than the "line of Britannicus" that he must follow (and herein resides the one flaw), he has no difficulty in perceiving the clear development of that line from its simple beginning to its inevitable ending.

The one flaw consists in the kind of dichotomy that I have noted, the division of interest between a tragic personage who is not the hero and a protagonist who is not tragic. The result is strongly sensible in the general effect produced by *Britannicus*. I think that I do not need to trace this effect in detail, for the overpowering impression produced by Agrippine and Néron dominates our emotions, and our sympathies for Britannicus and Junie are of lesser magnitude. Even our hatred for Narcisse exceeds our admiration for Burrhus. In a word, pity and its accompanying passions are made subordinate to the whole range of passions from contempt, to blame, to condemnation, to hatred. Our feelings will be mixed, and the "wrong" ones—in terms of any tragic effect—will predominate. I do not mean to say that this is necessarily bad art: we shall find that in every play we discuss there will be a mixture of emotions, since every play will combine a number of personages and a variety of actions, each one accompanied by its own proper emotion. I mean merely that we resist the admission that Britannicus is not the tragic hero and that the play is not a tragedy; we resist accepting the fact that we have before us a serious drama of another—and unnamed—kind whose proper emotional effect is not classifiable as tragic. But it is a very real and a very potent effect.

V

Bérénice

Bérénice was performed first a little less than a year after *Britannicus,* in November, 1670, and it was published early in 1671. Once again Racine drew his subject from Roman history, and at the beginning of his Preface he cited the source from Suetonius: "Titus reginam Berenicen, cui etiam nuptias pollicitus ferebatur, statim ab urbe dimisit invitus invitam."

He was, indeed, very proud of the fact that he had been able to derive a whole tragedy from so brief a statement, and he considered that (in the evolution of his art) the construction of so simple an action was a notable achievement. In the same Preface he says of his new subject: "... ce qui m'en plut davantage, c'est que je le trouvai extrêmement simple. Il y avait longtemps que je voulais essayer si je pourrais faire une tragédie avec cette simplicité d'action qui a été si fort du goût des anciens. Car c'est un des premiers préceptes qu'ils nous ont laissés." The statement is useful not only with respect to *Bérénice* but also as a revelation of the directions in which Racine had been moving in his earlier plays. We have, in fact, seen him reduce the number of events and episodes that went into the structure of his plots, just as he strove for a smaller number of personages and for greater concentration upon his protagonist. All these developments were part of a single purpose: to achieve the more tightly organized and the more highly unified structure, in order to achieve the greater and the clearer effect. In *Britannicus,* however, there were still a goodly number of events, both internal and external, and Racine sought in the following play a formula that would permit him to

130

diminish that number and, by so doing, to arrive at greater simplicity of action.

In that action as he finds it in Suetonius, Titus is the active subject and Bérénice is the passive object; and I think that that is an accurate representation of the plot as Racine constructs it in *Bérénice*. In spite of the title, Titus is the protagonist; the simple action that he performs is to send Bérénice away: "dimisit." Racine's problem was to expand upon this simple subject, to develop it to the point where it would have sufficient magnitude to create the effect that he sought. I suppose that one of the men-of-the-theater of today would solve the problem with dispatch. The curtain would go up on Titus and Bérénice; Titus would say "Bérénice, go away" (or even "Bérénice, go home"); Bérénice would leave and the curtain would fall. Cute as this might be supposed to be, the effect—if any—would be trivial; at any rate, it would in no way correspond to the effect that Racine was seeking and that he describes in the same Preface: "... il suffit que l'action en soit grande, que les acteurs en soient héroïques, que les passions y soient excitées, et que tout s'y ressente de cette tristesse majestueuse qui fait tout le plaisir de la tragédie."

The answer to the "tristesse majestueuse" was obviously to associate with the various personages the right kind of emotions through providing them with the right characters and actions. These would be of the "right kind" only under two conditions: if the characters and actions (and their interrelationship) were in themselves conducive to sadness and pity, and if they were developed with sufficient extension to implant, to nurture, and to consummate those emotions. In the case of *Bérénice*, simplicity within magnitude—or magnitude upon a simple substructure—became a very special kind of task. It needed to be completed and achieved with the greatest efficacy in the protagonist himself, in the treatment of the action that he had to do, and to this Racine gave his most careful thought. His solution was manifold, but in its essence very simple: the separation of Titus and Bérénice must be delayed as long as possible, and both he and she must be given alternative lines of conduct once the separation had been determined. That is, rather than saying immediately to Bérénice, "Rome demands that I abandon you and that you leave," Titus must say this only after a long struggle and various subterfuges to avoid saying it. And after he has said it, both he and Bérénice (and in a secondary way Antiochus) must consider various ways of acting before reconciling themselves to an inevitable situation.

Racine invented, for Titus, a number of successive steps that led to the ultimate announcement. First was of course the decision itself, the choice between love for Bérénice and faithfulness to the traditions of Rome. Racine chooses, for the beginning of his action, a time when Titus has already been in love with Bérénice for a period of five years and when he has been emperor for only eight days. During those five years his love was completely legitimate, violating no Roman law, and Titus might (if he failed to consider his political future) well look forward to the prospect of marrying Bérénice. For the last eight days, however, since the death of Vespasien and the proclamation of Titus as emperor, that marriage is no longer possible; Rome will not tolerate as wife to the emperor either a foreigner or a queen, and Bérénice is both. Now within those eight days, while presumably he was mourning his father, Titus has made the decision: he will order Bérénice to leave. The time of his decision is made clear in the long discussion with Paulin (II, 2):

> Mais à peine le ciel eut rappelé mon père,
> Dès que ma triste main eut fermé sa paupière,
> De mon aimable erreur je fus désabusé:
> Je sentis le fardeau qui m'était imposé;
> Je connus que bientôt, loin d'être à ce que j'aime,
> Il fallait, cher Paulin, renoncer à moi-même;
> Et que le choix des dieux, contraire à mes amours,
> Livrait à l'univers le reste de mes jours.   (459–66)

And again:

> Vingt fois, depuis huit jours,
> J'ai voulu devant elle en ouvrir le discours.   (473–74)

The decision has therefore been made before the opening of the play; Titus' problem, now, is to tell Bérénice.

However, as the play opens everybody assumes that Titus has decided in favor of Bérénice and that they will soon be married. So Arsace:

> Quoi! déjà de Titus épouse en espérance ... (15)

So Antiochus:

> Dois-je croire qu'au rang où Titus la destine
> Elle m'écoute mieux que dans la Palestine?
> Il l'épouse. (27–29)

And Arsace again:

> Peut-être avant la nuit l'heureuse Bérénice
> Change le nom de reine au nom d'impératrice. (59–60)

Most important of all, Bérénice has persuaded herself that her hopes are about to be realized:

> ... si de ses amis j'en dois croire la voix,
> Si j'en crois ses serments redoublés mille fois,
> Il va sur tant d'états couronner Bérénice,
> Pour joindre à plus de noms le nom d'impératrice.
> Il m'en viendra lui-même assurer en ce lieu. (173–77)

Only Phénice, at the end of Act I, interjects a note of caution by insisting upon the traditional attitude of the Romans; but she is not believed.

But why this delay in revealing a decision that has been made some time previously? This is, I believe, the first of Racine's inventions for complicating his simple plot. The decision is not a part of the action, but precedes it. By starting from the supposition that the opposite choice has been made, Racine makes possible a number of episodes that are necessary to his conception of the total structure. If Antiochus believes that Bérénice is about to become the empress, he may confess to her his love before a final leave-taking (I, 4). His confession will have important consequences: when Titus hints at her disgrace (II, 4), Bérénice is

able to withhold belief by supposing that Titus is jealous of
Antiochus; and when Antiochus carries Titus' cruel message to
her, she is able to dismiss it as an effect of his love and hence to
disbelieve it (III, 3). Furthermore, an initial assumption by
Bérénice that Titus is going to marry her will make even more
difficult his task of telling her that he is not, and it accounts in
part at least for his first failure (II, 4). Thus by starting with a
situation in which Titus' choice is not yet known, Racine complicates in a very useful way the state of feeling of each of the
personages and he renders probable a number of future episodes.

Racine's second invention for enriching his simple plot was
the integration, into Titus' character, of a fundamental inability
to face Bérénice and to announce his decision to her. We have
already seen this weakness confessed by Titus himself in one of
the passages quoted, which insists upon his failure as it continues:

> Mais par où commencer? Vingt fois, depuis huit jours,
> J'ai voulu devant elle en ouvrir le discours;
> Et dès le premier mot ma langue embarrassée
> Dans ma bouche vingt fois a demeuré glacée.   (473–76)

Titus calls this weakness "inconstancy," as he opposes it to his
sense of duty and patriotism that would constitute "constancy":

> Enfin j'ai ce matin rappelé ma constance.   (483)

> ... plus j'y pense,
> Plus je sens chanceler ma cruelle constance.   (547–48)

It would perhaps be more accurate, however, to regard it as one
peculiarity of his love, as a kind of excessive tenderness that will
not permit him to witness the suffering of his beloved:

> D'un amant interdit soulagez le tourment:
> Epargnez à mon cœur cet éclaircissement.
> . . . .
> Soyez le seul témoin de ses pleurs et des miens;
> Portez-lui mes adieux, et recevez les siens.

Fuyons tous deux, fuyons un spectacle funeste
Qui de notre constance accablerait le reste.   (741-48)

Yet in this appeal to Antiochus, as in his whole inability to face
Bérénice, there is undoubtedly an element of cowardice that must
be reckoned as a part of his character, and that he sees as a
"faiblesse" of his heart:

Aidez-moi, s'il se peut, à vaincre sa faiblesse,
A retenir des pleurs qui m'échappent sans cesse.   (1055-56)

This may be taken as an excellent example of how Racine
progressed in his understanding of the relationship of character
to action and in his capacity to endow his personages with the
needed traits. There was, in his source, no indication that Titus
possessed such a weakness as excessive tenderness or cowardice.
But in order to expand his simple plot to the right proportions,
he must multiply the episodes that would delay the announcement to Bérénice; and among these there must be a failure by
Titus in a first attempt, the delegation of the responsibility to
another, the internal struggle preceding the final success. Lest
such episodes be wooden and unconvincing, they must be given
a basis in Titus' character, and Racine therefore invented a Titus
who was all his own and who fitted his specific purposes in the
play. The traditional Titus disappears, an original man emerges,
the "invitus" of Suetonius is expanded into a whole character.
We shall find another such expansion, perhaps even more remarkable, in the character of Agamemnon as he created it for
Iphigénie.

Racine's third device for the enrichment of his plot was the
provision of a personage to whom the difficult task of telling
Bérénice might be delegated. Here, again, an unimaginative solution might have been found: Titus might have been made to send
Paulin, or Rutile, or even Phénice, to deliver his message. But
such a solution would fall far short of the aims that Racine had
in mind for the episode; it would provide very little expansion,
it would add nothing to the total emotional effect. It might solve

Titus' problem, but it would not solve Racine's. Therefore the poet sought and found an extremely difficult expedient: he entrusted the charge to another lover of Bérénice, hence to a rival of Titus but to one whom Titus did not recognize as such. In a word, he invented the personage, the character, the past history, and the role of Antiochus. Antiochus, of course, became useful to Racine in other ways, but his main function was to serve as Titus' spokesman; Racine created him largely as an instrument to this end, and gave great care to his development.

Antiochus is the first person to appear on the stage. In two brief lines—

> Vous, cet Antiochus, son amant autrefois?
> Vous, que l'Orient compte entre ses plus grands rois?—
>
> (13-14)

Arsace states the two essential phases of his role, as lover of Bérénice and as potential rival of Titus. The monologue that constitutes I, 2, recounts in summary his relationships with Bérénice, states the extent of his love, and tells what he expects to do in the forthcoming meeting:

> Hélas! je ne viens que vous dire
> Qu'après m'être longtemps flatté que mon rival
> Trouverait à ses vœux quelque obstacle fatal,
> Aujourd'hui qu'il peut tout, que votre hymen s'avance,
> Exemple infortuné d'une longue constance,
> Après cinq ans d'amour et d'espoir superflus,
> Je pars, fidèle encor quand je n'espère plus.   (40-46)

Arsace assures Antiochus, in I, 3, that everything is ready for the departure and, in I, 4, Antiochus tells him that he means to leave if Bérénice confirms the approaching marriage; but he does not as yet tell him why. Thus the long interview with Bérénice that occupies the fourth scene has been completely prepared (at the same time as other elements of the exposition have been included). In that interview, Antiochus does exactly what he had expected to do (in spite of some hesitation); but he also accomplishes other things important for the future evolution of the plot. He establishes his capacity to make a difficult statement under difficult circumstances—a capacity lacking in Titus—as he shows how, as a result of old friendship, he is able to talk to Bérénice. He states that he is about to depart and willing to die, both of which possibilities will furnish later arguments. And he gives to Bérénice the chance to declare her love for Titus and her expectation of their marriage.

When, therefore, Titus suffers his first failure, he naturally thinks of Antiochus as an intermediary. They are old friends; he has long been indebted to Antiochus for signal service as a military ally (105–14, 687–92); he knows that Antiochus is an old friend of Bérénice:

> Je sais que Bérénice, à vos soins redevable,
> Croit posséder en vous un ami véritable.
> Elle ne voit dans Rome et n'écoute que vous;
> Vous ne faites qu'un cœur et qu'une âme avec nous.
>
> (695–98)

What he does not know is that Antiochus is his rival, and this he must obviously not know until the very end of the action. Hence he is able to charge Antiochus with his message, and to reward him in advance by granting him additional territories (763–67); furthermore, to propose that Antiochus depart with Bérénice —a solution that Antiochus would eagerly wish for himself. The result of these proposals is first to place Antiochus in a state of violent emotional conflict; not only does his love for Bérénice reinforce his sense of duty to Titus, but his anticipation of the effect upon Bérénice presents itself as a deterrent. He would and he would not. Second, when Antiochus has delivered his message and received, for his pains, only incredulity on the part of Bérénice and an order never to appear before her again, he returns to his original resolve to leave; but to it is added a new hopelessness and a new concern for Bérénice's fate.

Now it is perfectly clear that Racine develops the role of

Antiochus far beyond what he needed merely to provide another
delay in Titus' declaration to Bérénice. It must have been obvious
to him very soon that, in this role, he might find possibilities for
certain emotional effects that he could not otherwise introduce,
for a kind of magnification in its own right. The situation was
ideal: a rival for Titus and another lover for Bérénice, with the
character and the stature that qualified him for both functions
and with a complex historical relationship to hero and heroine,
could support (and stimulate) a whole range of emotions that
might otherwise not be introduced into the tragedy. In addition
to his utility for the action, he could contribute his own feelings
of love, admiration, despair, faithfulness, even jealousy, and he
could make possible a complication of Bérénice's feelings. All
these might add to the "tristesse majestueuse" that Racine was
seeking, and so he extended the participation of Antiochus beyond the major episode and brought him into the denouement.
I shall have occasion to ask whether such an extension of the
role is in the long run advantageous for the total emotional effect
of *Bérénice*.

Perhaps we may think of the attribution of certain peculiar
traits to Bérénice as a fourth device for the expansion of Racine's
simple action. Roughly stated, we may say that just as it must be
difficult for Titus to make the announcement, it must be difficult
for Bérénice to believe it. Again a simpler solution would have
been possible: Titus might have delivered or sent his message,
Bérénice might have accepted her fate and left Rome. The effect
would have been inconsiderable—or at least far less considerable
than the one Racine achieved. He chose rather to introduce a
kind of parallelism in his two main characters, to make Bérénice
as incredulous as Titus was hesitant. This he did by assigning
to her certain special traits of character, rendering possible complex and subtle reactions. Bérénice remembers, in her past, certain changes and vicissitudes, which she speaks of as "mes tra-
verses ... mes fortunes diverses" (143–44). The remembrance leads

her to be wary of any semblance of permanent good fortune (she says, "le ciel *semble* me présager / Un honneur" [145–46]) and to be extremely sensitive to any signs of misfortune. Thus she tells Antiochus of her "alarmes" and her "douleur" during the past week when, as he mourned his father, Titus had failed to reaffirm his love for her (151–62). But by a kind of countermovement, and because she needs to boost her own confidence, she will overstate the case in her favor—even as she interjects all kinds of cautious formulas:

> Et même en ce moment, *sans qu'il m'en ait parlé,*
> Il est dans le sénat, par son ordre assemblé.
>
> . . . .
>
> Et, *si de ses amis j'en dois croire la voix,*
> *Si j'en crois ses serments redoublés mille fois,*
> Il va sur tant d'états couronner Bérénice,
>
> . . . .
>
> Il m'en viendra lui-même assurer en ce lieu.   (169–77)

She gives an excellent example of this tendency in the speech (I, 5) in which, replying to Phénice's expression of some doubt about the marriage, she obviously tries to talk herself into belief. Instead of facing the facts alleged by Phénice, she develops a dubious argument which consists merely in a long enumeration of the signs of Rome's respect and affection for Titus. This is rhetoric of self-persuasion, and her final lines can serve only to blind herself.

These traits account not only for Bérénice's response to the announcements (Titus' hints and Antiochus' clear statement), but in a way they contribute to Titus' failure. Bérénice takes the initiative in their meeting (II, 4). Still assuming, with aggressive confidence, that she will be empress, she declares her love and asks for a similar declaration from Titus; she places love before greatness; and she speaks of the suffering of uncertainty:

> Qu'un mot va rassurer mes timides esprits!   (581)

Then, concluding her first speech, she speaks words that have for the audience only a sharp dramatic irony, but that must be heartbreaking to Titus as he recalls what he has just said to Paulin:

> Mais parliez-vous de moi quand je vous ai surpris?
> Dans vos secrets discours étais-je intéressée,
> Seigneur? Étais-je au moins présente à la pensée? (582–84)

Titus is already disarmed; he is completely incapacitated when Bérénice, before he has told his story, anticipates what the effect upon her will be. The anticipation springs from her fears and her uncertainties:

> Et moi (ce souvenir me fait frémir encore),
> On voulait m'arracher de tout ce que j'adore;
> Moi, dont vous connaissez le trouble et le tourment
> Quand vous ne me quittez que pour quelque moment;
> Moi, qui mourrais le jour qu'on voudrait m'interdire
> De vous ...   (611–16)

Instead of bringing from Titus a promise of marriage, as Bérénice had hoped, her words merely reduce him to silence. After the conversation, from which she infers correctly that there are doubts about her marriage, she persuades herself that Titus' motive was jealousy and that the situation may still be repaired. Again, her aptitude for self-deception permits her to look forward to a clarification by Titus.

The same attitudes appear before and after Antiochus has spoken for Titus. At the mere intimation that Antiochus might have bad news for her, Bérénice confesses her fears:

> Prince, c'est trop cacher mon trouble à votre vue.
> Vous voyez devant vous une reine éperdue,
>
> . . . .
>
> Éclaircissez le trouble où vous voyez mon âme. (871–79)

This of course adds to Antiochus' hesitation, and it is only when Bérénice threatens him with her hatred that he delivers his mes-

sage. After he does so, and although she knows that he has
spoken the truth, she seeks an excuse and an explanation; she
finds it in Antiochus' love for her, and accuses him of deceit:

> Ce piège n'est tendu que pour nous désunir.   (910)

> Vous le souhaitez trop pour me persuader.
> Non, je ne vous crois point. Mais, quoi qu'il en puisse être,
> Pour jamais à mes yeux gardez-vous de paraître.   (914-16)

But to Phénice she reveals her real reaction, and her last lines in
the scene express all her weakness and all her knowledge of it:

> Ne m'abandonne pas dans l'état où je suis.
> Hélas! pour me tromper je fais ce que je puis.   (917-18)

Through an extremely elaborate preparation of character and
circumstances, Racine thus brings about a suitable complication
of the "simple" business of telling and believing. All three of the
personages involved (Antiochus, Titus, and Bérénice) are so
created as to make possible the hesitations, the fears, the disbe-
liefs, the flight from responsibility, that are necessary to prolong
the process of announcing the separation; and the long history
of the relationships among them is invented in order to add
probability to necessity.

There is, however, a final device conceived by Racine for the
enrichment of his simple plot. It belongs, in a way, to the other
side of the opposition. For in spite of his weakness and his hesitation, Titus does make a choice, he does stick by it firmly, and he
does ultimately communicate it to Bérénice. If he does so, it is
not merely because of the element of patriotism in his character,
because he is a Roman; it is also because the right "Roman" arguments and probabilities are provided for him at every important
juncture. We may say that this function is divided among three
instruments: first, Titus' own sense of the Roman tradition and
his attachment to' its history; second, the person of Paulin; and
third, the "person" of the Roman people as it makes itself felt
directly or through the senate. Titus is introduced to us at a time

when he has just completed a period of mourning for his father
(55–56) in favor of which he has put his love aside (153–54). We
learn that when he first appeared before Bérénice, five years before,
it had been as a representative of Rome (195–96); and throughout those five years his love had had to combat his patriotism:

> Rome, Vespasien, traversaient vos soupirs.   (246)

The combat became acute upon the death of Vespasien; but now
Titus has resolved it in favor of Rome:

> Je connus que bientôt, loin d'être à ce que j'aime,
> Il fallait, cher Paulin, renoncer à moi-même;
> Et que le choix des dieux, contraire à mes amours,
> Livrait à l'univers le reste de mes jours.
> Rome observe aujourd'hui ma conduite nouvelle.
> Quelle honte pour moi, quel présage pour elle,
> Si dès le premier pas, renversant tous ses droits,
> Je fondais mon bonheur sur le débris des lois!   (463–70)

Even Bérénice identifies Titus' "gloire" with Rome:

> Mais vos pleurs ont assez honoré sa mémoire:
> Vous devez d'autres soins à Rome, à votre gloire.   (603–4)

But her statement is full of ironic implications, since she refuses
to recognize that the "autres soins" demand Titus' desertion of
herself. Titus, driven to silence, can say only "Rome ... l'Empire ..." (623).

There are several lengthy statements in which Titus emphasizes
the particular effect of the Roman tradition upon his love for
Bérénice. In III, 1, he describes to Antiochus the interdict upon
royal and foreign blood, citing the example of Julius Caesar's
obedience (723–36). In the long monologue of IV, 4, in a crisis
of self-persuasion, he recalls the strength of the tradition and
his own intimate connection with it. And in his meeting with
Bérénice (IV, 5) he admits that it was only through his forget-
fulness of Roman law that he allowed himself to think that he
might ever marry her (1087–1102). Other shorter passages, al-

most everywhere in the work, restate the conflict between Roman lore and Titus' love; it is, indeed, one of the basic oppositions of the play. In spite of the strength of this sense in Titus, however, and in spite of the fact that he really never departed from his resolve, it was necessary to turn this permanent potential into an active force—to give him greater strength at each point where his resolve might possibly flag. This was done through the device of the "Senate and People of Rome" and, more specifically, through the role assigned to Paulin.

The Roman senate is present from the very beginning of the play, first as a vague body unconnected with Titus' affairs—

> Le sénat a placé son père entre les dieux— (166)

next as a group directly connected with them:

> Il verra le sénat m'apporter ses hommages,
> Et le peuple de fleurs couronner ses images. (299–300)

In the latter passage, it is associated with the people of Rome, and both are frequently lumped together as symbolizing "Rome":

> Rome vous voit, Madame, avec des yeux jaloux;
> La rigueur de ses lois m'épouvante pour vous.
> L'hymen chez les Romains n'admet qu'une Romaine;
> Rome hait tous les rois; et Bérénice est reine. (293–96)

Here senate and people are specifically related to the marriage of Titus and Bérénice, as they are in Titus' question—

> De la reine et de moi que dit la voix publique? (344)

and in the whole lengthy discussion between Titus and Paulin in II, 2. Especially in Paulin's reply, Rome is both an abstraction and a material entity; it is the latter aspect that becomes immediate—and a potential for action—in such lines as these:

> Et je ne réponds pas, avant la fin du jour,
> Que le sénat, chargé des vœux de tout l'Empire,
> Ne vous redise ici ce que je viens de dire;

Et que Rome avec lui tombant à vos genoux,
Ne vous demande un choix digne d'elle et de vous.

(414-18)

Both Bérénice and Titus recognize the importance of Roman opinion in their crisis, Bérénice in spite of her self-deception:

N'est-ce point que de Rome il redoute la haine? (639)

Titus as a loyal member of the body politic:

Que diront avec moi la cour, Rome, l'Empire? (671)

Je sais que le sénat, tout plein de votre nom,
D'une commune voix confirmera ce don. (765-66)

We should note that Racine does not restrict the presence of the senate to the problem of Titus and Bérénice; it is involved with Vespasien's burial, with the grants of territories to Bérénice and Antiochus, with all matters affecting the state. It must have this general function if it is to operate usefully in the particular case at hand.

In that particular case, Titus acknowledges the importance to himself of Roman opinion, even though he might delude himself into thinking that that opinion will approve his marriage:

Car enfin Rome a-t-elle expliqué ses souhaits?
L'entendons-nous crier autour de ce palais?
Vois-je l'État penchant au bord du précipice?
Ne le puis-je sauver que par ce sacrifice?
Tout se tait; et moi seul, trop prompt à me troubler,
J'avance des malheurs que je puis reculer.

. . . .

Rome peut par son choix justifier le mien. (1001-9)

He tries to convince Bérénice of that importance (1139-46), of the fact that he is held to conform to the wishes of the Romans, although she is prone to uphold the opposite position. And at the very point (1216) where he is tempted (all for love) to flaunt that opinion, its flattering effects are reported to him by Paulin:

> Ne troublez point le cours de votre renommée.
> Déjà de vos adieux la nouvelle est semée;
> Rome, qui gémissait, triomphe avec raison;
> Tous les temples ouverts fument en votre nom;
> Et le peuple, élevant vos vertus jusqu'aux nues,
> Va partout de lauriers couronner vos statues. (1219-24)

From this point on, the Roman people and senate will practically be present on the stage. Rutile announces their presence in an antechamber:

> Seigneur, tous les tribuns, les consuls, le sénat,
> Viennent vous demander au nom de tout l'État.
> Un grand peuple les suit, qui, plein d'impatience,
> Dans votre appartement attend votre présence. (1241-44)

Bérénice also waits in her apartment; Titus must choose, and the moral conflict between her and Rome is turned into a material and physical conflict; he chooses to meet the Romans (1251-52). In fact, Titus puts upon this announcement of the presence of his constituents the interpretation that the gods thus express their will—and bolster his failing courage:

> Je vous entends, grands dieux! Vous voulez rassurer
> Ce cœur que vous voyez tout prêt à s'égarer! (1245-46)

Arsace describes, in the last act, the extent to which this physical presence has become a moral force:

> Le peuple avec transport l'arrête et l'environne,
> Applaudissant aux noms que le sénat lui donne;
> Et ces noms, ces respects, ces applaudissements,
> Deviennent pour Titus autant d'engagements,
> Qui, le liant, Seigneur, d'une honorable chaîne,
> Malgré tous ses soupirs et les pleurs de la reine,
> Fixent dans son devoir ses vœux irrésolus. (1271-77)

Only a little later, the spectator himself is invited to hear the acclamations of the people, which—offstage or backstage or around the palace—shouts its joy at Bérénice's impending departure

(1313–19); Rome has been materialized even further. Bérénice deprecates the senate's applause (1328–29), but Titus defends himself against her. Although he has heard the applause—

> J'ai vu devant mes yeux Rome entière assemblée;
> Le sénat m'a parlé ...   (1375–76)

(Rome again materialized)—he has not allowed it to prevent his final decision, that is, that he will die.

The role assigned to the people and senate of Rome is another one of Racine's discoveries in *Bérénice*. To be sure, he had in the earlier plays sometimes alluded to the existence of public opinion or of a mass force, as in the people and army of *La Thébaïde*. But these had not in the same way been transformed into components of the action. In *Bérénice*, people and senate are among the important probabilities for the furthering of the action. They begin as fairly distant abstractions; as the time when they will be needed approaches, they are brought closer and made more physical; ultimately they exert their force as completely present and material elements. They have, in a word, all the qualities of another actor in the play, another member of the dramatis personae. The technique that Racine develops here will be used, with perhaps even greater success, in the case of the army in *Iphigénie*.

Just as Rome is transformed into a dramatic person, so one of the Romans, Paulin, is advanced from the subordinate role of confidant to that of spokesman for his countrymen. He not only listens, he speaks and advises; and in so doing he becomes an "incorporation" of the Roman spirit and a source of probabilities for Titus' actions. Titus himself gives Paulin this part to play:

> Je veux par votre bouche entendre tous les cœurs.
>
> . . . .
>
> Pour mieux voir, cher Paulin, et pour entendre mieux,
> Je vous ai demandé des oreilles, des yeux;
> J'ai mis même à ce prix mon amitié secrète:
> J'ai voulu que des cœurs vous fussiez l'interprète.
>   (358–64)

Paulin will provide, in II, 2, the lengthy interpretation of "la voix publique," assuming at the end all its authority when he says to Titus:

> Vous pouvez préparer, Seigneur, votre réponse.   (419)

In IV, 3 (this time in an aside addressed essentially to the audience), he states again the position of Rome:

> Grands dieux, sauvez sa gloire et l'honneur de l'État!
> (986)

Toward the end of the same act he enters still more directly into the action, first in a passage (1219–24, already cited) in which he reports to Titus on the current state of opinion about him, next in a speech which amounts to a reprimand to Titus in the name of Rome:

> Quoi! vous pourriez, Seigneur, par cette indignité,
> De l'Empire à vos pieds fouler la majesté?
> Rome....   (1249-51)

To which Titus capitulates, making his choice in favor of Rome rather than of Bérénice:

> Il suffit, Paulin, nous allons les entendre.   (1251)

Racine's handling of the part has the advantages both of tightening the "economy" of the play by making an instrumental personage into an active one and of furthering his intention to use Rome and Roman opinion as a means of establishing probability.

All the devices and inventions that I have discussed so far have been related primarily to the first (and major) part of the action, that part consisting in Titus' notification of Bérénice that she must leave Rome. But as Racine conceived of the total action (and we may ask later whether he should have done so), it also has a second part in which the consequences of the notification for each of the major personages are investigated. That is, after Titus has finally communicated his decision to Bérénice, he and she must decide what course of action to follow in the future; and so must Antiochus. For each one there are alternatives: Titus may remain and rule, or he may die; Bérénice may leave alone, or she may leave with Antiochus, or she may die; Antiochus' choices are identical with hers. Now Racine apparently realized the danger in having two "parts" to his dramatic action, the danger that, if they remained purely consecutive parts, the play at a given point would break in two and become two imperfect plays (like the *Hippolytus* of Euripides). The solution was to make the two parts simultaneous in so far as that was possible, with the conclusion of the one necessarily preceding the conclusion of the other. Specifically, the alternatives for each of the persons could be developed throughout the play, and long before the decision was announced; the choice among them could then be made after the announcement.

The simplest (and possibly the least interesting) case of the three is that of Antiochus. Two of Antiochus' alternatives are present from the beginning. When he appears at the opening of the first act, he assumes that Titus is about to marry Bérénice; he himself is ready to leave Rome—the first alternative (32, 72–78: "Je sors de Rome, Arsace, et j'en sors pour jamais"). His intention to do so remains constant throughout the play; the only delay is caused by Titus:

> Mais n'accusez que lui, si malgré mes adieux
> De ma présence encor J'importune vos yeux.
> Peut-être en ce moment je serais dans Ostie,
> S'il ne m'eût de sa cour défendu la sortie.   (853–56)

>   Et ne partais-je pas,
> Si Titus malgré moi n'eût arrêté mes pas?
> Sans doute, il faut partir.   (921–23)

He reiterates his determination after Bérénice has forbidden him to see her again (946). In each of these statements, he means to leave alone. Only when Titus orders him to leave with Bérénice, even suggesting that they might marry, does Antiochus consider this possibility:

> Prince, dans son malheur ne l'abandonnez pas.
> Que l'Orient vous voie arriver à sa suite;
> Que ce soit un triomphe, et non pas une fuite;
> Qu'une amitié si belle ait d'éternels liens. (758–61)

In the ensuing conversation, Arsace emphasizes the possibility:

> Vous partirez, Seigneur, mais avec Bérénice. (772)

> Puisque aujourd'hui Titus ne prétend plus lui plaire,
> Songez que votre hymen lui devient nécessaire. (819–20)

For a while Antiochus allows himself to be deluded; but as he foresees Bérénice's reactions, he realizes that departure and marriage with her is out of the question. The second alternative is short-lived.

So is the third; or in any case, it never enters very seriously into consideration until the end of the play. Very early, Antiochus sees it as one of several courses of action open to him:

> Allons loin de ses yeux l'oublier, ou mourir. (34)

At this point, we take his death as a commonplace solution—and not very seriously. We perhaps give it a little more credence when he tells Bérénice that he hopes to die, even though there is as yet no urgency or determination associated with it:

> Adieu. Je vais, le cœur trop plein de votre image,
> Attendre, en vous aimant, la mort pour mon partage.
> Surtout ne craignez point qu'une aveugle douleur
> Remplisse l'univers du bruit de mon malheur:
> Madame, le seul bruit d'une mort que j'implore
> Vous fera souvenir que je vivais encore. (279–84)

We are thus astonished when, in the last scene, Antiochus declares that, all other attempts to drive out his love having failed, he means now to die by his own hand:

> Il faut d'autres efforts pour rompre tant de nœuds;
> Ce n'est qu'en expirant que je puis les détruire;
> J'y cours. (1458–60)

This does not sound very convincing to us, and we may readily conclude that Racine introduces the gesture here for two reasons: to provide a parallel with Titus' offer to die, and to permit Bérénice to make her own final decision in terms of two noble offers—"Princes trop généreux" (1469). Bérénice dismisses two of Antiochus' alternatives in her final speech (1495–1501), and Antiochus' final "Hélas!" indicates that he finishes his action where he had started it, resigned to return alone to his own country.

Titus' offer to die is better prepared; it should be, since he is the protagonist and each of his acts is more important to the general structure of the work. When first he mentions the possibility of his death (to Antiochus), he thinks of it only remotely and as a termination to his suffering:

> Mon règne ne sera qu'un long bannissement,
> Si le ciel, non content de me l'avoir ravie,
> Veut encor m'affliger par une longue vie.   (754–56)

He speaks of it as a more real contingency, and with greater passion, when he says to Bérénice,

> Que sais-je? j'espérais de mourir à vos yeux,
> Avant que d'en venir à ces cruels adieux,   (1093–94)

and later in the same speech,

> Je sens bien que sans vous je ne saurais plus vivre.   (1100)

He is even more vehement in response to Bérénice's charges of ingratitude:

> Je n'aurai pas, Madame, à compter tant de jours.
> J'espère que bientôt la triste renommée
> Vous fera confesser que vous étiez aimée.
> Vous verrez que Titus n'a pu, sans expirer ...   (1122–25)

Thus when Bérénice threatens to take her life, he can only say to Paulin, "Paulin, je suis perdu, je n'y pourrai survivre" (1199).

Indeed, it is only after reading Bérénice's letter, in which he discovers that her proposed departure was merely a subterfuge to mask her suicide, that he also offers to die. He could not, as he had said, survive her, and only a promise by her to avoid suicide will make him change his resolve. Bérénice makes that promise in her last speech (1493–94), and we may assume that Titus will live and reign. It is important to note, for the general conception of the tragedy, that when Titus proposes suicide, he does so in terms that befit a Roman; his identification with country and tradition persists to the very end:

> Pour sortir des tourments dont mon âme est la proie,
> Il est, vous le savez, une plus noble voie.
> Je me suis vu, Madame, enseigner ce chemin
> Et par plus d'un héros, et par plus d'un Romain:
> Lorsque trop de malheurs ont lassé leur constance,
> Ils ont tous expliqué cette persévérance
> Dont le sort s'attachait à les persécuter,
> Comme un ordre secret de n'y plus résister.   (1407–14)

He will, like a Roman, die upon his sword.

Death thus presents for Titus a somewhat more real alternative than it had for Antiochus; it presents a very real alternative for Bérénice once she has a suggestion that her marriage with Titus may not take place. To a degree, her separation from Titus and her departure from Rome are not a matter of her own choosing; Titus decides for her. But the remaining problems are related to her departure: In what spirit will she accept the necessity of leaving? Will she leave alone, or accompanied by Antiochus? Or will she prefer death to an ignominious departure? As we have already seen, there is a wide range in her reactions to the news that Titus has rejected her; she passes from incredulity to despair, from a sense of the impossibility of her situation to anger, from fright to a final noble resignation. When she finally does agree publicly to depart (Arsace announces, "La reine part, Seigneur" [1262], and she herself confirms, "Je veux partir" [1304]), it is only because she is using a "stratagème" to cover up her intention to die. She ultimately agrees to leave and to live (1493).

Meanwhile, the thought that she might wish to die has accompanied throughout the notion of separation from Titus. She uses it as a means of forestalling the announcement:

> Moi, qui mourrais le jour qu'on voudrait m'interdire
> De vous ...   (615–16)

After Antiochus has delivered his message, she seems already to have in mind the stratagem:

> Mais que dis-je, mes pleurs? si ma perte certaine,
> Si ma mort toute prête enfin ne le ramène ...   (975–76)

When Titus at last succeeds in telling her his decision, she several times threatens to die:

> Je vous crois digne, ingrat, de m'arracher la vie.   (1176)

> Non, si le ciel encore est touché de mes pleurs,
> Je le prie en mourant d'oublier mes douleurs.
>
> . . . .
>
> Si, devant que mourir la triste Bérénice
> Vous veut de son trépas laisser quelque vengeur,
>
> . . . .
>
> Mon sang, qu'en ce palais je veux même verser ...
>   (1185–93)

Titus takes the threat seriously ("La reine veut mourir" [1200]) and is almost led to change his mind by it ("Je ne souffrirai point que Bérénice expire" [1215]). Indeed, Bérénice gives every sign of wishing to carry it out:

> Qu'avez-vous fait, Seigneur? L'aimable Bérénice
> Va peut-être expirer dans les bras de Phénice.
> Elle n'entend ni pleurs, ni conseil, ni raison;
> Elle implore à grands cris le fer et le poison.   (1227–30)

Hence Titus is fully justified in giving credence to the "strata-gème" and in attempting to counteract it by declaring that his own death would follow Bérénice's. The spectator also believes it, and I think that this is perhaps the only one of the three threats of suicide that carries conviction. For only Bérénice comes to a sufficient state of hopelessness to wish profoundly for death; Titus and Antiochus, having different kinds of characters and being in different situations, find other solutions completely acceptable. The spectator is apt to feel that their fifth-act offers to die are merely a means for bringing Bérénice around to her final decision not to die.

The conclusion from this study of alternatives and consequences seems to be evident: whereas Racine succeeded admirably in developing in a poetically convincing fashion the first part of his action (that concerned with Titus' struggle leading up to the announcement), he succeeded much less well in the second part (consequences and ultimate decisions). In the first part, where the problem was so to enrich the action that it would have the proper magnitude and the desired emotional effect, he found those characters, those circumstances, those devices that produced the needed complication. He built very carefully upon an initial situation (the necessity of sending Bérénice away), with useful traits of character (such as Titus' weakness in the face of Bérénice and her unwillingness to believe), and with sure probabilities from circumstance and argument (such as the senate and people of Rome). But when Titus' announcement to Bérénice had finally been made, these probabilities were in a sense exhausted. In spite of Racine's effort to establish, far back in the play, the bases for a development (after the announcement) of the consequences, these bases turn out to be insufficient in two of the cases (Titus and Antiochus). The second part of the action is never fully integrated with the first, even though the same persons are involved and the one follows upon the other. Its emotional effect is therefore less vigorous. I should point out, however, that Racine felt that this was not the case; he was aware of the difficulty, and he thought that he had conquered it. In his Preface, speaking of Bérénice in the last act, he says: "... le dernier adieu qu'elle dit à Titus, et l'effort qu'elle se fait pour s'en séparer, n'est pas le moins tragique de la pièce; et j'ose dire qu'il renouvelle assez bien dans le cœur des spectateurs l'émotion que le reste y avait pu exciter." This may be so; but we may ask whether the emotion is the same emotion, and whether "assez bien" is good enough.

It will be noted, also, that in his statement about the final scene Racine makes no mention of Antiochus. This may be a tacit admission of the possibility that Antiochus really has no function there, and that his presence is one of the evidences of the over-extension of his role. In the conception of the first part of the action, Racine needed Antiochus to do certain things (especially to deliver the message after Titus' first failure); to do them, he must stand in certain relationships to the two main personages. His role was conceived, properly, as a secondary one. I think, also, that it may have been conceived only as instrumental to the first part of the action, and that Racine's decision to use the personage as he did in the denouement was a part of his general wish to magnify his simple action. It may have been an unfortunate decision, as may also have been certain of the ways in which the role was used in the first part. I should like to propose two doubts with respect to the role of Antiochus in *Bérénice:* first, that both the character and its uses may be overextended in the first part; second, that they may really not be necessary at all in the second part.

In my discussion of the reasons why Racine invented the role of Antiochus, I indicated that basically he was needed for communicating the message and that, for him to be of the greatest use, it was well that he should be a lover of Bérénice as well as an ally of Titus. The first overextension of the role, it seems to me, comes in the degree to which his love for Bérénice is expressed. In his soliloquy of I, 2, and again in the long meeting with Bérénice (I, 4), Antiochus traces the history of his love and speaks of the violence of his passion. After Titus has charged him with the message, he exclaims upon the extent to which the new prospect arouses a torment of conflict within him (II, 3), and after Bérénice's rebuff he finds himself in a state of despair worse than before—and more than ever determined to leave Rome (III, 4). I do not say that these passions are unreal or unconvincing or excessive in themselves; but I wonder whether they might not be disproportionate to his contribution to the plot. That is, Antiochus and the affairs of Antiochus become a dominant center of interest in the play, especially since he is the first of the important personages to appear and his love is the first to move us. But after our interests have been attached rather to Titus and Bérénice (where they should be!), we resist the revival and the reintrusion of our concern for him. We feel that the repercussions of the major situation of the play upon a secondary personage receive too much attention and distract too much from the major emotional line.

After he has delivered his message, Antiochus' usefulness is really at an end. Yet Racine introduces him twice into the second part of the action, once at the end of Act IV when he intercedes for Bérénice and pleads her case against that of Rome (IV, 8), and again in Act V where (in scenes 1 to 4) he hears of Bérénice's plan to leave and (in scene 7) participates in the final scene of sacrifice and renunciation. All these appearances seem unjustified. In the first appearance, part of what Antiochus does might better have been done by a messenger (or possibly by Phénice), the rest represents a new function assigned to him; instead of representing Titus' case to Bérénice, he does the reverse. At any rate, he now speaks definitely against his own interests. (In an original scene 9, suppressed after the first edition, Antiochus was made to remark upon the incongruity of his action. Racine's decision to remove the scene may reflect his discontent with the whole intervention of Antiochus at this point.) Early in Act V, the report that Bérénice has decided to leave once more raises Antiochus' hopes; it should not, since Bérénice has made it clear, long since,

that there could be no question of his accompanying her. And
Titus' statement, immediately afterward (V, 3), returns Antiochus
to his state of hopelessness and tears. For his final confession to
Titus of their rivalry and his final statement that his only solution
lies in death, the probabilities are slight if not non-existent. The
denouement might well, might better have been brought about
without them.

If Racine chose to amplify Antiochus' role in these various
ways, it was undoubtedly because he thought of the process as one
of the means of expanding his simple action to the necessary
tragic magnitude. He may have emphasized the role of Bérénice
as he did, and incidentally entitled his tragedy for her, for the
same reason. I think that I have correctly identified Titus as the
protagonist; the number of personages and actions subordinated
to his action, the centrality of his problem to the rest, the dynamics provided by the successive steps toward his solution, might
be offered as substantiating evidence. Yet as the play progresses,
Bérénice becomes a very real rival to Titus for the central place
in the audience's feelings—if in fact (since she is a woman and
rejected) she does not hold that place undisputedly throughout.
Her position is just as fundamentally tragic as his. Both are in
an impossible situation not of their choosing, both through the
general nobility of their characters should merit better, both struggle against their circumstances until they are finally reconciled
to them. But it might be possible to regard Bérénice's lot as more
tragic in the sense that she is more clearly a victim, more completely passive. Titus' unhappy state results in large part from
a choice that he has made through his own will, in an active way;
Bérénice has no choice. As a result, the spectator's feelings are
divided between two personages, one of whom is the protagonist,
the other of whom is the tragic heroine.

Or perhaps we might better say that the spectator's feelings are
rather attached to a total situation, to the plight of Titus and
Bérénice, than specifically to either one of the two personages.
The "invitus, invitam" of Racine's source is made into a plural

that covers not only the state of soul of both actors but also the general situation in which both are caught up. I think that this is not an uncommon type of dramatic structure, and that, especially in the tragedy of the French Renaissance, poets sought to derive their emotional effect from the whole complex of a dramatic situation rather than to concentrate it upon the protagonist. Perhaps Jodelle's *Cléopâtre captive* works partly in this way. But the difficulty of such a structure in *Bérénice* is that it leads to that ambiguity, that ambivalence of feeling that we have seen in others of the early tragedies. While it is easy to cast Antiochus in a subordinate position and to make an adjustment of our feelings with respect to him, Titus and Bérénice appeal to us with almost equal force. And since one cannot, because of the nature of the situation, approve the one without blaming the other, we remain divided and hesitant. The total force of the play upon the passions is thus diminished.

I should like to suggest that these various weaknesses in the structure of *Bérénice*—inclusion of the second part, overdevelopment of the role of Antiochus, uncertainty with respect to the dominant personage and emotion—all come from one basic flaw in the conception of the play: the action that Racine wished to expand and complicate was in itself too simple, too bare, to permit of that development. He could well reply to his critics who maintained that simplicity was a sign of poverty of invention: "Ils ne songent pas qu'au contraire toute l'invention consiste à faire quelque chose de rien, et que tout ce grand nombre d'incidents a toujours été le refuge des poètes qui ne sentaient dans leur génie ni assez d'abondance ni assez de force pour attacher durant cinq actes leurs spectateurs par une action simple, soutenue de la violence des passions, de la beauté des sentiments, et de l'élégance de l'expression." But nevertheless the essential elements of the plot, the simple action from which he started, must be capable (through their number or their complexity) of undergoing the transformation that would make them dramatically effective. If they were not so capable, the play might resemble a Renaissance tragedy; the expansion might come solely through "the violence of the passions, the beauty of the sentiments, and the elegance of the expression." That is, it might be either a lyrical or a rhetorical tragedy. I do not think that this is the case in *Bérénice*. As I have tried to show, that much of the first part as relates to the difficulties which Titus had in telling Bérénice of her fate—and his ultimate telling—is completely properly constructed as an expansion of a simple action. It is the rest of the play, those weaknesses that I have pointed out, that seems to constitute an improper or an infelicitous expansion.

One of the qualities through which Racine sought to establish the merit of his play was "l'élégance de l'expression." I do not mean to comment, at this point, on the whole matter of the diction in *Bérénice*. But I should like to emphasize the way in which his clear conception of the central action leads him, not to "elegance of expression," but to two forms of clarity or perspicuousness that constitute a special excellence of the presentation. We have seen already, and we shall later see on various occasions, Racine's technique of summarizing or stating the action in a concise formula. This he does both to keep the line of the action perfectly clear and to direct or redirect the emotion. The best example of this in *Bérénice* occurs in the next to the last scene of the play. Titus is speaking to Bérénice:

> Lorsque j'envisageai le moment redoutable
> Où, pressé par les lois d'un austère devoir,
> Il fallait pour jamais renoncer à vous voir;
> Quand de ce triste adieu je prévis les approches,
> Mes craintes, mes combats, vos larmes, vos reproches,
> Je préparai mon âme à toutes les douleurs
> Que peut faire sentir le plus grand des malheurs;
> Mais, quoi que je craignisse, il faut que je le die,
> Je n'en avais prévu que la moindre partie.
> Je croyais ma vertu moins prête à succomber,
> Et j'ai honte du trouble où je la vois tomber.   (1364–74)

The passage revolves about Titus; it states the elementary situation and his problem with respect to it; it summarizes his own emotional conflict and his expectation of Bérénice's response— a response that has already been seen by him; and it expresses clearly his present state of feeling. As it does all these things, it re-creates the whole of Titus' role in the play and the whole progress of his emotions. Racine succeeds in reducing to a very concise statement (is it concision of "thought" or of "diction"?) the central plot of his tragedy, with a consequent recapitulation of both the action and the emotion for his spectator.

The second form of clarity is specifically present in the diction, and once again it is possible only because the "simple action" has been so clearly conceived. If that action reduces essentially to the notion of "dimisit," then a certain number of French equivalents for the concept will be used throughout to express it. Racine discovers and employs them in a very extraordinary way. Early in the poem, Titus epitomizes his problem in the formula, "Pour jamais je vais m'en séparer" (446). When Antiochus carries his message to Bérénice, he formulates it thus:

> Qu'à jamais l'un de l'autre il faut vous séparer.   (894)

Bérénice replies: "Nous séparer?" (895). A minute later she repeats: "Nous séparer!" (903). When, in IV, 5, Bérénice opens the scene with an attack upon Titus, she says at the end of her first speech:

> Il faut nous séparer; et c'est lui qui l'ordonne!   (1044)

Titus concludes his speech of reply with the formula:

> Car enfin, ma princesse, il faut nous séparer.   (1061)

And later in the scene, Bérénice asks in anguish:

> Ah! Seigneur, s'il est vrai, pourquoi nous séparer?   (1126)

Now this reiteration of various forms of "se séparer" reflects a wish to use diction for specific purposes. As the situation reduces to the word, the emotion connected with the situation comes to attach to the word; and as the action progresses, the context of feeling associated with the word becomes richer and more complex.

Several other equivalents to the "dimisit" are used in a similar fashion. One of them is "abandonner." Again, it is Titus who summarizes his action through the term; but, curiously enough, he first applies it (with a resultant dramatic irony) to Antiochus, as he charges him to protect Bérénice:

> Prince, dans son malheur ne l'abandonnez pas.   (758)

Antiochus echoes it as he refers to his forthcoming action:

> Allons lui déclarer que Titus l'abandonne,   (832)

only to realize, from his use of the term, all the implications of his action:

> L'aimable Bérénice entendrait de ma bouche
> Qu'on l'abandonne?   (836-37)

Bérénice herself (after twice saying, "Nous séparer") rephrases the catastrophe from her own point of view:

> Après tant de serments, Titus m'abandonner!   (906)

She again couples the two terms in her attack upon Titus:

> Hé bien, il est donc vrai que Titus m'abandonne?
> Il faut nous séparer; et c'est lui qui l'ordonne!   (1043-44)

Since the two verbs have varying meanings, the one stressing their mutual love and the results for both of Titus' action, the other pointing rather to the effect upon Bérénice, their coupling at various points tends to throw into relief the different aspects of the situation and the conflicting emotional consequences. The same is true for the use of "quitter." Titus announces his intention to Antiochus:

> Cependant aujourd'hui, Prince, il faut la quitter.   (714)

Antiochus replies in astonishment: "La quitter!" (715). (We should note here the parallelism to the echoing of "nous séparer" at 894–95 and 904, since both cases call the attention of the listener to the verbs and to the actions that they represent.) Once again, it is Bérénice who links two of the expressions:

> Après tant de serments, Titus m'abandonner!
> Titus qui me jurait ... Non, je ne le puis croire:
> Il ne me quitte point, il y va de sa gloire.   (906–8)

Titus takes up the term again in his conversation with Bérénice:

> Je sais qu'en vous quittant le malheureux Titus
> Passe l'austérité de toutes leurs vertus.   (1169–70)

Bérénice insists upon it in her last adieux to her two lovers:

> Prince, après cet adieu, vous jugez bien vous-même
> Que je ne consens pas de quitter ce que j'aime
> Pour aller loin de Rome écouter d'autres vœux.
> Vivez, et faites-vous un effort généreux.
> Sur Titus et sur moi réglez votre conduite.
> Je l'aime, je le fuis: Titus m'aime, il me quitte.
> Portez loin de mes yeux vos soupirs et vos fers. (1495–1501)

The statement is addressed specifically to Antiochus; but, once more, it gives one of those total summations of the action of the play and of its denouement that assist the spectator in keeping clear the general movement of the tragedy and in associating with it the proper emotions.

We might make a similar study of other passages and of the use of other words. But the point should be sufficiently clear without it: as Racine moved forward in the direction of a better control of his organizing plot, he also progressed toward a surer handling of the other elements of the play that are subordinated to plot. In *Bérénice,* his conception of the "simple action" enables him to reduce the number of active participants in the action; but it also permits him to assign to each personage the character needed for his participation, and in some cases to effect an expansion of his activity and hence of his traits of character. Similarly, the same conception carries on through such elements as thought and diction, producing effects of concentration and of precision that are witnesses to Racine's growing mastery of his art.

VI

Bajazet

SLIGHTLY MORE than a year after the first performance of *Bérénice*, the company of the Hôtel de Bourgogne produced Racine's sixth tragedy, *Bajazet*, in January, 1672. It was published in the same month. For the first time, Racine chose a subject from contemporary history, excusing himself on the basis of the "éloignement des pays" (Second Preface).

In certain ways, the artistic problem that Racine set for himself in *Bajazet* was the exact opposite of the one he had set in the preceding play. In *Bérénice*, he had selected so simple an action that he needed, in order to achieve the desired magnitude and the proper "tristesse majestueuse," to enrich his subject by the invention of appropriate personages and situations. Some of these contributed usefully to the total dramatic merit of the work, others did not. In *Bajazet*, his action was again simple, simple in the sense that it might be reduced to a few episodes, concerning a protagonist, and having a clear and necessary sequence. But now the subject was of such nature, its conditions and presuppositions were so extraordinary, that the poet needed to invent numerous complications in order to establish probabilities for the action and to render it credible. The problem was not enrichment but justification. That is, the reason for expansion of the simple action was not to increase its bulk (both material and emotional) but rather to introduce the many small parts that would make the mechanism work.

We may state the simple action in terms of the protagonist,

163

Bajazet. Bajazet, faced with the alternative of marrying Roxane or dying, refuses the marriage; yielding to the urgings of Atalide and Acomat, he acquiesces and accepts; but upon his discovery of Atalide's jealousy, he decides to refuse once again, he refuses, and he dies. Reduced to abstract terms, the organizing idea is one of a man who makes a decision that will cost him his life, who is persuaded by others to reverse it, but who returns to it when he sees the consequences of its alternative. Simple enough—in the abstract. But poems, and especially plays, do not exist in the abstract, and the bare statement of their organizing idea has little potential with respect to our emotions. When I make the kind of summary that I have just proposed for *Bajazet,* we feel nothing, unless we attach some vague response to such terms as "dying" and "jealousy." The idea needs to be made into the poem in order to produce its effect.

The general nature of the subject of *Bajazet* made it necessary for Racine to develop an extremely complicated situation in order to make his poem as he wanted it. Perhaps the most extraordinary element in the situation is Roxane's power to offer Bajazet marriage and an empire, and to threaten him with death if he refuses them. To reach this situation, a long list of antecedents is provided, constituting a fair part of the exposition. Roxane has long been the favorite of the sultan, Amurat, and in her behalf he has violated one of the customs of his empire and named her sultana:

> Car on dit qu'elle seule a fixé son amour.
> Et même il a voulu que l'heureuse Roxane,
> Avant qu'elle eût un fils, prît le nom de sultane.   (100–102)

Roxane states the exceptional nature of her title, after having defined the custom, but she points out that Amurat has not gone so far as to marry her:

> Amurat plus ardent, et seul jusqu'à ce jour,
> A voulu que l'on dût ce titre à son amour.
> J'en reçus la puissance aussi bien que le titre,
>
> . . . .

Mais ce même Amurat ne me promit jamais
Que l'hymen dût un jour couronner ses bienfaits.

(299-304)

The power that he has given to her, says Acomat, is absolute, and
among the prerogatives that he has delegated to her during his
absence is that of deciding whether Bajazet shall live or die:

Il partit, et voulut que, fidèle à sa haine,
Et des jours de son frère arbitre souveraine,
Roxane, au moindre bruit, et sans autres raisons,
Le fît sacrifier à ses moindres soupçons.   (129-32)

Thus the capacity of Roxane to threaten Bajazet with death is
firmly established at the outset.

Her ability to offer him marriage and an empire requires even
more complete justification. First, she must wish to marry him,
and her love for Bajazet must have certain unusual features.
Since she is the sultan's favorite, it could have developed only
during his absence; it must still remain clandestine. Acomat tells
how a false rumor of Amurat's death and bribery of Bajazet's
guards had permitted a first meeting between Bajazet and
Roxane (145-52), a meeting in which Roxane had not failed to
impress him with the strength of her position:

Roxane vit le prince. Elle ne put lui taire
L'ordre dont elle seule était dépositaire.
Bajazet est aimable. Il vit que son salut
Dépendait de lui plaire, et bientôt il lui plut.   (153-56)

This meeting has produced a violent love in Roxane, aroused
by Acomat's words before the meeting had taken place:

Que te dirai-je enfin? la sultane éperdue
N'eut plus d'autres désirs que celui de sa vue.   (141-42)

Roxane herself alludes to this love several times during her conversation with Atalide (I, 3), speaking of the many things that
she has already done for Bajazet and of her wish to marry him
if she can be assured that he really loves her.

If she has doubts about Bajazet's love, it is again because of the peculiar circumstances in which they find themselves. Bajazet is a prisoner, in effect, and since their first meeting (the "s'entrevoir" of line 152 is significant) they have not spoken. Atalide has served as an intermediary between them, communicating the love of one to the other; in order that she might be able to do so, it has been publicly assumed that she was Bajazet's beloved. As a result, whereas Roxane's love for Bajazet has been a certainty, his love for her has been a matter of assumption and conjecture. Acomat assumes that it is mutual:

> Tout conspirait pour lui. Ses soins, sa complaisance,
> Ce secret découvert, et cette intelligence,
> Soupirs d'autant plus doux qu'il les fallait celer,
> L'embarras irritant de ne s'oser parler,
> Même témérité, périls, craintes communes,
> Lièrent pour jamais leurs cœurs et leurs fortunes.   (157–62)

Only Roxane has doubts and suspicions about it; in spite of Atalide's assurances (269–73), she finds the direct evidences of Bajazet's passion less convincing than the indirect. In a long speech (274–86), she expresses her concern over what seem to her to be inadequate witnesses to Bajazet's love, indicating that she cannot give herself and the empire to him on the basis of "ces gages incertains" (286). It is thus imperative that she meet with Bajazet and seek a clarification, and such a rendezvous has been arranged.

In order to make it possible for Roxane to offer an empire to Bajazet along with her love, Racine had to create even more complex circumstances. The absence of Amurat on a military expedition and the "absolute powers" granted to Roxane would not in themselves have been sufficient; he had to invent, besides, a conspiracy and a prime conspirator. Again, certain details must go far back into the past. One of these is the long resentment of the Janissaries against Amurat, for past wrongs, and their loyalty to their grand vizier, Acomat; the resentment is augmented, now, by the fact that Acomat has been left in Constantinople and excluded from the expedition (35–48, 87–91). The position of the Janissaries, however, is ambiguous: if Amurat wins his war against Babylon, they will remain loyal; if he loses it, they will turn against him and take up the cause of Acomat (53–68). The way is thus prepared for changes in the state of the conspiracy depending upon the reports (true or false) that arrive from Babylon. Another antecedent to the action is the whole plan that Acomat has pursued ever since Amurat's departure. Acomat has decided to support Bajazet against Amurat and has fostered the love between Roxane and Bajazet as a means to his ends:

> Pour moi, demeuré seul, une juste colère
> Tourna bientôt mes vœux du côté de son frère.
> J'entretins la sultane, et cachant mon dessein,
> Lui montrai d'Amurat le retour incertain,
> Les murmures du camp, la fortune des armes.
> Je plaignis Bajazet, je lui vantai ses charmes. (133–38)

He alludes, in a veiled way, to his activity:

> Mais j'ai plus dignement employé ce loisir:
> J'ai su lui préparer des craintes et des veilles,
> Et le bruit en ira bientôt à ses oreilles. (92–94)

At one moment, he circulated the rumor of Amurat's death, in order to bring Bajazet and Roxane together (145 ff.), at another he succeeded in arranging secret meetings between himself and Roxane (201–9); the latter accounts for his presence, now, in the seraglio (3–7). Finally, he has aroused the people in favor of Bajazet and has obtained the support of the priests; the time is now ready, he tells Roxane, to proclaim Bajazet sultan:

> Pour moi, j'ai su déjà par mes brigues secrètes
> Gagner de notre loi les sacrés interprètes:
> Je sais combien crédule en sa dévotion
> Le peuple suit le frein de la religion.
>
> . . . .

Les peuples, prévenus de ce nom favorable,
Savent que sa vertu le rend seule coupable.
D'ailleurs, un bruit confus, par mes soins confirmé,
Fait croire heureusement à ce peuple alarmé
Qu'Amurat le dédaigne, et veut loin de Byzance
Transporter désormais son trône et sa présence.   (233–46)

The time of Amurat's absence has thus been used by Acomat
to bring Roxane and Bajazet together and to prepare for the
coup d'état that would give the empire to Bajazet. It has been
used by Roxane to pursue her love for Bajazet and to make plans
to marry and crown him. It has been used by Amurat himself to
bring his military campaign close to its conclusion; he now
awaits the arrival of the Persian reinforcements for Babylon,
hoping to achieve final victory by defeating them (17–24). The
battle, indeed, may already have been won or lost: Osmin indicates the lapse of time since his departure from the camp:

Mais comme vous savez, malgré ma diligence,
Un long chemin sépare et le camp et Byzance;
Mille obstacles divers m'ont même traversé,
Et je puis ignorer tout ce qui s'est passé.   (25–28)

This fact permits Acomat to urge haste upon Roxane:

Ce combat doit, dit-on, fixer nos destinées;
Et même, si d'Osmin je compte les journées,
Le ciel en a déjà réglé l'événement,
Et le sultan triomphe ou fuit en ce moment.   (221–24)

It also permits the arrival, later on this same day, of another
messenger from the camp who will be able to report the true outcome of the battle and to bring orders from Amurat. Meanwhile,
during his absence Amurat has not been unattentive to affairs in
Constantinople. He has, three months before, sent a slave with
orders that Bajazet be killed; but the orders were ignored and
the slave himself murdered. It is thus likely, now, that another

inquiry will be made by Amurat into the compliance with his orders (70–83); it will also be possible for Roxane to use the "cruel order" as a weapon against Amurat (248).

To bring about this initial situation, in which a woman could offer a man the choice between herself and an empire on the one hand and death on the other, Racine had to invent a whole elaborate past history for his personages and a complicated present state of affairs. He needed to prepare the backgrounds of Roxane, of her co-conspirator Acomat, of the sultan; he needed to imagine a war, a prolonged absence, events at home and abroad. But even so involved a set of probabilities was not sufficient for his purposes; he must also assign to his personages those traits of character that would permit them to move from the initial situation, through a developing action, to its denouement.

Most important of all, in this part of his task, was what he could do with the character of his protagonist, Bajazet. For the man faced with the choice must make it, and depending upon the choice (or the choices) that he made, the action would take one turn or another. Racine had conceived of his action as made up of refusal–acceptance–refusal–death; the man's character must have within it the potential for these successive parts of his action. A difficult task in the case of Bajazet, as difficult as was the provision of the complex probabilities for Roxane's action. Once again, the subject itself contained certain of the conditions, if not of character, at least of the peculiar circumstances that had contributed to the formation of character. Racine is at great pains to emphasize the special traits that accrue to Bajazet through his natural position as brother to the sultan. Acomat (again) makes the first statement:

> Tu sais de nos sultans les rigueurs ordinaires:
> Le frère rarement laisse jouir ses frères
> De l'honneur dangereux d'être sortis d'un sang
> Qui les a de trop près approchés de son rang.
> L'imbécile Ibrahim, sans craindre sa naissance,

Traîne, exempt de péril, une éternelle enfance.
Indigne également de vivre et de mourir,
On l'abandonne aux mains qui daignent le nourrir.

(105–12)

Bajazet, as the sultan's brother, may therefore pretend to the throne; but he also stands in constant danger of death at Amurat's hands—or through the authority delegated by him to Roxane. His is a particular situation that fits into a general pattern. But his own character is entirely individual, and he is distinguished from the category of "sultan's brothers":

Car enfin Bajazet dédaigna de tout temps
La molle oisiveté des enfants des sultans.
Il vint chercher la guerre au sortir de l'enfance,
Et même en fit sous moi la noble expérience.
Toi-même tu l'as vu courir dans les combats,
Emportant après lui tous les cœurs des soldats,
Et goûter, tout sanglant, le plaisir et la gloire
Que donne aux jeunes cœurs la première victoire.

(115–22)

These military virtues are accompanied by other qualities admired by the people (242).

The most important parts of Bajazet's character, however, are those that affect his relationships with Roxane and Atalide. He loves Atalide, and this is a love that depends upon a long history; Atalide describes it:

Dès nos plus jeunes ans, tu t'en souviens assez,
L'amour serra les nœuds par le sang commencés.
Elevée avec lui dans le sein de sa mère,
J'appris à distinguer Bajazet de son frère;
Elle-même avec joie unit nos volontés.
Et, quoique après sa mort l'un de l'autre écartés,
Conservant, sans nous voir, le désir de nous plaire,
Nous avons su toujours nous aimer et nous taire.

(359–66)

During Amurat's absence this love has grown, since the two have been able to see each other as a result of Atalide's intermediation for Roxane. Bajazet's love for Atalide precludes his loving any other woman; this means that his relationship to Roxane must be on another basis, and that the whole elaborate device of the indirect courtship must be developed in order to induce Roxane into error. Bajazet's attitudes toward her are characterized as "respects" (374), "soins, complaisance" (157); Roxane complains of a coldness that belies Atalide's description of his feelings:

> L'ingrat ne parle pas comme on le fait parler!
>
> . . . .
>
> Peut-être trop d'amour me rend trop difficile;
> Mais sans vous fatiguer d'un récit inutile,
> Je ne retrouvais point ce trouble, cette ardeur
> Que m'avait tant promis un discours trop flatteur.
>
> (276–84)

If Roxane thinks that he loves her, it is only because Atalide and Acomat have told her that he does—and because of the wishful thinking derived from her own ardor.

From Bajazet's own point of view, his attitudes toward Roxane have involved no hypocrisy: he has made no declaration of feelings that he did not possess. He has been misrepresented to her, but he himself has made no misrepresentation. Racine gives him a concern for his own safety—

> Bajazet est aimable; il vit que son salut
> Dépendait de lui plaire, et bientôt il lui plut—   (155–56)

which is also expressed in his behavior toward Acomat (189–92). Because of this concern (and Roxane has told him that his life is in her hands, that his death has been ordered by Amurat), he has agreed, at Atalide's urging, to "feign" (388; cf. 666, 670) and his feigning has consisted in his acceptance of Roxane's love—not in any declaration of his own. His love for Atalide has played a large part in his willingness so to act. When, however, Roxane

demands that he marry her, his love for Atalide will prevent him
from accepting; and his honor, his general moral nobility, will
make him turn aside Acomat's suggestion that he commit a
"perfidy" (654). Acomat characterizes Bajazet:

> O courage inflexible! O trop constante foi,
> Que, même en périssant, j'admire malgré moi!   (655–56)

The courage that Acomat ascribes to him means that he does
not fear death, that he will not for fear of death be led into an
ignoble action. He himself states his feelings:

> Je me plains de mon sort moins que vous ne pensez.
> La mort n'est point pour moi le comble des disgrâces;
> J'osai, tout jeune encor, la chercher sur vos traces;
> Et l'indigne prison où je suis renfermé
> A la voir de plus près m'a même accoutumé.
> Amurat à mes yeux l'a vingt fois présentée.
> Elle finit le cours d'une vie agitée.   (608–14)

Here again, a past history, a special set of circumstances, and
permanent traits of character are made to bring about an important decision on the part of the protagonist.

The same traits of character account for Bajazet's later decisions. We may say, I think, that his acceptance of the marriage
comes from his love for Atalide—a decision as strange as are the
circumstances that produce it—and that his final acceptance of
death comes from his fearlessness, from his virtue and honor,
along with that same love. His character does not need to be
complex (and surely it does not need to change) in order to
bring about these seemingly conflicting actions. A few strong
traits suffice—but only when they are conjoined with the multiple
and complicated circumstances that we have seen. More important still, they must operate in connection with other traits,
some of them unusual or unusually efficacious, assigned to the
other personages. Perhaps the best example of such a trait in
Bajazet is Atalide's jealousy. Without this jealousy, Roxane could
not learn of Bajazet's real love, nor could Bajazet be brought to
a realization of the futility of his feigning. Therefore Racine takes

care to emphasize, from the beginning, the nature and the vigor of Atalide's jealousy, and his treatment of this trait is one of the most consistently pursued developments in the play.

Atalide's role as intermediary between Roxane and Bajazet ("Atalide a prêté son nom à cet amour" [168]) makes it possible for her to see Bajazet frequently during Amurat's absence; but it also puts her in a position where she can witness the growth and extent of Roxane's passion. An ideal situation for jealousy. She gives the first indication of her own capacity for doubt when she says to Roxane:

> Et pourquoi de son cœur doutez-vous aujourd'hui? (267)

In her scene with Zaïre (I, 4), she confesses her weakness—after recognizing that her jealousy is unfounded:

> Avant que dans son cœur cette amour fût formée,
> J'aimais, et je pouvais m'assurer d'être aimée.
> Dès nos plus jeunes ans, tu t'en souviens assez,
> L'amour serra les nœuds par le sang commencés.
> . . . .
> Zaïre, il faut pourtant avouer ma faiblesse:
> D'un mouvement jaloux je ne fus pas maîtresse.
> Ma rivale, accablant mon amant de bienfaits,
> Opposait un empire à mes faibles attraits;
> Mille soins la rendaient présente à sa mémoire;
> Elle l'entretenait de sa prochaine gloire.
> Et moi, je ne puis rien. Mon cœur, pour tous discours,
> N'avait que des soupirs, qu'il répétait toujours. (357–84)

This last passage also indicates one of the ingredients of her character, her self-pity that convinces her that others possess all kinds of superiorities over her; it is partly responsible for her willingness to think that Bajazet might be unfaithful to her, might prefer Roxane or his safety:

> Penses-tu mériter qu'on se perde pour toi?
> Peut-être Bajazet, secondant ton envie,
> Plus que tu ne voudras aura soin de sa vie. (404–6)

In the same scene Zaïre (who knows her mistress well) reproaches her with undue anxiety, predicting the exact mistake
that Atalide will later make:

> Toujours avant le temps faut-il vous affliger?
> . . . .
> Suspendez ou cachez l'ennui qui vous dévore.
> N'allez point par vos pleurs déclarer vos amours.
> La main qui l'a sauvé le sauvera toujours,
> Pourvu qu'entretenue en son erreur fatale,
> Roxane jusqu'au bout ignore sa rivale.   (408–14)

Atalide recognizes in herself this capacity for jealousy and
struggles against it. After Bajazet's first refusal, she offers to
sacrifice herself in order to save his life; but the very words that
she uses, relating how the image of her "rivale heureuse" has
affected her, prepare for her later mistake:

> Il est vrai, je n'ai pu concevoir sans effroi
> Que Bajazet pût vivre et n'être plus à moi;
> Et lorsque quelquefois de ma rivale heureuse
> Je me représentais l'image douloureuse,
> Votre mort (pardonnez aux fureurs des amants)
> Ne me paraissait pas le plus grand des tourments.
>   (683–88)

Bajazet is convinced (with the aid of Acomat); but as soon as it
is reported that he has been spared, Atalide's jealousy begins to
assert itself. There is a long series of passages in which the passion is expressed with growing violence; they all must be cited
if we are to see with what attention Racine prepared the final
fatal action, Atalide's accusation of Bajazet. The first one follows
upon Zaïre's announcement that Bajazet has been recalled to the
palace:

> Ainsi, de toutes parts, les plaisirs et la joie
> M'abandonnent, Zaïre, et marchent sur leurs pas.
> J'ai fait ce que j'ai dû; je ne m'en repens pas.   (802–4)

The next one, in reply to Zaïre's "S'il l'épouse, en un mot,"
begins to show Atalide's despair: "S'il l'épouse, Zaïre!" (814).
Atalide attempts to combat and conquer this jealousy, knowing
what its consequences could be:

> Sentiments trop jaloux, c'est à vous de vous taire.
> Si Bajazet l'épouse, il suit mes volontés;
> Respectez ma vertu qui vous a surmontés;
> A ses nobles conseils ne mêlez point le vôtre;
> Et, loin de me le peindre entre les bras d'une autre,
> Laissez-moi sans regret me le représenter
> Au trône où mon amour l'a forcé de monter.
> Oui, je me reconnais, je suis toujours la même.   (818–25)

She thinks of death as the solution to her dilemma, but would
not wish it thought that jealousy was the cause. When Acomat
comes to tell what has happened (giving, incidentally, an inaccurate report of Bajazet's reactions during the meeting), she
inquires curiously into the details:

> Mais quels sont ces transports qu'ils vous ont fait paraître?
>   (862)

After Acomat's description, she can say only "Hélas!" (889);
when he has gone, she gives the first signs of her resentment,

> Allons, retirons-nous, ne troublons point leur joie,   (901)

and then, in two long speeches, she displays the full extent of her
jealousy. In the first, she doubts Bajazet's capacity to resist
Roxane, while repeating again her feelings of self-denigration:

> Que veux-tu que je croie?
> Quoi donc? à ce spectacle irai-je m'exposer?
> Tu vois que c'en est fait, ils se vont épouser.
> La sultane est contente; il l'assure qu'il l'aime.
> Mais je ne m'en plains pas, je l'ai voulu moi-même.
> Cependant croyais-tu, quand, jaloux de sa foi,
> Il s'allait plein d'amour sacrifier pour moi;
> Lorsque son cœur, tantôt m'exprimant sa tendresse,

> Refusait à Roxane une simple promesse;
> Quand mes larmes en vain tâchaient de l'émouvoir:
> Quand je m'applaudissais de leur peu de pouvoir,
> Croyais-tu que son cœur, contre toute apparence,
> Pour la persuader trouvât tant d'éloquence?
> Ah! peut-être, après tout, que sans trop se forcer,
> Tout ce qu'il a pu dire, il a pu le penser.
> Peut-être en la voyant, plus sensible pour elle,
> Il a vu dans ses yeux quelque grâce nouvelle.
> Elle aura devant lui fait parler ses douleurs;
> Elle l'aime; un empire autorise ses pleurs.
> Tant d'amour touche enfin une âme généreuse.
> Hélas! que de raisons contre une malheureuse!   (902–22)

In the second, these feelings of hurt pride and neglect are developed even further:

> Mais après les adieux que je venais d'entendre,
> Après tous les transports d'une douleur si tendre,
> Je sais qu'il n'a point dû lui faire remarquer
> La joie et les transports qu'on vient de m'expliquer.
> Toi-même, juge-nous, et vois si je m'abuse.
> Pourquoi de ce conseil moi seule suis-je excluse?
> Au sort de Bajazet ai-je si peu de part?
> A me chercher lui-même attendrait-il si tard,
> N'était que de son cœur le trop juste reproche
> Lui fait peut-être, hélas! éviter cette approche?   (929–38)

One of the reasons for the incorrect and exaggerated report by Acomat is of course to permit Atalide, in this scene with Zaïre, to reach a high point of anger, self-pity, and jealousy.

All these passions culminate in her statement to Bajazet that she means to die, accompanied by the strong reproach for his infidelity:

> Mais vous n'auriez pas joint à ce titre d'époux
> Tous ces gages d'amour qu'elle a reçus de vous.
> Roxane s'estimait assez récompensée,
> Et j'aurais en mourant cette douce pensée,

Que, vous ayant moi-même imposé cette loi,
Je vous ai vers Roxane envoyé plein de moi;
Qu'emportant chez les morts toute votre tendresse,
Ce n'est point un amant en vous que je lui laisse.

(967–74)

This is, of course, the point in the action at which Racine wished
to arrive. All the lengthy and careful unfolding of Atalide's
character, and above all of her jealousy, was needed so that she
could make this speech: for from it comes, to a degree, the rest
of the action of *Bajazet*. In the speech that follows (975–1011),
the protagonist not only defends himself against the unjustified
accusations, but he also decides to clarify his situation in relationship to Roxane. In III, 5, therefore, he tells Roxane that he does
not mean to marry her. This declaration, added to Atalide's attempt to defend Bajazet, arouses Roxane's suspicions about the
two lovers; she determines to inquire further, to set a trap for
Atalide:

Ils ont beau se cacher. L'amour le plus discret
Laisse par quelque marque échapper son secret.
Observons Bajazet; étonnons Atalide.   (1119–21)

But Atalide, again through jealousy, betrays both herself and
Bajazet; she exacts a letter from him, in which he says specifically
that he never loved Roxane. When she reads it, she realizes how
dangerous her action has been:

De quelle crainte encor me laisse-t-il saisie?
Funeste aveuglement! Perfide jalousie!
Récit menteur! Soupçons que je n'ai pu celer!
Fallait-il vous entendre, ou fallait-il parler?   (1149–52)

As for Roxane, she plans and executes her trap by telling Atalide
that she means to hand over Bajazet to Orcan to be murdered;
by so doing she is able to confirm her hypothesis, which is fully
corroborated when she comes into possession of Bajazet's letter
(IV, 5). This she uses both to inform Acomat (IV, 6) and to

accuse Bajazet (V, 4); and when Bajazet refuses to accept
Roxane's cruel conditions, she speaks the "Sortez" that means his
death. To conclude the whole matter of Atalide's jealousy, Racine
provides again one of those summarizing statements that clarify
the plot for the spectator and help to direct his feelings. Atalide
characterizes her own role:

> Jalouse, et toujours prête à lui représenter
> Tout ce que je croyais digne de l'arrêter,
> Je n'ai rien négligé, plaintes, larmes, colère,
> Quelquefois attestant les mânes de sa mère.
> Ce jour même, des jours le plus infortuné,
> Lui reprochant l'espoir qu'il vous avait donné,
> Et de ma mort enfin le prenant à partie,
> Mon importune ardeur ne s'est point ralentie,
> Qu'arrachant, malgré lui, des gages de sa foi,
> Je ne sois parvenue à le perdre avec moi.   (1595–1604)

Such a sequence of passages relevant to a single trait of character, Atalide's jealousy, and its consequences indicates the degree
of complication that Racine thought necessary for the unwinding
of his "simple action," as well as his meticulous attention to the
providing of every needed detail. If such complication was provided, it was because of the importance of the single trait in the
working-out of the whole action. Once again, the simplest conception of the initial situation will help us to appreciate this importance: Roxane offers Bajazet either death or her love and an
empire. As far as she is concerned, her offer of life and an empire
depends upon assurances that Bajazet really does love her. (She
states this clearly as a condition—

> Je veux que, devant moi, sa bouche et son visage
> Me découvrent son cœur sans me laisser d'ombrage—
>
>   (329–30)

and reiterates it at several points.) If it should turn out that he
does not love her, he must die; and what better proof of this than

his love for another? Such proof, again, might come to Roxane directly, through a confession by Bajazet or by Atalide; but Bajazet must continue to feign if he is to save his life (until that moment when he decides that he can no longer do so), and Atalide promotes and continues the deception for the sake of her lover. Thus only an indirect, unwitting, accidental proof will serve the purpose, and Racine arrives at it through the device of Atalide's jealousy. Roxane, convinced, orders Bajazet's death.

The complications introduced into *Bajazet* thus have two main sources: the desire of the artist to render credible and acceptable an essentially extraordinary situation, and the need to justify, by giving them a firm basis in character, certain difficult turns in the action. The result is a play that has a more involved exposition than most of Racine's and that gives the impression of being comprised of many more external acts. Yet the action does remain simple; we may appreciate its simplicity if we note the way the action is conducted through the successive acts:

Act I. Roxane's alternatives for Bajazet. He may marry her and become sultan, or he may die.

Act II. Bajazet's first refusal of Roxane. But at Acomat's urging and after Atalide's threat that she will die, Bajazet agrees to save himself.

Act III. As a result of Atalide's jealousy, Bajazet refuses Roxane a second time. Roxane suspects that he loves Atalide.

Act IV. When Roxane's suspicions are confirmed, she decides that Bajazet must die.

Act V. Bajazet, given a third chance to save himself, refuses and is killed.

Stated in this way, the action might seem to have a major flaw; we should be justified in asking: Are not Bajazet's three refusals repetitions of the same action? If they were, we should have a play whose dynamics were deficient, that is, one in which probabilities already exhausted were called upon to provide new actions. Another way of saying this is that the actions would tend to derive from permanent elements in character without a proper basis in probability. We should have the kind of action that might be expected from Corneille, but not from Racine.

I think that this is not the case. Bajazet's first refusal (II, 1) is motivated not by the respect for Turkish tradition that he alleges but by several permanent dispositions: his love for Atalide (which means that he cannot at the same time love Roxane), the fact that he does not fear death, his sense of honor that would not tolerate a "lâcheté" (596). If he agrees to consent, it is less because of arguments of expediency offered by Acomat than because of Atalide's threat (should he continue to refuse) to confess their complicity and then to die. His second refusal (III, 5) has an entirely different source; Atalide's jealous interpretation of his consent as unfaithfulness, even as love for Roxane, and her repeated threat to die show him the futility of his feigning, of his "silence perfide" (997), and he resolves to act in accordance with his honor and honesty. This decision could not have been made without Atalide's prior action, and thus to his permanent moral character is added the probability of circumstances. His third refusal is different again, primarily because the conditions stated by Roxane have now changed: she demands that he witness the murder of Atalide and then promise to marry her. Impossible conditions for Bajazet ("L'horreur et le mépris que cette offre m'inspire" [1550]), and he refuses above all because of his love but also because of his honor. Thus each of Bajazet's four decisions goes back—as it must—to stable elements of his character; but each depends also upon changing circumstances and new antecedent actions. There is an order in time that cannot be violated. The first refusal is made upon the basis of the conditions with which the play opens; he alone is responsible for it. The acceptance depends, however, on the intervention of Acomat and Atalide, the second refusal on the effects of Atalide's jealousy, the third refusal (basically) on the effects of Roxane's consequent jealousy.

We should also take into account, in explaining the dynamics of the simple action, a certain number of new events that had to be invented if personages were to be led to make the proper decisions: the discovery of the letter, Amurat's victory, the arrival of Orcan with the letter, the secret orders issued to Orcan, and others of the same kind. All these are of the nature of external or material actions, and they complicate the external plot, they augment the number of episodes, without necessarily affecting the simplicity of the essential action as I have described it. We may, indeed, see in *Bajazet* a kind of dual development: on the one hand, a moral action centering upon Bajazet's fate and the decisions that lead to his death; on the other hand, a multiplicity of circumstances, episodes, and moral characteristics assigned to all the personages, all of them needed to bring about the simple action. The first is a typically "Racinian" development. What is important in it is the moral choices of the protagonist, the conflict within himself and with his circumstances, the order of his decisions and their ultimate result. But because of the very nature of this moral action, because of the extraordinary situation that he had chosen to exploit, Racine had to elaborate the second. And this is not "Racinian" or neo-classical in any sense. It is too intricate, too external, too highly intrigued.

Indeed, as we think about the kinds of problems that Racine was setting himself, one after another, as he sought to improve his art and extend its powers, we may think of *Bajazet* as a kind of *gageure*. Having developed, through *Andromaque,* then *Britannicus,* then *Bérénice,* the art of the simple plot and especially the art of the moral plot, and having moved successively closer to the plot revolving about an active protagonist, he now saw the possibility of combining such a plot with a multiplicity of external, non-moral elements. If he could do this, he might achieve at once the interest of the drama of the passions and that of the drama of intrigue. In a way, he might combine two tendencies of the Renaissance theater that had hitherto remained separate. The early Renaissance playwrights, the Jodelles and the Grévins, had insisted upon the passions; they had written plays in which "nothing happened" and in which (unfortunately) the passions were manifested in a non-dramatic, rhetorical fashion. Their successors at the end of the sixteenth century, especially Hardy, had foregone passion for action, thereby creating a characterless drama that came close to melodrama. Would it be possible to preserve the domination of character and passion—hence to write a Racinian tragedy—and at the same time attract and hold the spectator through a lively and adventurous plot? That was the artistic problem of *Bajazet*.

The two devices that we have studied so far would seem to have been invented in order to attain this double goal. The contrivance of a diversified set of circumstances made possible certain complexities of the action, at the same time as it provided the probabilities for exploiting an extraordinary situation. The development of given traits of character for the main personages established the basis in necessity for the moral choices they had to make. We have seen the latter in a general way in Bajazet, in a highly particularized way in the case of Atalide's jealousy. We might see it in an interesting fashion in the whole career of Acomat through the play. But perhaps the best example of a joining of the two devices in one personage is that of Roxane.

The role of Roxane is analogous to that of Andromaque in the sense that it is "pivotal"; that is, the total situation alters with each change in her intentions. The difference would be that such changes, in the case of Roxane, affect primarily the protagonist, whereas Andromaque's decisions had had their repercussions upon all the other actors; and Andromaque was herself the protagonist. As I have pointed out, Bajazet's moral dilemma throughout results from alternatives offered him by Roxane; it is she, not he, who is responsible for his plight at the beginning and in each successive phase of the action. With respect both to situation and to character, Roxane must therefore be the most flexible of all the personages; were she to remain in a static situation, or were she to have a limited capacity for reaction, nothing much could happen in the play. The many and varied details of the situation, stated in the first act, are largely a means for ascribing to her the power of offering life and an empire or death to Bajazet; they create the extraordinary situation. It is not sufficient, however, for Roxane to be in this unusual situation; she must have, as well, all the possible traits of character that will enable her to act appropriately as the unusual situation develops.

In his creation of Roxane's character, Racine paid strict attention to this multiplicity of needs. He gave to her, first and foremost, her great love for Bajazet. All the other personages recognize the quality of this love, but she herself gives the best testimony. Her love for Bajazet has caused her to desert Amurat—

> Bajazet, il est vrai, m'a tout fait oublier—   (308)

and she confesses its vigor to him:

> De toi dépend ma joie et ma félicité.   (556)

She recognizes the extent to which it is a blind love—

> De mon aveugle amour seraient-ce là les fruits?—   (1071)

as well as the degree to which she has been dominated by it:

> Mais, hélas! de l'amour ignorons-nous l'empire?   (1085)

For the purposes of the action, her love must be of this nature, not only so that she may propose the initial alternatives, but also so that she may understand (and resent) the love of Bajazet and Atalide. It is responsible for her capacity to pardon Bajazet, even when the evidence is strong against him (777, 946). It is responsible, also, for her uncertainty about Bajazet's love for her: the disproportion is a source of concern for her. She complains of it to Atalide, wishing that she might believe all that Atalide had told her, pointing out that Bajazet himself has given her no satisfactory evidence (274–86). She now makes positive assurances of his love one of the conditions of her willingness to save his life (255–56, 285–86). These must come from Bajazet himself, not from an intermediary, since she is mistrustful of Atalide (327–32).

Such mistrust is, indeed, one of the signal accompaniments of her love and one of the main traits of her character. It should be, since she has been the victim of a deception in which Acomat, Atalide, and Bajazet have participated—more or less willingly, and for different reasons. In any case, Roxane has been slowly moved toward an extreme action that will lead her, for Bajazet's sake, to violate the traditions of the empire, to turn against Amurat in spite of his love and his generosity, to disobey (again) his firm orders. She is aware of all these sacrifices, for which she has had no return. Once she has been "désabusée," once she suspects that she is "méprisée" (389–90), she must have the capacity to react appropriately. Zaïre points to the necessity of keeping up the deception if Atalide and Bajazet would avoid a crisis:

> N'allez point par vos pleurs déclarer vos amours.
> La main qui l'a sauvé le sauvera toujours,
> Pourvu qu'entretenue en son erreur fatale,
> Roxane jusqu'au bout ignore sa rivale. (411–14)

Roxane herself insists that her sacrifices be compensated; in a speech to Bajazet (505–12) she tries to impress upon him the extent of his obligation to her. Should he fail to return her love, he will earn the title of "ingrat"—and this is the epithet that she applies to him on numerous occasions (cf. 276, 323, 523, 527, 1089, 1311). This extreme sensitivity about the return of favors, about gratitude, leads Roxane to suspect readily that she is being deceived. Hence when Bajazet displays reticence about marrying her, she immediately calls the guards, closes the harem, and announces that the whole conspiracy will be dropped (II, 2). After the second refusal, when Atalide attempts to defend him, she quickly becomes suspicious of their love (III, 6).

This readiness to suspect (which in a way is built into the general situation) is accompanied by other useful characteristics. Roxane is jealous, as Bajazet recognizes when he refers to her "soupçons jaloux" (751) and as she herself shows in her prompt suspicion of Atalide (1060). Her monologue in III, 7, is devoted to an analysis of this sentiment, which leads her, in another monologue (IV, 4), to fix upon a course of action. A third monologue (IV, 5)—Zatime is present, but Roxane is speaking to herself and to Bajazet—distinguishes some of the by-products of her jealousy, such as her attempts at self-deception:

> Tu ne remportais pas une grande victoire,
> Perfide, en abusant ce cœur préoccupé,
> Qui lui-même craignait de se voir détrompé.   (1298–1300)

Like her suspicion, it is a quick jealousy that brings into play her tendency to anger. We note how, in her first long conversation with Bajazet, she flares up, passing to the *tu* form and engaging in rash invective (520 ff.). She calls herself "une amante en furie" (541), speaks of "ma tranquille fureur" (1276). Others accord her the same trait: Atalide and Acomat both call it "colère" (729, 845) and "fureur" (781, 809, 1388).

But sensitivity, jealousy, and anger all exist, in Roxane's character, as handmaidens to her vindictiveness. This is a fundamental disposition for the plot; for if her great love would lead her to forgive Bajazet, would prompt her to clemency and to disobedience of Amurat's order, it must be counteracted by another passion that will cause her to order his death. Otherwise the second alternative cannot exist, either at the beginning or at any other point in the action. This passion has many facets, some of which we have already seen; but at its center is a powerful desire for revenge once she feels she has been wronged. As is so frequently the case, it is Roxane who gives the first insight into this aspect of her character:

> Malgré tout mon amour, si dans cette journée
> Il ne m'attache à lui par un juste hyménée,
> S'il ose m'alléguer une odieuse loi;
> Quand je fais tout pour lui, s'il ne fait tout pour moi;
> Dès le même moment, sans songer si je l'aime,

> Sans consulter enfin si je me perds moi-même,
> J'abandonne l'ingrat, et le laisse rentrer
> Dans l'état malheureux d'où je l'ai su tirer.   (317–24)

She will, however, go farther than "abandon," and she early tells
Bajazet that she could have him killed:

> S'il m'échappait un mot, c'est fait de votre vie.   (542)

(The word that "escapes" her is of course the "Sortez" of line
1564.) Bajazet warns Acomat about this quality in Roxane (577),
Acomat speaks of it a little later (638), Roxane at various points
ascribes her actions to it. For the trait does result in a number of
indispensable acts. When Roxane discovers Bajazet's love for
Atalide, she decides immediately upon his death:

> Qu'il meure. Vengeons-nous. Courez. Qu'on le saisisse.
>   (1277)

But she will torture him first in various ways:

> Qu'il me voie, attentive au soin de son trépas,
> Lui montrer à la fois, et l'ordre de son frère,
> Et de sa trahison ce gage trop sincère.
> Toi, Zatime, retiens ma rivale en ces lieux.
> Qu'il n'ait, en expirant, que ses cris pour adieux.
>   (1316–20)

The desire for revenge is here accompanied by an element of
cruelty that is even more distinct in the following lines, where
she imagines the joys of showing Bajazet's corpse to Atalide:

> Quel surcroît de vengeance et de douceur nouvelle
> De le montrer bientôt pâle et mort devant elle,
> De voir sur cet objet ses regards arrêtés
> Me payer les plaisirs que je leur ai prêtés!   (1325–28)

Cruelty, again, in the conditions that Roxane wishes to impose
upon Bajazet as she gives him his final chance to save his life,

> Dans les mains des muets viens la voir expirer,   (1544)

and in her final proposal to "unite" Bajazet and Atalide:

> Loin de vous séparer, je prétends aujourd'hui
> Par des nœuds éternels vous unir avec lui.
> Vous jouirez bientôt de son aimable vue.   (1623–25)

For she knows that Bajazet is already dead.

These are extreme traits of character. To them we might add her excessive ambition, her delight in the possession of power, her readiness to resort to artifice, her unscrupulousness. When we see Roxane's character in the composite, we realize that it is extraordinary, striking, vigorous. It has a complexity that gives it both life and distinctiveness. We must conclude, also, that all its features are in direct proportion to the uses to which it will be put in the plot. If Racine here creates a multifaceted personage of generally violent dispositions, it is because he has a multi-episodic plot in which many of the episodes involve violent action. Again, Roxane's character is one of the instruments for the justification of what happens as a result of the unusual suppositions from which he begins.

This is both a quality and a defect in the general construction of *Bajazet*. It is a quality in so far as Racine achieves, in the role and in the character of Roxane, not only a device ideally suited to the purposes of his plot, but also an action and a personage interesting in themselves. From the beginning, Roxane is a dominating figure in the play and what she decides, says, and does is of passionate interest to the spectator. We perhaps do not go so far as to approve of her, but we find her character highly "intelligible" in the sense that we can understand her predicament, follow her reactions as her situation changes, become increasingly fascinated by the intricacies of her personality as they reveal themselves to us. Herein lies the defect. Because of the striking nature of Roxane's character, because of the crescendo of cruelty and violence in her action, she comes to occupy a disproportionate share of the plot and thus of the audience's attention. She does not threaten to become the protagonist; Bajazet remains firm in that position. But she tends to overshadow him as a center of the spectator's passions.

Somewhat the same thing had happened in the case of Agrippine in *Britannicus* and of Bérénice; perhaps there are analogies in all the plays we have seen so far. As Racine progressed toward the mastery of his dramatic art, he moved constantly in the direction of the clear definition and isolation of the protagonist and of the action built around him. But as he did so he found it necessary, for one reason or another, to expand the role of one of the other characters; in *Bérénice,* the reason may have been to enrich and augment the somewhat sparse action of Titus; in *Bajazet,* to give credibility to the statement and the development of an extraordinary situation. Whatever the reason, he found himself devoting a goodly proportion of each poem to the expansion and exploitation of personages other than the hero or heroine. (In the case of *Bajazet,* the question might also be asked whether the same does not happen with Acomat and Atalide.) In part, such expansion would be necessary in any dramatic poem: we cannot imagine a good tragedy in which only the protagonist would be presented in a fully developed form while all the other actors were merely puppets. Each personage needs to have as much character, to play as much of a part, as is required by the general structure of the plot. The question is one of proportion —above all of the proportions within the spectator's feelings. If these "other" personages come to demand an excessive amount of the spectator's attention or involvement or emotion, they detract from the hold that the protagonist should have upon him, hence from the clarity and the concentration of the central emotion belonging to the play.

I think that there may be, in *Bajazet,* another element that contributes to the confusion of the emotion—the quantity and the intricacy of material detail and physical action. If there is an "oriental flavor" about the tragedy, it is not because Racine was seeking any local color (even though he claims faithfulness to the "mœurs et coutumes de la nation"), but because his general conception of the plot demanded that he invent palace revolutions, a letter lost and found, the arrival of slaves from a distant army, and all the rest. This is not in itself objectionable; but as Racine added interesting personage to interesting personage, as he multiplied the amount of expository detail necessary to establish the situation and the number of episodes needed to accomplish the action, his simple action tended to be overwhelmed, almost to be lost from sight. His protagonist, whose role is fairly straightforward and who was meant to arouse a relatively direct emotion of pity, pales in comparison with more striking figures. In a word, the typically "Racinian" aspect of his tragedy falls into relative obscurity. This may be why, having attempted the *gageure* of *Bajazet*—the founding of a simple moral action upon a complex material action—he moved on to plays in which complication and enrichment were sought through other means.

VII

ℳithridate

ALMOST EXACTLY a year separated the first performances of *Bajazet* and of *Mithridate,* which was produced at the Hôtel de Bourgogne in January of 1673 and published in March of the same year. The one-a-year rhythm of Racine's compositions is at this point in his career fairly regular. For his seventh tragedy Racine chose a subject out of Roman history, although his hero and principal personages were among the Eastern enemies of the Romans.

"His hero" is perhaps not an inaccurate description of Mithridate's role in the tragedy, if we understand "hero" not in the dramatic but in the epic sense—in the sense in which we would use it for a modern novel or any narrative poem. We might also think of Mithridate as the central figure in a history; for Racine himself seems to have thought of him in that way. A statement in the Preface is highly revealing: "... excepté quelque événement que j'ai un peu rapproché par le droit que donne la poésie, tout le monde reconnaîtra aisément que j'ai suivi l'histoire avec beaucoup de fidélité. En effet, il n'y a guère d'actions éclatantes dans la vie de Mithridate qui n'aient trouvé place dans ma tragédie. J'y ai inséré tout ce qui pouvait mettre en jour les mœurs et les sentiments de ce prince, je veux dire sa haine violente contre les Romains, son grand courage, sa finesse, sa dissimulation, et enfin cette jalousie qui lui était si naturelle, et qui a tant de fois coûté la vie à ses maîtresses." To think of the play as demonstrating the "striking actions," the "character and the feelings" of its hero, is to conceive of it as would any narrator

—poet or historian—who meant to organize his narrative around the "life" or the "personality" of his subject.

This is not necessarily an improper or a wrong way to organize a narrative. I point to Racine's statement merely because it may provide us with a first hypothesis in the light of which we might read *Mithridate,* namely, as a serious drama constructed according to a schematism that would permit the "display" of the hero's life and character. Such a schematism would need, in large part, to provide the appropriate occasions for the display, that is, a certain number of circumstances conducive to the hero's action and of personages who might be the objects of his passions. This is the basis of organization of a large group of episodic, picaresque, or biographical novels. Since we are here, however, dealing with a dramatic treatment, the schematism would have to supply devices for the concentration and the ordering of the materials, that is, a centralizing action and some sequential principle other than the mere chronology of a "life." It should be noted that the problem is radically different from that in a "poem of praise" such as *Alexandre le Grand.* In the latter, action and episodes and personages were devised in such a way as to render possible the progressive and climactic glorification of the hero; in *Mithridate* (if indeed it is made as I am here suggesting), that kind of progression and result would be replaced by another order, essentially more dramatic, and by a willingness to display weakness as well as strength, vice as well as virtue, in both actions and passions. The potential for a truly tragic action would be greater in the case of a *Mithridate* so conceived.

In another passage of his Preface, Racine identified the central action of his play as the death of Mithridate: "sa mort, qui est l'action de ma tragédie." A death, however, is not an action, at least not in the poetic sense; it is at best a subject or a theme or an event in a dramatic action. We must suppose that Racine meant it in one of these senses, that he wished to include in the idea of "sa mort" the whole complex of circumstances and incidents that led up to it. Our first reading of the play, act by act, might thus consist in the testing of two hypotheses, both suggested by the poet: that *Mithridate* is written in such a way as to present a "display" of its hero's life and character, that its action is composed of all the elements necessary to bring about the death of the hero.

Act I. Mithridate does not himself appear in the first act; but as far as he is concerned it is divided into two parts. A first (longer) part involves essentially the reactions to his reported death by three persons, his two sons and his intended bride, already proclaimed his queen. A second (shorter) part is given over to the response of his sons to the news of his return. Both parts serve to characterize him and to relate a portion of his life. For forty years Mithridate has opposed the power of the Romans:

> Ainsi ce roi, qui seul a durant quarante ans
> Lassé tout ce que Rome eut de chefs importants,
> Et qui dans l'Orient balançant la fortune,
> Vengeait de tous les rois la querelle commune,
> Meurt ...   (9-13)

The opposition to Rome has constituted the core of his military career. That career, meanwhile, has been accompanied by his adventures as a lover, and we learn that many mistresses have served his passion (86–88); latest of these is Monime, betrothed and crowned but as yet unwed. For both careers, as soldier and as lover, Mithridate has been given the requisite traits of character. His courage and determination, mentioned constantly, are the basis of his military success, along with great patriotism and an unending hatred for Rome; "transport" and "tendresse" (353, 87) mark him as a lover, but they are frequently tempered by cruelty and jealousy (86–87, 353). Other traits belong to the whole man; they are best summarized by Pharnace in the last scene of Act I:

> Mithridate revient, peut-être inexorable:
> Plus il est malheureux, plus il est redoutable.
> . . . .

Rarement l'amitié désarme sa colère;
Ses propres fils n'ont point de juge plus sévère;
Et nous l'avons vu même à ses cruels soupçons
Sacrifier deux fils pour de moindres raisons.

. . . .

Amant avec transport, mais jaloux sans retour,
Sa haine va toujours plus loin que son amour.
Ne vous assurez point sur l'amour qu'il vous porte:
Sa jalouse fureur n'en sera que plus forte.　　(343–56)

Le Roi, toujours fertile en dangereux détours,
S'armera contre nous de nos moindres discours.
Vous savez sa coutume, et sous quelles tendresses
Sa haine sait cacher ses trompeuses adresses.　　(369–72)

Perhaps cruelty and ruse are the dominant characteristics accorded the father by the son.

Such a realistic appraisal of Mithridate's character would be in keeping with any intention to "display" the man and his acts as history had preserved them. But each of the traits is also rendered useful by Racine for the action of the play as he develops it; each thus serves his poetic purposes. Their first usefulness lies in determining, within this same Act I, the two sets of reactions already mentioned. The initial report of Mithridate's death elicits from Xipharès a statement of his own opposition to the Romans and his faithfulness to his father's cause; from Pharnace a suggestion that he takes the opposite side; from Arbate, required to choose between the two, a preference for the person and the position of Xipharès. It thus sets the half-brothers in clear opposition one to the other, on the score of the division of Mithridate's estates, on the matter of avenging their father, and on the important issue of their attitude toward Rome. All these probabilities will be called upon in the later development of the action.

So much for the military consequences of the report; it also has important repercussions for the amorous affairs of all the parties. Pharnace had declared his love for Monime a week before, when the first rumors of his father's death had been heard. Now that more substantial reports arrive, Xipharès makes an open declaration to her; the two brothers thus become rivals in love as well as in all the rest. Moreover, Monime rejects overtly all thought of marriage with Pharnace, suggests covertly that Xipharès' love might be acceptable to her. Once again, the probabilities so established will later be useful: Pharnace will use his knowledge of his brother's love against him, Monime will be tricked into implicating Xipharès (about whose love she must know in order to do so), Xipharès and Monime will ultimately be contented.

Mithridate, of course, is not dead, and from the beginning —in the very way in which the report is made—the spectator is led to guess as much. The very first lines of the play seem to make an unequivocal affirmation:

> On nous faisait, Arbate, un fidèle rapport;
> Rome en effet triomphe, et Mithridate est mort.   (1–2)

But a few lines later Xipharès betrays the nature of his information:

> Et j'ai su qu'un soldat dans les mains de Pompée
> Avec son diadème a remis son épée.   (7–8)

Moreover, in the fourth scene of this act the personages (and the spectator with them) will be informed of Mithridate's return. Racine thus uses the dramatic device of the false report in order to permit revelations of the passions and statements of positions that would not otherwise have been possible. He had used the device, with some awkwardness, in the case of Étéocle in *La Thébaïde* and of Porus in *Alexandre;* he was to use it later in *Mithridate* in connection with Xipharès and, most successfully of all, for Thésée in *Phèdre*. The great virtue of the device in *Mithridate* (as later in *Phèdre*) is that it introduces mobility into a hitherto static situation, serving in a sense to upset the balance of conflicts and oppositions that had prevailed previously.

After the report has been rectified and Mithridate's return announced in scene 4, a new set of reactions becomes possible. Pharnace immediately evinces disappointment; Monime and Xipharès, shame and guilt over what they have done. In scene 5, Pharnace reveals (in an aside) that he awaits the arrival of the Romans, and (openly to Xipharès) he proposes to his brother an alliance against their father; they should, he suggests, obtain control over Nymphea and prevent their father from entering it. When Xipharès refuses, moved by love of his father and a sense of atonement for his mother's past treachery, Pharnace urges that they agree to keep each other's secrets. It is of course he who will first break his trust.

Although Mithridate has been absent from the first act, he has in a way been constantly present. The act has been used to reveal the situations and the passions of three personages who will either determine his actions in the rest of the drama or whose actions will be determined by him. It has also been used, and very effectively, to characterize Mithridate with some completeness. The "display" of his character has run parallel to the creation of probabilities for his subsequent actions and for those of the other actors.

Act II. Whereas Mithridate had been entirely absent from the first act, he is constantly present in the second act except for the first and the last scenes. The first scene, in which Monime confesses (to her servant) her love for Xipharès, serves to inform the spectator of Monime's passion and to make him understand, in scene 4, the reasons why she behaves as she does toward Mithridate. The final scene is devoted to a parallel revelation of her love, this time to Xipharès himself, a revelation essential if we are to appreciate fully what happens later in III, 5, where Mithridate tricks Monime into the third confession of her love. The last scene of Act II also advances the action as it concerns Xipharès and Monime; in it, Monime states that she will marry Mithridate out of a sense of duty, and out of a sense of her own incapacity to resist Xipharès she orders him not to see her again.

The rest of the act is Mithridate's. The brief scene 2, where he makes his first appearance, permits the direct display of his character as it had been previously described. The "faux bruit de sa mort" of which Phædime had spoken (329) turns out, now, to have been started by himself (428), thus attesting to his capacity for ruse; and the new project that he promises to detail to his sons is a witness, as he himself says, to his "courage" (432). Besides, his initial lines in the play (423–26) are an expression of his suspicious nature. The same traits are developed in scene 3, in which he discusses his situation with Arbate. His courage is stressed several times (438, 440), he refers again to the "bruit" of his death (450), he dwells at length on his suspicions relating to his sons. But many more things are introduced: Mithridate admits that he is vanquished (439), thus confirming the "Rome en effet triomphe" of line 2; he has suffered a setback in his military career. He suspects also that he has lost out in his love; war, love, and suspicion are interrelated in such lines as the following:

> Toujours du même amour tu me vois enflammé:
> Ce cœur nourri de sang, et de guerre affamé,
> Malgré le faix des ans et du sort qui m'opprime,
> Traîne partout l'amour qui l'attache à Monime,
> Et n'a point d'ennemis qui lui soient odieux
> Plus que deux fils ingrats que je trouve en ces lieux.
>
> (457–62)

Love, hatred, and suspicion combine in the closing words of the scene:

> Dieux, qui voyez ici mon amour et ma haine,
> Epargnez mes malheurs, et daignez empêcher
> Que je ne trouve encor ceux que je vais chercher.
>
> (524–26)

In the last of these passages, as in other places (455–56, 537, 558), Mithridate speaks of his "malheurs." This is a general way of characterizing his situation—both in war and in love—and of establishing the probabilities for his future action within the play. It may also be a way of identifying him as a "tragic" hero

by pointing up his circumstances of misfortune and by eliciting
the audience's sympathy for them. Such potentialities for action
begin to be realized in this third scene; in an Oedipus-like quest,
Mithridate urges Arbate to give him information that he really
does not wish to hear. As he gets this information, he is confirmed in his preference for Xipharès over Pharnace, and his
statement in scene 2, "Mais vous avez pour juge un père qui vous
aime" (427), comes to be specified and limited. This preference
leads him to suspect Xipharès less readily than he suspects
Pharnace and to approve what knowledge he has of Xipharès'
pretensions to certain parts of his estates.

Although, in scene 4, Mithridate alludes in passing to the new
military exploits that will serve his glory (544-46), his main subject of conversation with Monime is naturally his love for her
and his wish to marry her immediately. He recognizes, in her
presence, the same situation of "malheur" to which he had earlier
referred, tending to ascribe it now to destiny and fortune (e.g.,
"mon infortune" [534]; "le sort ennemi" [561]; "au destin qui
m'outrage" [575]). His misfortunes are those of war, but they
also comprise the treachery of Pharnace, whose character Mithridate sketches (602-3), and hence involve his love. The scene
comprises several events for which Mithridate is responsible:
he proposes immediate marriage to Monime, he rebukes her for
accepting only as a matter of duty, he accuses her of loving
Pharnace—but only after allowing her to think, because of his
ambiguous statements, that he might be accusing Xipharès; he
indicates the distinction that he makes between the two brothers.
It is possible that the unclear allusion to "un fils perfide" (589),
wilful or not, and Monime's reaction to it may have furnished to
Mithridate the pattern for his later testing of Monime.

In any case, the same pattern is repeated at the beginning of
scene 5, where Mithridate tells Xipharès that "un fils audacieux"
(607) has betrayed him. Both statements would seem to constitute examples of the king's capacity for ruse. But here Xipharès'
fears are soon quieted as Mithridate points to Pharnace. In the

same scene, after affirming his confidence in Xipharès, Mithridate entrusts Monime to his care; meanwhile, he refers guardedly again to the "grands desseins que mon cœur se propose" (616) and, in the closing lines, shows the extent to which he is capable of revenge:

> En un mot, c'est assez éprouver ma faiblesse:
> Qu'elle ne pousse point cette même tendresse,
> Que sais-je? à des fureurs dont mon cœur outragé
> Ne se repentirait qu'après s'être vengé.   (631–34)

Then he leaves Monime to confess her love to Xipharès, and Xipharès with the dilemma of obeying his father or obeying his beloved. Throughout Act II, then, Mithridate has continued to manifest his capacities for war and for love and he has pursued both strains in his actions; at the same time, he has given witness to the other traits of character that will underlie the major episodes of the play.

Act III. The third act is again marked by the constant and dominating presence of Mithridate. Since the previous acts had sufficiently displayed his character, Act III can now display character in action and, in so doing, can further the major development of the tragedy. It does so by exploiting the military and the sentimental potential of the hero, alternatively and sometimes simultaneously. In the first scene Mithridate at last explains in detail his "grands desseins," justifying them as a means of countering "la fortune ennemie" (759). They include, beside the great campaign against the Romans, an act of revenge: because Pharnace has loved Monime and proposed marriage to her, he will be married (in a military alliance) to the king of Parthia's daughter (849–54). When Pharnace resists and suggests instead an alliance with Rome, Mithridate's anger against him grows; and when the son definitely refuses to obey, the father openly accuses him of the betrayal. Xipharès, speaking only of military matters, rejects any turn toward Rome and offers, instead, to share with his brother the task of carrying out Mithridate's designs; he says nothing of love.

But Pharnace, when Mithridate has him arrested (in scene 2), not only confesses his own guilt but implicates also both Xipharès and Monime:

> Il aime aussi la Reine, et même en est aimé. (998)

For Mithridate, this means a return of suspicion about his favored son, suspicion that he resists initially (scene 3) but that grows as he ponders upon it. His soliloquy in scene 4 alternates between his unwillingness to believe the perfidious Pharnace and his fears that Xipharès may indeed have played false; these doubts are resolved in his determination to obtain the answer from Monime herself. He will work through ruse and dissimulation:

> S'il n'est digne de moi, le piège est digne d'eux.
> Trompons qui nous trahit; et pour connaître un traître,
> Il n'est pas de moyens.... Mais je la vois paraître:
> Feignons; et de son cœur, d'un vain espoir flatté,
> Par un mensonge adroit tirons la vérité. (1030–34)

And he does. In scene 5, his ruse consists in urging Monime, three times in succession, to accept marriage with Xipharès rather than with himself—alleging his age and his misfortunes—and in threatening her, should she refuse, with the necessity of marrying Pharnace. Monime, duped, discloses her love and Xipharès':

> Avant que votre amour m'eût envoyé ce gage,
> Nous nous aimions ... (1111–12)

Mithridate is shocked to anger (in scene 6), now calls Xipharès "ingrat" and "perfide," quickly decides upon his revenge in the form of Xipharès' death; he is sufficiently composed, however, to realize the usefulness of continued dissimulation: "Dissimulons encor" (1126).

Thus the third act has carried Mithridate through a discovery to others of his military intentions, to a knowledge of the guilt of both his sons and of his queen, finally to a condemnation to death of his favorite son. (He had previously, as we know from line 350, sacrificed two other sons.) For the accomplishment of these actions, all the traits earlier associated with his character have been exploited, and a number of stated probabilities have been realized; note that a quickness to revenge, resident in character, is conjoined with his earlier killing of two sons to bring about his determination to kill a third.

Act IV. The fourth act is fairly equally divided between two functions, that of pursuing (in the first three scenes) the consequences of Mithridate's actions in the preceding act, and that of adding new episodes to the central action (in the rest). The interruption of the main thread by a set of "consequences" is essential; as the play is constructed, the actions of the other persons depend, in part at least, upon decisions made and actions taken by Mithridate, and time must be taken out to develop probabilities for these other persons. In addition, Mithridate's own actions will be given new directions by the attitudes, the responses, and the decisions of the secondary personages. Scene 1 is a derivative scene of this kind. Speaking to Phædime, Monime expresses her fears that Mithridate may have been "feigning" (1134), her hopes that she may at last be married to Xipharès. There are further allusions to Mithridate's "dessein" (1155); there is news of the harsh treatment being given Pharnace (1162).

In scene 2, Monime's fears (rather than her hopes) are shown to have been justified. Xipharès knows that he has been betrayed, and he has been warned by Arbate to leave at once. That is, Mithridate's second act of vengeance is about to be accomplished, with Xipharès as the victim (1192). In this connection, such traits of Mithridate's as would appear in his revenge are stressed:

> Vous dépendez ici d'une main violente,
> Que le sang le plus cher rarement épouvante;

> Et je n'ose vous dire à quelle cruauté
> Mithridate jaloux s'est souvent emporté.
> Peut-être c'est moi seul que sa fureur menace ...
>
> (1203–7)

These traits had been ascribed to Mithridate before; they are now repeated as applicable to a particular situation. "Display" of character is now subordinated to justification of action. There is further characterization of Mithridate by Monime, who, when she learns of the trick played upon her, can speak only of the "barbare" and of his "barbarie" (1251, 1255). Her estimate of Mithridate accounts for her rejection, in this scene, of Xipharès' proposal that she marry Mithridate, and later (scene 4), of Mithridate's own proposal. Finally, scene 2 gives more insights into the love of Xipharès and Monime—her desperate guilt at having betrayed him, his willingness to pardon her as long as love was the motive—and describes Xipharès' situation in the same terms used for Mithridate's:

> Je suis un malheureux que le destin poursuit.   (1218)

As he continues in the same speech, Xipharès gives one of those summary statements that Racine tended more and more to introduce into his plays:

> C'est lui qui m'a ravi l'amitié de mon père,
> Qui le fit mon rival, qui révolta ma mère,
> Et vient de susciter, dans ce moment affreux,
> Un secret ennemi pour nous trahir tous deux.   (1219–22)

Scene 3 merely announces Mithridate's arrival and allows Monime to send a warning and a message of caution to Xipharès.

There is some question, I think, about the probability of Mithridate's proposal of an immediate marriage in scene 4. He had made the same offer in II, 4, only to learn that Monime's obedience would be a result of her sense of duty, not of her love. In the feint of III, 5, he had obtained the information that Monime loved his son rather than himself. His own plans to marry her before embarking on the Roman expedition have apparently not changed, and he seems willing to take her as merely dutiful:

Songez que votre cœur est un bien qui m'est dû.   (1281)

But is it poetically probable that, given the antecedents and the circumstances, he should again make the same proposal in almost the same terms? Or has the poet here re-exploited an old probability without sufficiently renewing and refreshing it? In any case, Monime's answer is necessarily and categorically negative. As Mithridate makes his case, he stresses his former glory as an argument in his favor, urges his present misfortunes ("le sort ennemi" [1304]) as a basis for Monime's sympathy; but he also indicates that anger and revenge will follow upon her refusal. Before refusing, Monime blames Mithridate for having reawakened her love for Xipharès and revived her hopes; she also condemns him for the trick. Afterward, taking full responsibility for her refusal of Mithridate, she begs him to spare Xipharès.

Mithridate's monologue in scene 5 (like the one in III, 4) represents his vacillation among several passions and various courses of action. His anger, his fury, his desire for revenge would now have him "immolate" all three of his enemies. But his love for Xipharès, and especially the need he feels for his support, would have him spare this son, while his love for Monime suggests two alternatives: cede her to Xipharès, or persist in wishing to keep her for himself. No decision is made; but a number of rival probabilities have been introduced, and the choice among them will be determined by what new arguments or events are subsequently added. Scene 6 makes such additions: Arbate's news that Pharnace's intervention has endangered the march on Rome induces Mithridate to call upon Xipharès for help; but the report (later proved false) that Xipharès has joined the rebels leads the old king to resolve, once more, to kill both his sons. The last announcement, in scene 7, that the Romans have arrived sends Mithridate off with vague threats of revenge.

With respect to Mithridate, then, the fourth act has brought him to a sharper realization of the treachery of one son, Pharnace, and to a supposition about the treachery of the other; it has informed him of the hopelessness of his love for Monime, who has refused to marry him; and it has brought to a critical point his war with the Romans—here in Nymphea rather than at Rome itself. In a sense, the last event has negated his plans for the Roman conquest and reduced his line of action to a defensive one. His "malheurs" in war have become more immediate and more desperate, partly through the treason of Pharnace; his "malheurs" in love have reached a climax in Monime's vigorous rejection of him. What lines of action still remain open to him? Negatively, revenge; positively, steps to avert complete disaster at the hands of the Romans.

Act V. Both the negative and the positive actions taken by Mithridate in the last act occur at a distance from the stage and are reported through a *récit;* he himself appears only in the final scene. This arrangement is necessary for two reasons: messages, reports, and orders from the king, if they are to have their maximum effectiveness, must follow a fixed chronology and must be spaced at proper intervals; this would not be possible if he were constantly present. Second, the military action in which he participates, involving large numbers of men and many vicissitudes, must be located at the port of the city—not in the omnibus palace. The first of the reports, to the effect that Xipharès had been killed and that Mithridate was in a desperate situation, had reached Monime during the interval between Acts IV and V; it had led to her "fureur" and to her attempt to kill herself, using Mithridate's diadem as an instrument. These events are summarized early in scene 1, where Phædime points out the likelihood that the report about Xipharès is false: an earlier rumor that he had defected to the rebels had been disproved, and the new one is subject to denial. As for the king, the report indicates that he had responded to the news of the Romans' arrival by going out to attack them, and that so far he has been the loser; but at least one of his "enemies," Xipharès, has become his ally. Monime's response to the dual report is her "fureur," despair toward her own situation, and especially a feeling that she herself has been guilty and responsible in both disasters. She wishes only to find some means to die.

The means are provided in scene 2, when Mithridate sends her a poison—for obvious uses. This is his way of avenging himself upon the third of his "enemies." Given her dispositions at this point, Monime is ready and willing to take it—as expiation for her own guilt, as a sacrifice to her lover—and is about to do so when, in scene 3, Arbate arrives with a counterorder and saves her life. Mithridate, although we can know it only indirectly, has changed his mind; hence his own situation and his state of knowledge must also have changed. The function of scene 4, devoted largely to Arbate's *récit,* is to explain the change and the events behind it. Arbate first reports the current situation: Xipharès is alive, Mithridate close to death, and both are now approaching. Then Arbate relates a whole series of offstage actions, some of them involving Mithridate, others Xipharès: the report of Xipharès' death; Mithridate's attempts at suicide, first by taking poisons (he had alluded to his immunity in IV, 5), then by engaging in a hopeless battle against the Romans—seconded and encouraged by Pharnace, finally by using his own sword to prevent a dishonorable capture; the victory of Xipharès over Pharnace and the Romans; last of all, Xipharès' grief on discovering his father's state, and his own attempted suicide.

Scene 5, concluding the tragedy, returns Mithridate and Xipharès to the stage; but the action will be entirely the father's. Since he is close to death and can foresee no future action for himself, Mithridate is limited to two kinds of activity in this scene; he may justify what he has done, and he may arrange the lives of those who will survive him. His justification constitutes the last "display" of character, recalling as it does his glory, his long struggle against the Romans, his avoidance of the ignominy of capture, and—even if it was Xipharès' rather than his own—

the final victory. Such lines as these represent his character as it
had been from the beginning:

> ... j'ose me flatter qu'entre les noms fameux
> Qu'une pareille haine a signalés contre eux,
> Nul ne leur a plus fait acheter la victoire,
> Ni de jours malheureux plus rempli leur histoire.
> Le ciel n'a pas voulu qu'achevant mon dessein
> Rome en cendre me vît expirer dans son sein.
> Mais au moins quelque joie en mourant me console:
> J'expire environné d'ennemis que j'immole;
> Dans leur sang odieux j'ai pu tremper mes mains,
> Et mes derniers regards ont vu fuir les Romains.
>
> (1657–66)

That other kind of "display" that consists in action according to
character resides, here, in two acts: Mithridate pardons Xipharès
and advises him to go into hiding, and he gives Monime to him
in marriage. For both these acts probabilities had been established in Mithridate's long soliloquy of Act IV; for the pardon,
in lines 1394–1400, for the "ceding" of Monime, in lines 1401–3.
Only the intervening circumstances had been necessary to bring
about these choices rather than their alternatives. As for the
last of his "enemies," the dying Mithridate leaves his punishment
to the perfidious Romans.

The fifth act of *Mithridate* brings to conclusion all the lines of
action pursued throughout the play. Some, such as Mithridate's
plans of conquest and marriage, end negatively with his death;
they cannot possibly come about. Others, involving the revenge
upon his "enemies," take a negative turn because of changes in
circumstances and in his state of knowledge. The rest, consisting
largely in the favorable resolutions for Xipharès and Monime
and in the local defeat of the Romans, are the realization of alternative probabilities, or, as in the last example, the result of
Xipharès' activity rather than of Mithridate's.

Such a study of Mithridate's role in the tragedy indicates, first
and clearly, that Racine has succeeded in making of his hero a

truly central personage. Central, first, in the sense that Mithridate is almost constantly present on the stage, speaking and acting before the spectator, and much more so than any of Racine's earlier heroes. With the exception of Act I, there is no act in which the king does not appear; in Acts II, III, and IV, he is present much of the time, and in Act V he arrives for the crucial events of the denouement. Moreover, at such times as he is absent, the dialogue relates to his character and his affairs, the actions of other persons are preparations for or consequences of his own. Central, therefore, in the sense that he is the hero of the main action of the play. Since Pharnace's love and treason are patently auxiliary to the progress of Mithridate's affairs, there is really only one other action in the tragedy that might be considered to rival Mithridate's and to be a contender for the place of organizing action in the work; that is, of course, the love and fortunes of Xipharès and Monime.

Mithridate opens with a set of circumstances that would seem to favor the general improvement of Xipharès' situation. Mithridate is dead, Xipharès may succeed both to a part of his estates and to his queen; hence his declaration of love to Monime. It closes with these potentialities realized; Mithridate is dead, having left as a legacy to Xipharès both his betrothed and his dominions, and the lovers are contented. Only the revenge upon Rome and upon Pharnace need still be accomplished. The direction of the action could thus be interpreted as a movement from statements of probability about Monime and Xipharès to the ultimate exhaustion of that probability. Besides, the sympathies of the spectator, attached to the two lovers from the beginning, seems throughout the play to accompany their vicissitudes and to be satisfied, at the end, especially by their success. There are a number of reasons for this attachment: the noble characters of the two young lovers, their closeness in age (as contrasted with the disparity between Monime and Mithridate), the fact that they had loved before the interposition of Mithridate; the general antipathy to Xipharès' rival, Pharnace; the tendency of the audience to regard Mithridate as soldier and king rather than as lover. Apparently, Racine worked carefully to direct the sentiments of his audience toward Xipharès and Monime, not only by the way in which he built their own characters, but also through the establishment of the whole complex of emotional reactions to the various personages.

Yet the fate of Monime and Xipharès does not come to constitute the central action of the play. In spite of our interest in their destinies, we are aware always of the fact that what happens to them is subordinate to Mithridate's career of conquest and revenge. This is because he has been given, in the play, the power of decision and command, and as long as he is alive no change can come about in the situation of Monime and Xipharès except through his wish. Monime and Xipharès never challenge this power; only Pharnace does so, and in so doing becomes the antagonist, the only real "enemy." The dramatist uses this device—of resting in his protagonist the capacity to direct the action—as a means of establishing that same protagonist in a position of centrality and domination. Monime may wish to marry Xipharès, but she will marry Mithridate—up to the point of the trick—through a sense of duty and obedience. Xipharès may blame fortune for his misfortunes, but he will remain submissive and subservient to his father in matters of love as of war, going so far as to urge Monime to marry Mithridate (IV, 2), espousing his ambitions of conquest, fighting in his cause. Only Mithridate, in the closing scene, can bring about the adjustments in the situation that will lead to the lovers' happiness.

There is a parallel, I think, between the centrality of Mithridate and that of Andromaque; but there is also an important difference. In *Andromaque,* Racine devised a complicated interrelationship of personages of such nature that the decisions and the fortunes of all the others depended, ultimately, upon decisions by the heroine. Each change or seeming change in Andromaque's intentions led to alterations in the situations of Pyrrhus, Hermione, and Oreste; and, contrariwise, the responses of these per-

sonages, dictated by their passions, affected Andromaque's own
activity. The device was fairly mechanical; and since it involved
necessarily long systems of action and reaction, much of the play
had to be devoted to the lives and loves of the secondary actors.
Andromaque was largely absent. In *Mithridate,* Racine achieves
simultaneously presence and centrality; his protagonist dominates the stage as he dominates the action. This comes about
partly as a result of the reduction in the number of tightly interrelated personages to three—Mithridate, Xipharès, and Monime;
Pharnace remains essentially distant and auxiliary. Partly it
comes from the nature of the interrelationship: Whereas Mithridate's decisions affect the destinies of the other two, what they do
has little effect upon his will; the system of "reverse" passions
and actions does not apply. And whereas the others may have
their ups and downs, the vicissitudes of their fortunes do not
change in any important way the essentially unilinear character
of Mithridate's career.

This means, really, that the action of *Mithridate* is constructed
on a different basis from that of *Andromaque.* A look at the
basic nature of this action will suffice to clarify the point. Assuming (as we must) that Mithridate is still alive at the beginning of the tragedy—the report of his death serves supplementary purposes—we see his problems as really very limited in
number: he must continue his opposition to the Romans; he
must marry Monime; he must avenge himself upon all those
who, when his death was rumored, took action contrary to his
interests. For each of these problems, varying or even opposite
solutions are possible, and the course of the action, as well as its
conclusion, will depend upon which of the alternatives is realized and at what point. In the case of the Romans, there is no
alternative with respect to the end: Mithridate must continue to
oppose them as he has for the last forty years; this is a fundamental element of his character. Only the ways of opposing them
remain subject to choice: he may continue to meet their attacks,
he may go out against their Asian legions, or—and this is his

great "dessein"—he may attempt the conquest of Rome herself. The last of these constitutes his primary military intention until the end of the fourth act, where Pharnace's treason prevents the departure of Mithridate's forces and where, shortly thereafter, the arrival of attacking Roman troops obliges him to resort to defensive action. We should note that it is not Mithridate's will but rather circumstance and the deeds of others that determine the ultimate direction of his action.

His project to marry Monime follows a similar development. Again, this is a long-term plan of Mithridate's, antedating by months or years the opening of the drama, and, again, he remains unswerving in his determination through most of the play. In reality, there are no alternatives for Mithridate; he means to marry Monime. Hence his reiterated proposals after his return, including the last one at a time when it would seem neither probable nor likely to succeed. His failure to marry her must depend upon others—upon her refusal (which ultimately does take place), upon her preference for another (which she does state), or upon the victory of a rival (and one of the two rivals does win, at the end, with Mithridate's blessing and because of his imminent death). His own responsibility for his failure is limited to the trick, which wins for him the judgment of "barbare" from Monime, and which determines her refusal. The mutual love of Monime and Xipharès is none of his doing, and their marriage comes only as a side effect of his suicide, which results rather from his "gloire" than from his thwarted love. All this means that, as in the case of his military defeat, outside events and the will of others produce the outcome of his relationship with Monime.

The necessity for revenge is the only one of his three problems that has its origins within the tragedy itself; for only when he returns does he learn of Pharnace's defection to the Romans and his proposal to Monime, and only much later does Pharnace accuse Xipharès (III, 2) and does Monime substantiate the accusation (III, 5). Mithridate's character will lead him to seek revenge upon all three guilty parties, to try to establish their guilt through devious means, and to avenge himself in extreme ways; on the other hand, his magnanimity is such that he will pardon and reward when these acts are merited. What, then, determines the outcome of his vengeful intentions in each of the three cases? For Pharnace, circumstances make it necessary for Mithridate to renounce his revenge, which he leaves to his son's Roman allies. Xipharès, through his loyalty to his father's military cause and through his active role in the battle (which indeed reverses Mithridate's fortunes), disproves the suspicion of disloyalty and gains Mithridate's gratitude; he is therefore pardoned for having loved Monime and proposed marriage to her. It is Xipharès' action here that leads Mithridate to choose the opposite of revenge; yet he does make the choice and, in so doing, acts. Revenge upon Monime becomes a necessity for Mithridate when, first, he learns that she loves Xipharès and when, second, she refuses to marry him; the latter event results from Mithridate's trick. Once more, Mithridate acts, sending poison to Monime as the means to his revenge; but his counteraction through Arbate's message shortly afterward spares her life. Changes in circumstances—his approaching death, Xipharès' victory—bring about the reward rather than the punishment of Monime. There is no revenge.

In none of the three cases, then, does Mithridate's wish for revenge come to fulfillment, and mostly this is because external events or circumstances not within his control—or the initiatives of other persons—intervene. There is a negative solution to each of the probabilities, at rare times because he changes his mind and selects an alternative probability, usually because he is powerless to act. In a way, this situation is representative of Mithridate's whole progress through the tragedy. His problems are not solved by himself or as a result of his action, but by "fate" or "fortune"—which we must take as meaning the activity of the world outside himself. What he does is in perfect keeping with his character: his bitter opposition to the Romans and his suicide, his condemnation and then pardoning of Monime and Xipharès. But it does not solve all his initial problems, and when it does it is *in extremis*—in a way that really represents defeat and disaster for him.

Now this is a strange way of conceiving and organizing the tragic action. What is "tragic" about Mithridate is his status of misfortune throughout the play and his defeat and death at the end, perhaps even the fact that, in some respects, his character is such that misfortune is not merited. The tragedy is one of situation, or of character in situation, without becoming one of action. I mean by this that the "tragic" events at the end do not grow, progressively and dynamically, out of the hero's attempts to right his unfortunate state. The action does not advance, in an orderly way, from an initial statement of problems for the protagonist to an ultimate solution, through his own agency, of those same problems.

I might suggest the possibility that the play is organized on a different basis. At the beginning, Rome is reported triumphant, Mithridate dead, Monime and Xipharès may express their love and hope to marry; Pharnace is known to be the ally of the Romans against his father. At the end, the Romans have suffered a local defeat, but the long and effective opposition of Mithridate has come to an end; Mithridate is dying; Monime and Xipharès receive Mithridate's sanction to marry; Pharnace has fled with his Roman allies. There is thus a kind of symmetry between the beginning and the end, a pattern that makes of the end an actualization of events and situations that were merely a matter of rumor or hope at the beginning. And in between? In between, a series of events—revelations or discoveries, victories or defeats, manifestations of loyalty or of treachery—is introduced in order to make it possible for Mithridate to "display" all the traits of character that had been assigned to him by others or that he himself had admitted as part of his essential constitution. The choice and introduction of such events is not random, for all relate at once to the main personages and to the central situation—and to their interrelationship. All have an order to the degree that they lead, one by one, to the worsening of Mithridate's situation—to the point where the suicide becomes necessary and the pardon possible.

Such an interpretation of the plot would corroborate my original thesis that *Mithridate* was organized in a way to "display" the life and the character of its hero and that its structure was directed toward bringing about his death. At the present time I see no other reading that explains as well various puzzling features of the play. But if we read *Mithridate* thus, we must conclude that the work is more effective as rhetoric than as drama. What is really imposing and impressive and moving about it is the figure of Mithridate—central, present, and manifesting with equal vigor and clarity the weaknesses and the strengths of his character. The others, much as we may approve and like them, are less monumental; but they help us to achieve the right degree of emotion and the right passions with respect to Mithridate. When Monime judges that he is a "barbare," we make the same judgment; when Xipharès supports his father's ambitions for conquest, they seem more legitimate and admirable to us. When Mithridate himself condemns, or pardons, or fights against great odds, or kills himself, we feel strongly the justification in his character and in circumstances for these actions. In all this, we are responding more clearly to a man, to his character and his acts, than to the emotional potential of a developing action.

If the effect is rather epideictic than tragic, it is so in a way different from the one we noted in *Alexandre le Grand*. In Racine's earlier play, not only was the "centrality" of the main personage less definite—tempered as it was by the strong personalities and actions of other personages—but the emotion attaching to him was of a different order. *Alexandre* is a poem of praise; either directly or indirectly, everything in the play contributes to the creation and development of "admiration" for the hero, who is "grand" in every respect. *Mithridate* is, rather than a poem of praise and blame, a poem of understanding and sympathy, per-

haps even of wonder. As such, it presents defects along with qualities, vices with virtues. It is the existence of these defects and
vices that gives to the hero some of the marks of a tragic hero;
for we may see him as at least partly responsible for his misery
through his violence, his jealousy, his vindictiveness, his habit of
dissimulation. Nevertheless, his final actions are of a nature to
establish the superiority of the positive aspects of his character, and
the fact that "destiny" and "fate" (in their special way) bring so
many of his misfortunes upon him leads us to accord him that
sympathy that we give to victims.

As compared with both *Andromaque* and *Alexandre,* where
the problem of the protagonist had been solved in two separate
ways, *Mithridate* makes some progress in dramatic technique,
shows some retrogression. It is less successful than *Andromaque*
in creating a central person about whom a truly dramatic action
was actually organized; but it succeeds better in bringing its
protagonist onto the stage and keeping him there constantly
enough to make his character the source of a vigorous emotional
response in the audience. In so far as it returns to the pseudo-
rhetorical structure of *Alexandre,* there is retrogression; Racine,
struggling with his permanent problem of bringing a protagonist
and an action together in the right relationship, reverts to a form
in which action is sacrificed to character. As a consequence, the
emotions induced result primarily from rhetorical, secondarily
from poetic, devices. Yet there is progress over *Alexandre,* since
the plot more closely revolves about the protagonist in *Mithridate,*
comprises a smaller number of rival persons, and better maintains the presence of its hero. For the act of "générosité" that
constitutes the denouement, similar to that of *Alexandre,* the
preparation is better in the later play; and because it evinces a
more striking reversal from the alternative probabilities, and a
more rapid one, it is better capable of producing wonder in the
audience.

In the treatment of some of the secondary developments in
Mithridate Racine also gives witness of increasing sureness in his

dramatic technique. We may take as an example the gradual revelation of Monime's love for Xipharès. In the first act, after Xipharès' confession, Monime gives only the most ambiguous intimation that this affection may be returned. At the beginning of the second act, she makes full announcement of her love; but it is to her servant, Phædime, that she speaks. Xipharès himself does not learn about it until her declaration to him at the end of the same act. And the person most affected by knowledge of it, in the working-out of the play, does not achieve that knowledge until the end of the third act; Monime's account to Mithridate, resulting from the trick, is the one that most adversely influences her own fortunes and most nearly leads to a successful revenge by Mithridate. Several purposes are served by this progressive revelation, so unlike the clear-cut positions of the personages in the early plays. For one thing, it allows the audience to have knowledge of the fact before the interested parties do, thus creating the possibility of suspense and anxiety on its part. For another, it allows the persons in the play to act diversely in terms of ignorance and of knowledge, according to a chronology that best fits the realization of the major pattern. Finally, it permits of a kind of dramatic climaxing that introduces movement and dynamic qualities into the plot.

In *Mithridate,* this device is used in relationship to a passion belonging to a secondary personage; in *Phèdre,* Racine will use it for the dominant passion of the protagonist. There is a strong similarity of pattern between the two plays; Phèdre discloses her love progressively to her servant, to the man she loves, and to that man's father—who in this case is the man she is married to rather than the one she is destined to marry. A fourth person, Phèdre's rival, is also informed of her love, which in a way becomes a matter of common knowledge; this further complication is necessary, in *Phèdre,* because of the way in which the complex plot is achieved. We may assume that Racine learned, through his experience with *Mithridate,* the advantage of the person-by-person communication of facts, just as he learned the usefulness of the false report in several successive plays. He probably came to some conclusions, also, about the virtues of the kind of centrality and presence that he had obtained for Mithridate, along with some doubts about the effect that such an arrangement might have upon the construction of a properly dramatic action.

VIII

Iphigénie

ALTHOUGH ITS first public performance did not come until early in 1675, *Iphigénie* was presented to the court at Versailles in August of 1674, thus maintaining the one-a-year sequence of Racine's tragedies during this period. In the new tragedy, published in 1675, he returned to a Greek subject and to the imitation of Euripides.

The plot of *Iphigénie* is a testimonial to many of the things that Racine had learned about dramatic structure through his experience with his earlier plays. It is a complex plot, not only in the Aristotelian sense of having a recognition and a reversal, but in any current sense that would describe it as comprising many episodes, involving many persons in a rather intricate interrelationship. These episodes follow one upon the other in an order at once convincing and suspenseful. It has, in Iphigénie herself, a protagonist who seems to have no rival for the central role in the play, even though we might have some questions about the nature of her activity. It depends, for its evolution and conclusion, upon personages who are clearly differentiated from one another and who are vigorously presented individually; these varied personages evoke a variety of strong emotions from the audience. Finally, the complexities of its structure are reflected in a presentation, through speeches and through the diction, that is as effective as it is subtle.

The action as it concerns the protagonist might be stated thus: Iphigénie arrives in Aulis, ostensibly to be married to Achille, really to be sacrificed; the efforts to save her, including her own, fail; but she is saved by the discovery of the "Iphigénie" demanded by the gods, and her marriage to Achille is arranged. The movement is complex: it is away from ignorance and toward knowledge with respect to the true reason for Iphigénie's presence in Aulis; from ignorance (and of even greater duration) to knowledge of the identity of the "Iphigénie" who must be sacrificed to the gods; from improbability to probability—that is, from a very remote potential to a near-realization—for the marriage of Iphigénie to Achille. It is complex, also, in the nature of the intermediate steps that must be taken to save Iphigénie from the sacrifice; a number of persons will intervene in her favor, they will appeal to varied emotions and use diversified means, they will be impeded and obstructed by an equally large number of persons who will oppose them because they wish to see the sacrifice accomplished.

Such a division of the personages into two opposing groups, taking sides on a central problem, recalls Racine's practice in earlier works—for example, in *La Thébaïde*. But the use of the device in *Iphigénie* is much more subtle and hence more effective. In *La Thébaïde,* for one thing, the opposition is stated unequivocally from the beginning of the play and remains unchanged throughout: there are those who would like to see the battle, even the single combat, take place, and those who strive to prevent it. Racine proceeds less bluntly in *Iphigénie*. Early in the first act, Agamemnon informs Arcas that Calchas, in the name of the gods, has demanded the sacrifice of Iphigénie; that Ulysse has become the most important human agent insisting upon it; and that he himself has yielded to Ulysse's arguments only after a great and protracted struggle of paternal love against patriotism. At the end of the scene, he sends Arcas with a second message countermanding the first, a message (he would have Arcas believe) that represents the triumph of love over patriotism. This ambivalence of Agamemnon, this apparent vacillation, is noteworthy, for it will render possible a certain number of later developments in the action; besides, it will characterize at least one other person in the group that has as its motto: "Iphigénie must be sacrificed."

In scene 1 of Act II a person who ultimately allies herself with this group is introduced, the young Ériphile. At first she is presented as a friend and protégée of Iphigénie; but it soon becomes clear that she is a rival through her love for Achille. Gradually as her spite and envy grow, fed by episodes in the action, she becomes Iphigénie's enemy; she provides the information that prevents Iphigénie's escape, thus joining definitely the group of the opposition. At the same time, it is she who effects the transformation of another "person" into an enemy; this is the camp at Aulis, a kind of natural enemy of Iphigénie even before it knows that she is to be the victim. For the camp—the armies and soldiers of the Greeks—will remain inactive and useless until the sacrifice again raises the winds in the port of Aulis; it must therefore demand the sacrifice, whoever the victim. By enabling the camp to pass from ignorance to knowledge of the fact that Iphigénie is to be the victim, Ériphile makes of it the enemy of her rival. In both cases, the fact of "becoming" an opponent of Iphigénie adds a dynamic dimension to the total structure.

The same is true, to a certain extent, for the persons who say, "Iphigénie must be saved"; but the dynamicism is of a special kind. Clytemnestre and Achille, her strongest defenders, are always on her side, never on the other—always, that is, after they have discovered that a defense is needed. But there is a long period during the play when they believe that a marriage is to take place, not a sacrifice; all their efforts are directed toward the consummation of the marriage. With the final arrival of Agamemnon's second letter, delivered too late by Arcas, Clytemnestre passes from ignorance to false knowledge, to the belief that Achille has rejected her daughter; a new line of action is necessary. It is not until the middle of Act III that both Clytemnestre and Achille—and Iphigénie—learn that the sacrifice is intended. The defenders can then begin the series of attempts to save Iphigénie, a series that had begun, in a curious way, at

the very beginning of the play. The last member of this group,
Arcas, also evolves. He begins as Agamemnon's supporter and
messenger and long continues in that role; indeed, it is while
delivering a final message that Arcas, through a long fidelity to
Clytemnestre and through general humanitarian feelings, exposes Agamemnon's plan to all the interested parties. The change
is prepared from the outset and should not surprise; it constitutes
another element of dynamicism at a critical point in the plot.

This alignment of the forces within the play leaves only one
primary personage unassigned, and that is the protagonist herself. Iphigénie, upon careful consideration, must be classified
with those who hold that "Iphigénie must be sacrificed"—with
her enemies. For her character is built in such a way that, once
she learns of Agamemnon's project, she must necessarily approve of it. Her love for Achille, her tenderness for her mother,
her charity toward Ériphile, are secondary emotions as compared with her filial piety and her sense of duty. Agamemnon
himself is the first to recognize them:

> Je plains mille vertus, une amour mutuelle,
> Sa piété pour moi, ma tendresse pour elle,
> Un respect qu'en son cœur rien ne peut balancer,
> Et que j'avais promis de mieux récompenser.   (117–20)

Iphigénie admits the primacy of her love for her father:

> C'est mon père, Seigneur, je vous le dis encore,
> Mais un père que j'aime, un père que j'adore,
> Qui me chérit lui-même, et dont jusqu'à ce jour
> Je n'ai jamais reçu que des marques d'amour.
> Mon cœur, dans ce respect élevé dès l'enfance,
> Ne peut que s'affliger de tout ce qui l'offense.   (1001–6)

Thus when the necessity to die is presented to her, she accepts:

> Quand vous commanderez, vous serez obéi.
> Ma vie est votre bien. Vous voulez le reprendre:
> Vos ordres sans détour pouvaient se faire entendre.
> D'un œil aussi content, d'un cœur aussi soumis

Que j'acceptais l'époux que vous m'aviez promis,
Je saurai, s'il le faut, victime obéissante,
Tendre au fer de Calchas une tête innocente,
Et respectant le coup par vous-même ordonné,
Vous rendre tout le sang que vous m'avez donné.

(1176–84)

And when all other expedients fail, she leaves voluntarily to present herself at the altar (V, 3).

I do not mean that Iphigénie is exclusively her own enemy, nor that she accedes immediately and without protest to her father's wishes; in the long speech in IV, 4 (quoted above), she defends her life, arguing largely from the effect that her death would have upon her mother and her lover. Yet her role in the play does not demand of her many actions beyond the ultimate compliance with Agamemnon's order. She arrives originally in order to marry Achille. In her first conversation with her father, she congratulates him on his present glories and asks to be present at the sacrifice. When told that Achille is deserting her in favor of Ériphile, she accuses Ériphile, refuses to speak with Achille, and prepares to leave Aulis (II, 2–6). In the third act, Achille's intentions having been clarified, she intercedes for Ériphile (scene 4); then, after Arcas' revelation, when Achille threatens to avenge himself upon Agamemnon, she makes a plea for her father rather than for herself (scene 6) while at the same time emphasizing her love for Achille. The last scene of the act brings a final concession from her that she will try to save her own life. Iphigénie appears twice in Act IV: in scene 4, face-to-face with her father, she indicates her willingness to die (in the terms I have already quoted); and in scene 10, after Agamemnon has decided to spare her, she and Clytemnestre agree to leave. The fifth act accomplishes what is necessary to bring Iphigénie to the sacrifice: Iphigénie, now forbidden to marry Achille, tells him that she no longer means to oppose Agamemnon's order ("Où serait le respect? Et ce devoir suprême" [1577]) and willingly follows Eurybate to the altar.

In proportion to the total activity of the play, the total action accorded to Iphigénie is extremely meager. Even some of the things that she does would seem not to be necessary to the central plot, such as the defense of her father, her intercession for Ériphile. Essentially, her first acceptance of her fate, her rejection of it, and her second acceptance of it are the only acts that she needs to accomplish in order to contribute her part to the action. As Racine conceives of that action, Iphigénie is a victim; for those who would "save Iphigénie" as for those who would "sacrifice" her, she is a victim; her role is passive rather than active; she is acted upon rather than acting. Throughout, the others have the initiative, propose and dispose. All that she can do is accept or reject a fate that others determine for her; and this she does. Indeed, it would almost seem as if the other actions ascribed to her are added and invented in order to supplement a relatively slim sum of necessary action by the protagonist. Just as her action is slight, so is her character. It is composed of those few passions and dispositions that I have mentioned; and whereas, because of these, it is wholly admirable, it is pale as compared with the vigorous and full-blown characters of Agamemnon, Achille, Clytemnestre, or even Ériphile.

Racine's conception of the plot of *Iphigénie,* while it enabled him to produce a tightly constructed action and one that was lively and interesting for the audience, imposed upon him a role for his protagonist that was passive and a character that was pale. That is, I believe, the principal weakness in the tragedy. It means, as far as the spectator is concerned, that his attention is upon a central problem rather than upon a central person, and that his emotions are consequently involved with personages other than the heroine—or at least more so than with her. We have seen this difficulty in others of Racine's plays: the problem of attaching firmly the audience's emotions to the protagonist was just as constant—and just as frequently unsolved—as was the problem of building the action around the protagonist. In the case of *Iphigénie,* he may have hoped to augment our sympathy for his heroine through two devices: by stressing the positive qualities of those who were determined to "save Iphigénie," especially Achille and Clytemnestre, and by blackening the characters of those who were intent upon her sacrifice, Agamemnon and Ériphile.

Agamemnon's character is one of Racine's great creations, not so much because of its vigor as because of its subtlety—not so much because of its apparent duality as because of its real unity. In appearance, Agamemnon is caught in a struggle between paternal affection, which would lead him to save Iphigénie, and patriotism, which would lead him to sacrifice her so that the mission against Troy might get under way. In reality, there is no such struggle: Agamemnon is moved only by fear and ambition, and the other passions are disguises for sentiments that he is ashamed to admit to because he recognizes them as reprehensible. Such a situation is easy to present in the novel, where the novelist may describe and discuss the apparent versus the real character. In the drama, difficulties arise because discussion is impossible and both sides of the character must be presented directly. Racine uses all the techniques available to the dramatist; not only statements about Agamemnon's "real" character by other personages, but unwitting revelations by Agamemnon himself, direct expressions in his monologues, and—perhaps most telling of all—his actions.

It was the necessities of the action as he conceived it that imposed upon Racine the task of devising as complex a character for Agamemnon as he did. He needed one man to lead and direct the campaign for the sacrifice of Iphigénie. That man had to have the authority to order the sacrifice—therefore Agamemnon —and at the same time the blood relationship that might make Iphigénie accept it—therefore Agamemnon. Since this man was the victim's father, he needed to have such passions as might overcome his natural paternal love; yet paternal love (real or apparent) must still be present if, on the one hand, the daughter was to do the father's bidding, and if, on the other hand, certain turns in the action were to take place. Moreover, the father had to be equipped with such passions as would make his attitudes and his responses toward the mother and the lover of a kind adequate, again, to the furthering of the action.

Agamemnon is called upon to do the following things:

1. He orders the sacrifice.
2. He summons Iphigénie to Aulis.

(These two events have happened before the beginning of the play; they are reported in lines 90 and 94.)

3. He countermands the summons (129).
4. He wavers, but yields to Ulysse's arguments (I, 3).
5. He forbids Clytemnestre to approach the altar (III, 1).
6. He tells Achille that the marriage will take place (III, 3)
7. He sends for Iphigénie (III, 5).
8. He avoids Clytemnestre, bars her access to the altar (III, 7).
9. He comes to fetch Iphigénie (IV, 3).
10. He admits that he means to sacrifice her (IV, 4).
11. He argues with Achille and breaks their ties (IV, 6).
12. He remains committed to the sacrifice (IV, 7).
13. He decides to spare Iphigénie, but to deny her the marriage with Achille (IV, 8).
14. He sends Iphigénie away from Aulis (IV, 10)
15. He informs her that she may not marry Achille (V, 1).
16. He agrees to the marriage of Iphigénie and Achille (V, 6).

So stated, the action of Agamemnon in *Iphigénie* is extensive and constant; what is more, it is really an action in the sense that he does a great many things, either in the form of decisions or of overt acts. It seems, as an action, to follow a clear and straightforward line; except for the countermanding of the summons and the hesitation in Act I, and for the decision to spare Iphigénie in Act IV, it is directed to the single end of sacrificing Iphigénie and it progresses in an orderly fashion toward that end. If we would determine how a father can pursue such a goal with respect to his daughter, and why he wavers and ultimately changes his mind, we must ask what basis in character, what passion, is responsible for each of these acts.

Agamemnon orders the sacrifice of Iphigénie. This act, although it precedes the action of the play proper, is reported in I, 1, and the report is the occasion for one of the most complete characterizations of Agamemnon. Calchas has demanded the sacrifice. Agamemnon, as he relates his struggle to Arcas, would have us believe that he had long hesitated between paternal love and patriotism before making the decision; the appeal of Ulysse to his pride and his ambition had finally persuaded him:

> Il me représenta l'honneur et la patrie,
> Tout ce peuple, ces rois, à mes ordres soumis,
> Et l'empire d'Asie à la Grèce promis:
> De quel front immolant tout l'état à ma fille,
> Roi sans gloire, j'irais vieillir dans ma famille!
> Moi-même (je l'avoue avec quelque pudeur),
> Charmé de mon pouvoir, et plein de ma grandeur,
> Ces noms de roi des rois et de chef de la Grèce
> Chatouillaient de mon cœur l'orgueilleuse faiblesse.
>   (74–82)

Moreover, his own fear of the gods had contributed to his decision:

> Pour comble de malheur, les dieux toutes les nuits,
> Dès qu'un léger sommeil suspendait mes ennuis,
> Vengeant de leurs autels le sanglant privilège,
> Me venaient reprocher ma pitié sacrilège,
> Et présentant la foudre à mon esprit confus,
> Le bras déjà levé, menaçaient mes refus.   (83–88)

This admission that vainglory, pride, ambition, love of power, egotism, confusion, and childish fear—rather than patriotism— had led him to his decision causes us to wonder about the profundity and the sincerity of the paternal love that he had alleged as opposing these qualities. As we recall his statement of his

love, we are impressed by its exaggeration, its bombast, its seeking for rhetorical effect, rather than by its sincerity:

> Surpris, comme tu peux penser,
> Je sentis dans mon corps tout mon sang se glacer.
> Je demeurai sans voix, et n'en repris l'usage
> Que par mille sanglots qui se firent passage.
> Je condamnai les dieux, et sans plus rien ouïr,
> Fis vœu sur leurs autels de leur désobéir.
> Que n'en croyais-je alors ma tendresse alarmée?
> Je voulais sur-le-champ congédier l'armée. (63-70)

Agamemnon seems here to be playing at self-justification in order
to obtain Arcas' approval; but we can also see him as trying to
justify himself to himself. The terms in which he phrases his acquiescence, with the "en pleurant" as an obvious modification,
confirm our suspicion:

> Je me rendis, Arcas; et vaincu par Ulysse,
> De ma fille, en pleurant, j'ordonnai le supplice. (89-90)

His description of his second act, the *summoning of Iphigénie,*
displays other passions. Fear of Clytemnestre causes him to resort
to artifice and lies:

> Mais des bras d'une mère il fallait l'arracher.
> Quel funeste artifice il me fallut chercher! (91-92)

And fear of Achille causes him to choose a time to send the summons when his daughter's fiancé is absent. The wary Arcas, always suspicious of his master through devotion to his mistress,
suspects Agamemnon's motive when he hears of the circumstances:

> Et ne craignez-vous point l'impatient Achille? (97)

Agamemnon's "Achille était absent" (102) provides an affirmative answer, upon which he elaborates when he says,

> Et cette guerre, Arcas, selon toute apparence,
> Aurait dû plus longtemps prolonger son absence.
>   (105-6)

The real reason why he now *countermands the summons* lies in the return of Achille:

> Et ce vainqueur, suivant de près sa renommée,
> Hier avec la nuit arriva dans l'armée.   (109–10)

He fears the action that Achille might take when Calchas attempts to sacrifice Iphigénie—action against himself, of course. There is no change of mind or heart; he still wants the sacrifice. Yet once again he pretends that paternal love underlies his action:

> Ma fille.... Ce nom seul, dont les droits sont si saints,
> Sa jeunesse, mon sang, n'est pas ce que je plains.
> Je plains mille vertus, une amour mutuelle,
> Sa piété pour moi, ma tendresse pour elle,
> Un respect qu'en son cœur rien ne peut balancer,
> Et que j'avais promis de mieux récompenser.   (115–20)

And once again the oratorical quality of his peroration gives away his insincerity and his pretense:

> Non, je ne croirai point, ô ciel, que ta justice
> Approuve la fureur de ce noir sacrifice.
> Tes oracles sans doute ont voulu m'éprouver;
> Et tu me punirais si j'osais l'achever.   (121–24)

As he lists his recommendations to Arcas, Agamemnon makes one of those confessions of motives—and of weakness—that are the best keys to his character. He speaks of what would happen should Iphigénie and Clytemnestre now arrive; but he is thinking of all those fears that have haunted him ever since he ordered the sacrifice. Fear of Calchas:

> ... Calchas, qui l'attend en ces lieux,
> Fera taire nos pleurs, fera parler les dieux;
> Et la religion, contre nous irritée,
> Par les timides Grecs sera seule écoutée.   (135–38)

What Greek more timid than he, if we are to believe lines 83–88? Fear of the twenty kings who might have ambitions similar to his own:

> Ceux même dont ma gloire aigrit l'ambition
> Réveilleront leur brigue et leur prétention,
> M'arracheront peut-être un pouvoir qui les blesse....
>
> (139-41)

Fear of himself:

> Va, dis-je, sauve-la de ma propre faiblesse. (142)

Fear that Iphigénie will discover his project:

> Mais surtout ne va point, par un zèle indiscret,
> Découvrir à ses yeux mon funeste secret.
> Que, s'il se peut, ma fille, à jamais abusée,
> Ignore à quel péril je l'avais exposée. (143-46)

Fear—and not the least of all—of Clytemnestre:

> D'une mère en fureur épargne-moi les cris. (147)

The fact that these, rather than paternal love, have all along been his true motives is emphasized in his revelation to Arcas of the contents of his letter. He has told another lie, used another subterfuge, informing Iphigénie that Achille now wishes to delay their marriage; he authorizes Arcas to add that Achille's love for Ériphile is the real cause of the delay. We are justified in asking, I believe, what kind of paternal love this might be, that is insensitive and unscrupulous with respect to a daughter's feelings and future. The last line of the scene,

> C'est Achille. Va, pars. Dieux! Ulysse le suit, (160)

adds Achille and Ulysse to the list of those whom Agamemnon fears.

In scene 3 of the first act, after Achille's departure, Ulysse tries to bolster Agamemnon's failing resolve; *Agamemnon wavers, but he yields to Ulysse's arguments.* The wavering, we may be sure, is a consequence of Achille's arrival and what he has said in the preceding scene; and Ulysse's arguments are based on his knowledge of all the other persons and things that Agamemnon fears:

Pensez-vous que Calchas continue à se taire;
Que ses plaintes, qu'en vain vous voudrez apaiser,
Laissent mentir les dieux sans vous en accuser?
Et qui sait ce qu'aux Grecs, frustrés de leur victime,
Peut permettre un courroux qu'ils croiront légitime?
Gardez-vous de réduire un peuple furieux,
Seigneur, à prononcer entre vous et les dieux.   (290–96)

Just as Arcas had recognized—and appealed to—Agamemnon's
fear of Achille, Ulysse founds his rhetoric on his awareness of
the existence of these other fears. In his reply, Agamemnon dis-
simulates again. He cannot of course tell Ulysse that his summons
has been countermanded; but, hoping for the success of his message, he speaks vaguely of "le destin" and "un dieu" intervening
to save Iphigénie:

Mais malgré tous mes soins, si son heureux destin
La retient dans Argos, ou l'arrête en chemin,
Souffrez que sans presser ce barbare spectacle,
En faveur de mon sang j'explique cet obstacle,
Que j'ose pour ma fille accepter le secours
De quelque dieu plus doux qui veille sur ses jours.

(331–36)

Agamemnon will need to derive much of his later action in the
play from this capacity for lying and dissimulation, and Racine
is careful to establish the capacity through several examples in
the first act.

Arcas and his message, however, have gone astray, Clytemnestre and Iphigénie arrive at the camp, and Agamemnon proceeds with his plans for the sacrifice. In the second act, during
his first conversation with Iphigénie, Agamemnon admits that a
sacrifice is to take place; but he fails, courage lacking, to tell her
that she is to be the victim, and the famous "Vous y serez, ma
fille" (578) gains part of its effectiveness from the fact that
it is another example of his dissimulation. When, in the third
act, *he forbids Clytemnestre to approach the altar,* he prepares
for his order by another series of ambiguous statements—

> Vous pouvez à l'autel envoyer votre fille;
> Je l'attends—   (782–83)

and of false reasons—

> Daignez à mon amour accorder cette grâce.   (810)

It is perhaps surprising that, weak as he is, he should have the strength to utter his "Obéissez" (819); only the fear of what "une mère en fureur" might do at the altar gives him the force to command. As she accedes to his wish, Clytemnestre shows her penetration into his character, speaking of him as "injuste," "fier," "timide," "cruel" (scene 2).

Meanwhile, Agamemnon *has told Achille that the marriage will take place.* Another lie springing from fear. We see Agamemnon's whole attitude through Achille's words:

> Il en croit mes transports; et sans presque m'entendre,
> Il vient, en m'embrassant, de m'accepter pour gendre.
> Il ne m'a dit qu'un mot.   (833–35)

If he has said "only one word," it was because he was planning another act that would further his major intention; in scene 5, *he sends for Iphigénie*—ostensibly to be married, in reality to be sacrificed in the ambiguous "cérémonie" to which Arcas refers. The persons who hear the announcement identify various of Agamemnon's traits. Achille speaks of his "aveugle fureur" (914), Clytemnestre of his "ordre cruel" (923), Arcas of his deceitfulness:

> Le Roi, pour vous tromper, feignait cet hyménée.
> Tout le camp même encore est trompé comme vous.
> (926–27)

Clytemnestre calls him "mon perfide époux" (944). The fullest indictment of his character comes in the following scene, where Achille uses such terms as "cruel stratagème," "barbare, sanguinaire, parjure," "trahison," "le cruel"—terms which Iphigénie, because she loves her father, will reject. Like these last two acts

of his, Agamemnon's next, when *he avoids Clytemnestre and
bars her access to the altar,* takes place far from the stage and
is made known afterward. This is a technique, it should be
noted, that permits commentary on an act along with the telling
of it, and such commentary is useful for the disclosure of the
emotions of all persons concerned. Here Iphigénie is able to expand upon another of her father's failings:

> ... mon père est jaloux de son autorité.
> On ne connaît que trop la fierté des Atrides.   (1064–65)

The next three or four of Agamemnon's acts spring from the
same impulses that I have been listing. In IV, 3, because Iphigénie
has failed to appear, *he comes to fetch her,* still pretending that
the marriage is his reason. We hear him call his orders "mes
justes désirs" (1159), in striking contrast to the epithet of "injuste" applied to him by the others; this is another attempt at
self-defense, and his dissimulation continues. When he is exposed in scene 4, he finally admits his guilt—but not as such, and
without admitting any of its real bases. His statement of the
recent events to Iphigénie is a masterpiece of self-condemnation:

> Cette nuit même encore, on a pu vous le dire,
> J'avais révoqué l'ordre où l'on me fit souscrire.
> Sur l'intérêt des Grecs vous l'aviez emporté.
> Je vous sacrifiais mon rang, ma sûreté.
> Arcas allait du camp vous défendre l'entrée:
> Les dieux n'ont pas voulu qu'il vous ait rencontrée,
> Ils ont trompé les soins d'un père infortuné,
> Qui protégeait en vain ce qu'ils ont condamné.
> Ne vous assurez point sur ma faible puissance.   (1229–37)

The audience, knowing why the order was revoked and being
aware of the magnitude of the present sham, judges Agamemnon
more severely than ever—almost as severely as does Clytemnestre
in her next speech, where she contrasts what her husband has
done with what he might have done. She knows him well, condemns him utterly, blames part of his weakness on his blood:

> Vous ne démentez point une race funeste.
> Oui, vous êtes le sang d'Atrée et de Thyeste.   (1249-50)

The epithets she applies to him are the usual ones: "bourreau," "barbare," "cruel," and certain of her insights are extremely penetrating:

> Pourquoi feindre à nos yeux une fausse tristesse?
> Pensez-vous par des pleurs prouver votre tendresse?
>   (1257-58)

> Mais vous, quelles fureurs vous rendent sa victime?
>   (1273)

> Cette soif de régner, que rien ne peut éteindre,
> L'orgueil de voir vingt rois vous servir et vous craindre,
> Tous les droits de l'empire en vos mains confiés,
> Cruel, c'est à ces dieux que vous sacrifiez.   (1289-92)

> Trop jaloux d'un pouvoir qu'on peut vous envier.   (1295)

> Aussi barbare époux qu'impitoyable père.   (1313)

Agamemnon's monologue of reply—he replies only to himself—occupies all of scene 5, and consists of two parts. His fears are the subject of the first four lines:

> A de moindres fureurs je n'ai pas dû m'attendre.
> Voilà, voilà les cris que je craignais d'entendre:
> Heureux si dans le trouble où flottent mes esprits,
> Je n'avais toutefois à craindre que ses cris!   (1317-20)

Another attempt at self-deception occupies the remaining two lines:

> Hélas! en m'imposant une loi si sévère,
> Grands dieux, me deviez-vous laisser un cœur de père?
>   (1321-22)

Agamemnon's characterization is by now complete and firm, having been made so by every device at the dramatist's disposal, and having already manifested itself in a whole series of revelatory acts. None of the acts that he now does as the play moves toward its ending will be out of that character.

The first of these comes in IV, 6, where *he argues with Achille and breaks their ties.* Agamemnon starts by answering Achille's questions in a tone worthy of his dignities:

> Seigneur, je ne rends point compte de mes desseins.
> Ma fille ignore encor mes ordres souverains;
> Et quand il sera temps qu'elle en soit informée,
> Vous apprendrez son sort, j'en instruirai l'armée.
>
> (1335-38)

He continues with the same evasions, asserting his authority rather than supplying answers:

> Mais vous, qui me parlez d'une voix menaçante,
> Oubliez-vous ici qui vous interrogez?   (1346-47)

> Et qui vous a chargé du soin de ma famille?   (1349)

> Plaignez-vous donc aux dieux qui me l'ont demandée.
>
> (1358)

As Achille develops his case and his accusations, Agamemnon turns to insult and to a coward's show of strength:

> Fuyez. Je ne crains point votre impuissant courroux,
> Et je romps tous les nœuds qui m'attachent à vous.
>
> (1415-16)

Achille desists from a violent reaction only because of Iphigénie's pleadings. After he leaves, another monologue shows Agamemnon's efforts to overcome his fear, efforts that seem at first to be successful:

> Et voilà ce qui rend sa perte inévitable.   (1425)

But as he goes on through the soliloquy, expressing his fear at every line, it is clear that his resolve is weakening:

> Ma fille toute seule était plus redoutable.
> Ton insolent amour, qui croit m'épouvanter,
> Vient de hâter le coup que tu veux arrêter.
> Ne délibérons plus. Bravons sa violence.
> Ma gloire intéressée emporte la balance.
> Achille menaçant détermine mon cœur:
> Ma pitié semblerait un effet de ma peur.   (1426–32)

Therefore, while at the beginning of the scene he seems to *remain committed to the sacrifice,* in the following scene *he decides to spare Iphigénie, but to deny her the marriage with Achille.*

This decision may appear to be a reversal, a change of mind. It is not. It merely represents the triumph of one set of fears over another, a triumph that had been in the making ever since the arrival in Aulis of Achille and then of Clytemnestre. All that was needed to establish it was the set of strong statements of opposition by Clytemnestre and then by Achille. Agamemnon, still talking to himself, begins once more by alleging paternal sentiments. Then fears:

> Une mère m'attend, une mère intrépide,
> Qui défendra son sang contre un père homicide.
> Je verrai mes soldats, moins barbares que moi,
> Respecter dans ses bras la fille de leur roi.
> Achille nous menace, Achille nous méprise ...   (1437–41)

These fears, rather than the father's love that he persists in flaunting, underlie his decision to spare Iphigénie; but as a form of revenge, as a means of salving his wounded pride, he declares himself against the marriage. The fond father again shows his affection. His next two acts are the results of these decisions. In IV, 10, Agamemnon *sends Iphigénie away from Aulis,* recommending the utmost secrecy so that Calchas, Ulysse, and the camp will not discover his action; meanwhile, he will lie to Calchas:

> Par de feintes raisons je m'en vais l'abuser.   (1484)

In V, I, we learn that *he has informed Iphigénie that she may not marry Achille;* or rather, one should say that "he has had her informed," for his usual lack of courage has led him to entrust Arcas with the message.

Agamemnon's action in the play is now complete. We will hear later of a further act of his, when, after Iphigénie has been saved by another means, *he agrees to the marriage of Iphigénie and Achille.* There is then nothing else for him to do, the action is out of his hands, and he can only accept conditions that are imposed upon him. He has been brought to the end of a long action that pursued, through most of the tragedy, the line that he had wished it to follow, but that concluded with the victory of the opposing forces: Calchas, Ulysse, and the camp have had their victim, Iphigénie has been saved, and Achille has been promised her in marriage. Throughout that long action, Agamemnon has acted in accordance with his major passions: fear, pride, ambition, love of power and authority, deceitfulness; but he has pretended always, and even to himself, that he was following the dictates of patriotism and paternal love. Racine assigns the true passions to him at the very beginning of the play, develops them through statements and activity, calls upon them as the basis for each act done by Agamemnon. They are unchanging and unfaltering, as is the opposition between the "apparent" motives that Agamemnon everywhere displays and the "real" ones that lie behind his actions. That opposition is just as essential to the movement of the plot as are the "real" passions themselves, and Racine is careful to exploit it at each appropriate juncture.

Developed as they are in this way, Agamemnon's character and his actions in *Iphigénie* gain a prominence that far surpasses that of the protagonist. Such prominence is necessary; for Agamemnon is active in a variety of ways throughout the drama, Iphigénie is largely passive. That is how the plot is constructed. It is also constructed in such a way that the denouement, instead of resulting from the will either of Agamemnon

or Iphigénie, comes about through the intervention of another
personage, Ériphile. The problem of Ériphile and the denouement was a dual one for Racine; he needed, on the one hand,
to give her the kind of character that would lead her, at the
right time, to tell Calchas of Iphigénie's intended flight; and
he needed, on the other hand, to provide her with the precise
history and circumstances that would make it possible to bring
about, at the right time and in the right place, the metamorphosis
of Ériphile into "Iphigénie." That is, the problem was both one
of character and one of situation or "thought." As a consequence, Racine had to give to this seemingly secondary personage a degree of attention and expansion that made of her,
also, a rival of the protagonist in the interest—but not in the
emotional attachment—of the spectator.

Ériphile is "une fille du sang d'Hélène" and her real name is
Iphigénie; she thus matches the requirements laid down in the
oracle (57–62), as does also Agamemnon's daughter. This coin-
cidence will of course not be known, must not be known, until
the very end of the play. From the time that she is first mentioned by Agamemnon (154) as "cette jeune Ériphile"—in the
opening scene of the tragedy, it should be noted—she is merely
a young princess whom Achille has brought captive from Lesbos.
Agamemnon invents the tale that Achille was in love with her,
thus making her a rival of Iphigénie; he could not have known
that she was really a rival because she loved Achille. Similarly,
he could not have known the degree to which he was right when
he spoke of her in these terms to Achille:

> Que dis-je? les Troyens pleurent une autre Hélène
> Que vous avez captive envoyée à Mycène.
> Car, je n'en doute point, cette jeune beauté
> Garde en vain un secret que trahit sa fierté;
> Et son silence même, accusant sa noblesse,
> Nous dit qu'elle nous cache une illustre princesse.
>
> (237–42)

Such descriptions as "une autre Hèléne," "un secret," "sa noblesse," "une illustre princesse," introduce the necessary ambiguity (in a sense oracular) to provide the probabilities for the ultimate identification. Still in the first act, Eurybate states the reasons for Ériphile's presence in Aulis, exactly as they will be stated through much of the work:

> Elle amène aussi cette jeune Ériphile,
> Que Lesbos a livrée entre les mains d'Achille.
> Et qui de son destin, qu'elle ne connaît pas,
> Vient, dit-elle, en Aulide interroger Calchas.   (345–48)

This much has been circumstance; delineation of character will begin when Ériphile makes her first appearance at the beginning of Act II. Envy is her first characteristic, "Laissons-les dans les bras d'un père et d'un époux" (396); a predisposition to sadness, her second, "Mettons en liberté ma tristesse et leur joie" (398); the latter is emphasized by Doris:

> Quoi, Madame? toujours irritant vos douleurs,
> Croirez-vous ne plus voir que des sujets de pleurs?
>
> (399–400)

> Votre douleur redouble et croît à chaque pas.   (416)

Ériphile calls herself "triste," speaks of her "chagrins" and her "dangers"; then she begins the accumulation of facts about her history that will permit of the final identification:

> Remise dès l'enfance en des bras étrangers,
> Je reçus et je vois le jour que je respire
> Sans que mère ni père ait daigné me sourire.
> J'ignore qui je suis; et pour comble d'horreur,
> Un oracle effrayant m'attache à mon erreur,
> Et quand je veux chercher le sang qui m'a fait naître,
> Me dit que sans périr je ne me puis connaître.   (424–30)

Doris adds two necessary details:

> En perdant un faux nom vous reprendrez le vôtre.
>
> . . . .
>
> Songez que votre nom fut changé dès l'enfance.   (434–37)

Other indications follow, stressing Ériphile's noble origins and her ignorance of them.

In order that she may accomplish her final criminal revelation, two more passions are necessary for her, her love for Achille (recounted in 477 ff.) and her vindictiveness—her determination to spoil the happiness of Achille and Iphigénie. She recognizes the latter trait in herself:

> Triste effet des fureurs dont je suis tourmentée!
> Je n'accepte la main qu'elle m'a présentée
> Que pour m'armer contre elle, et sans me découvrir,
> Traverser son bonheur que je ne puis souffrir.   (505–8)

And again:

> ... peut-être approchant ces amants trop heureux,
> Quelqu'un de mes malheurs se répandrait sur eux.
>
> (519–20)

Her characterization is completed by the statement that she is willing to die if Achille and Iphigénie marry:

> S'il s'achève, il suffit: tout est fini pour moi.
> Je périrai, Doris; et, par une mort prompte,
> Dans la nuit du tombeau j'enfermerai ma honte.   (524–26)

This is the factor that will lead to her suicide. Racine has sketched the character rapidly in the scene of her first appearance; as the plot moves forward and as the circumstances of Achille and Iphigénie evolve, he will provide her with the motivations and the acts that will bring her gradually toward the denouement.

It is important to recognize that, as in the case of Agamemnon, the character of Ériphile is meant to be essentially unsympathetic. We will at first sympathize with her misfortunes; but as we become progressively attached to the fate of Achille and Iphigénie,

as we hope increasingly for a happy outcome for them, each indication that Ériphile means to prevent it will set us all the more
against her. We feel the same way toward her excessive self-pity,
apparent again in II, 3. When, in scene 4, she is accused by
Clytemnestre of having "secret designs" on Achille, and when,
in scene 5, Iphigénie makes the accusation more directly, Ériphile responds in several ways: first, with a conventional denial
—for which we cannot blame her; next, with an assertion of her
dignity and a counteraccusation of Iphigénie for her unjust
suspicions. Here we do blame her, for the suspicions are justified
and there is deception involved in denying them. In scene 7, she
commits her first disloyalty, telling Achille of the reason that
Agamemnon had given for summoning Iphigénie to Aulis. Our
feelings are divided; for we want Agamemnon exposed, we wish
to have Achille informed, yet we disapprove of this early figure
of Ériphile as talebearer—a role that will lead to her most significant action in the tragedy. Her last speech in Act II shows three
things about her. In the broken phrase, "Ah! plutôt ... ," she indicates her propensity to consider—without naming them—alternative possibilities of action that will harm her rival; then,
in the lines beginning with "J'ai des yeux," her clairvoyant penetration into the realities of the situation, making it possible to
act to her advantage; finally, her vindictiveness:

> Et si le sort contre elle à ma haine se joint,
> Je saurai profiter de cette intelligence
> Pour ne pas pleurer seule et mourir sans vengeance.
>
> (764–66)

Our choices are now clear, and we choose Iphigénie against
Ériphile.

Iphigénie's act of kindness toward Ériphile as she begs Achille's
clemency for her has a dual effect. As an act of *générosité* on the
part of Iphigénie, it further improves her credit with us; at the
same time, making Ériphile's intentions toward her still more

despicable, it serves to solidify our antipathy for the "young princess." As one personage moves up, the other moves down. Ériphile's speech in lines 881 ff., mingling self-pity with a deceptive statement of her motives and intentions, further contributes to this effect. In the important scene of Arcas' revelation, she speaks only once: "O ciel! quelle nouvelle!" (913); we need to see in this phrase not essentially surprise, but a sudden realization of all the implications for herself and a vague premonition that the new state of affairs will more readily produce her revenge.

The means to that revenge are suddenly discovered by Ériphile at the beginning of Act IV. She has become fully aware, in the preceding act, of the extent of Achille's love for Iphigénie, and her envy has reached paroxysm; she discloses her state to Doris. Clairvoyant again, she realizes Agamemnon's position and what may be expected of him:

> Et que fera-t-il donc? Quel courage endurci
> Soutiendrait les assauts qu'on lui prépare ici:
> Une mère en fureur, les larmes d'une fille,
> Les cris, le désespoir de toute une famille,
> Le sang à ces objets facile à s'ébranler,
> Achille menaçant, tout prêt à l'accabler? (1119–24)

Her conclusion, self-pitying again, is that "Je suis et je serai la seule infortunée" (1126). From her conspectus of the total situation comes an inspiration concerning what she might do about it, intimated first in another broken phrase: "Ah! si je m'en croyais" (1127), then fully outlined:

> Je ne sais qui m'arrête et retient mon courroux,
> Que par un prompt avis de tout ce qui se passe,
> Je ne coure des dieux divulguer la menace,
> Et publier partout les complots criminels
> Qu'on fait ici contre eux et contre leurs autels. (1128–32)

After gloating over the trouble that she might cause, she formulates her plan more succinctly:

> Rentrons. Et pour troubler un hymen odieux,
> Consultons des fureurs qu'autorisent les dieux.   (1143-44)

But the time has not yet come for her disclosure; Agamemnon has not yet called off the sacrifice, Iphigénie is still in peril. Meanwhile, some additions will be made to the probabilities for the denouement. In Clytemnestre's long rant against Agamemnon (IV, 4), as she inveighs against Hélène's immorality she says:

> Avant qu'un nœud fatal l'unît à votre frère,
> Thésée avait osé l'enlever à son père.
> Vous savez, et Calchas mille fois vous l'a dit,
> Qu'un hymen clandestin mit ce prince en son lit,
> Et qu'il en eut pour gage une jeune princesse,
> Que sa mère a cachée au reste de la Grèce.   (1281-86)

Even the wariest spectator will not yet see in the formula "une jeune princesse" a combination of two phrases earlier used by Agamemnon, "cette jeune Ériphile" (154) and "une illustre princesse" (242). But the other half of the broken slate has now been brought into existence; we know that Ériphile is the daughter of illustrious if unnamed parents, we know that Hélène and Thésée have had such a daughter. Calchas will later fit the pieces together.

Ériphile is present when Agamemnon announces to Iphigénie that he intends to spare her and orders her to leave; she thus is a witness to the accomplishment of her worst fears about Agamemnon and to the ostensible removal of Iphigénie from danger. This is the time for revenge. Instead of following her mistress and Clytemnestre as before, she settles upon the particular form of vengeance that had suggested itself in the first scene of Act IV:

> Ah! je succombe enfin.
> Je reconnais l'effet des tendresses d'Achille.
> Je n'emporterai point une rage inutile.
> Plus de raisons. Il faut ou la perdre ou périr.
> Viens, te dis-je. A Calchas je vais tout découvrir.
>
> (1488-92)

As a result, her first significant intervention in the plot is accomplished, and she successfully prevents the escape of Iphigénie and her entourage. Ægine (in V, 4) informs Clytemnestre that Ériphile has indeed "discovered all" to Calchas, calling her a "serpent inhumain" as Clytemnestre calls her a "monstre." These epithets are necessary to fix firmly the sentiments of the spectator. As in the case of Agamemnon, Ériphile's important acts happen away from the stage; so for the disclosure to Calchas, so for her final appearance at the altar recounted in the last scene of the play. The battle at the altar has been interrupted by Calchas, who, having recognized in Ériphile "Un autre sang d'Hélène, une autre Iphigénie" (1749), and having brought together (through his unique knowledge) all the information necessary to identify Ériphile, declares that her death will satisfy the oracle. Before the sacrifice can be made, however, she takes her own life (1776). The last of her dispositions is thus brought to fulfillment.

If the treatment of Agamemnon in *Iphigénie* represents, on the part of Racine, a triumph in the presentation of a character and its consequences in action, the treatment of Ériphile represents a similar triumph in the handling of character and probability. Agamemnon's action was more complex and more varied, hence he needed to have a more fully developed character; Ériphile's action was more simple and restricted, hence fewer traits of character would suffice to produce it. But, on the one hand, the timing of her discoveries and her actions needed to be more carefully contrived; on the other hand, a whole elaborate set of probabilities had to be developed in order to bring about the final identification—constituting a true recognition—and with it the denouement of the play—constituting a true reversal. Racine proceeds with great deftness in the creation of these probabilities, beginning very early in the play, stating them subtly but with sufficient clarity, spacing them at the right intervals so that the mystery might be maintained but at the same time its clarification might not be unprepared.

In order to be driven to the point of telling Calchas that

Iphigénie was to be spared, Ériphile needed to witness Agamemnon's order to his daughter to flee; the sight of his weakness became the occasion for her strength. But in order for her revenge to succeed, for the flight to be impeded, another "enemy" of Iphigénie had to be brought into the action as Ériphile's collaborator. This was the "person" of the camp, the body of Greek soldiers assembled at Aulis. It would hardly be correct to say that this person has a character; all that it requires is an eagerness to set sail for Troy and sufficient violence to avenge itself upon anybody who might try to prevent it from leaving. That is, it must be able to await the sacrifice (once it knows about it) with enthusiasm, and to react sharply when it learns that the sacrifice might not take place. Racine's problem in inventing and developing the notion of the camp was thus a problem not in character but in "thought." He had to suggest first the presence of the camp, then provide it with the attitudes I have mentioned, then make it pass from ignorance to knowledge with respect to the coming sacrifice (thanks to Calchas) and with respect to Iphigénie's intended flight (thanks to Ériphile), finally cause it to prevent that flight.

Since several kinds of movement in the plot depend, as we have seen, upon a passage from ignorance to knowledge, Racine introduces a similar progression for the camp; that is, the camp is among those persons who at the outset do not "know" and who at the end (or close to it) do "know." He complicates the progression by adding to it a gradual change from immobility to mobility. There is, I believe, more than a metaphorical statement involved in the opposition of the line at the beginning,

> Mais tout dort, et l'armée, et les vents, et Neptune,   (9)

and the lines at the end,

> Les vents agitent l'air d'heureux frémissements,
> Et la mer leur répond par ses mugissements;

La rive au loin gémit, blanchissante d'écume;

. . . .

Tout s'empresse, tout part. (1779–89)

For if Agamemnon's concern is to "sacrifice Iphigénie" and that of his opponents to "save Iphigénie," the camp is determined essentially to "sail for Troy"; indeed, the sacrifice is demanded only as a means of raising the winds so that the army may sail. Without the sacrifice there will be no winds, without the winds no departure for Troy; hence the initial inactivity of the camp at Aulis. Racine begins with this situation—this *stasis*. Agamemnon and Arcas of course know about the standstill from the start, but only Agamemnon knows the remedy. He stresses the seriousness of the situation when he refers to the "mille cris de joie" (45) uttered by the soldiers when they were about to leave, before the winds had failed. Ulysse speaks of it to Achille:

Tandis qu'à nos vaisseaux la mer toujours fermée
Trouble toute la Grèce et consume l'armée. (185–86)

He also tells Agamemnon of the state of the camp's knowledge at this time:

Calchas, par tous les Grecs consulté chaque jour,
Leur a prédit des vents l'infaillible retour.
A ses prédictions si l'effet est contraire,
Pensez-vous que Calchas continue à se taire ... ? (287–90)

Before the camp learns that the departure depends upon a sacrifice, it learns of the arrival of Ériphile and Iphigénie:

Déjà de leur abord la nouvelle est semée;
Et déjà de soldats une foule charmée,
Surtout d'Iphigénie admirant la beauté,
Pousse au ciel mille vœux pour sa félicité. (349–52)

Once they have arrived, there is the danger that Calchas may identify his victim to the soldiers; thus Agamemnon's prayer to Ulysse: "Mais cependant faites taire Calchas" (392). It is from the camp that Achille learns of Iphigénie's arrival—

> Je soupçonnais d'erreur tout le camp à la fois—   (724)

and it is the camp's opinion of him that he fears:

> Suis-je, sans le savoir, la fable de l'armée?   (754)

Agamemnon, still hiding his plan, speaks vaguely to Clytemnestre of "le tumulte d'un camp" (787), "vous êtes dans un camp" (803); Achille tells her that the camp has been informed of the sacrifice:

> Mais vous a-t-il conté
> Quel bonheur dans le camp vous avez apporté?
> Les dieux vont s'apaiser. Du moins Calchas publie
> Qu'avec eux, dans une heure, il nous réconcilie;
> Que Neptune et les vents, prêts à nous exaucer,
> N'attendent que le sang que sa main va verser.   (835-40)

As a result of this news the soldiers, now fully aroused, again begin their preparations to leave for Troy. But they are still in the dark about the victim, as Arcas indicates to Clytemnestre —in the presence of Ériphile—when he exposes Agamemnon's plan,

> Tout le camp même encore est trompé comme vous,   (927)

and as Ériphile later repeats to Doris:

> ... quoique le bûcher soit déjà préparé,
> Le nom de la victime est encore ignoré:
> Tout le camp n'en sait rien.   (1115-17)

Ériphile's knowledge of this fact leads her to her first intimations of a revenge:

> ... si de tout le camp mes avis dangereux
> Faisaient à ma patrie un sacrifice heureux!   (1139-40)

Such formulas as "toute la Grèce," "tous les Grecs," and especially "tout le camp" recur frequently, indicating the extent to which

we are meant to think of the thousand shiploads of soldiers and
their twenty kings as a unit, as a person.

Agamemnon had early referred to this person as "les timides
Grecs" (138); now, as the time for their action approaches, Clytemnestre calls them "une foule cruelle" (1301). Agamemnon
admits to Achille his constant awareness of their influence:

> Accusez et Calchas et le camp tout entier.   (1359)

> Vous, qui vous offensant de mes justes terreurs,
> Avez dans tout le camp répandu vos fureurs.   (1363–64)

Therefore his main concern, as he spares Iphigénie, is that the
soldiers should not know:

> Tout dépend du secret et de la diligence.
> Ulysse ni Calchas n'ont point encor parlé;
> Gardez que ce départ ne leur soit révélé.
> Cachez bien votre fille; et que tout le camp croie
> Que je la retiens seule, et que je vous renvoie.   (1474–78)

These words, spoken in the presence of Ériphile, convince her
that her first inspiration was the right one, and she leaves to
warn Calchas. Her warning is immediately effective, and Iphigénie's escape is prevented:

> Vois comme tout le camp s'oppose à notre fuite;
> Avec quelle insolence ils ont de toutes parts
> Fait briller à nos yeux la pointe de leurs dards.
> Nos gardes repoussés, la reine évanouie ...   (1498–1501)

The dormant camp has been awakened, brought to activity, made
to defend its right to Iphigénie as sacrificial victim. Even after
Iphigénie's return, it remains aggressive in its opposition, which
Achille will now attempt to render ineffective:

> Ne craignez ni les cris ni la foule impuissante
> D'un peuple qui se presse autour de cette tente.
> Paraissez; et bientôt sans attendre mes coups,
> Ces flots tumultueux s'ouvriront devant vous.   (1517–20)

But he will be obliged to carry the fight to the very scene of the sacrifice; Eurybate describes the resistance:

> Ce n'est plus un vain peuple en désordre assemblé;
> C'est d'un zèle fatal tout le camp aveuglé.
> Plus de pitié. Calchas seul règne, seul commande.
>
> (1623–25)

Consequently Iphigénie realizes that she must herself go to the altar and tries to persuade her mother of the uselessness of accompanying her:

> Mais que pouvez-vous faire en l'état où nous sommes?
> Vous avez à combattre et les dieux et les hommes.
> Contre un peuple en fureur vous exposerez-vous?
> N'allez point, dans un camp rebelle à votre époux,
> Seule à me retenir vainement obstinée,
> Par des soldats peut-être indignement traînée,
> Présenter, pour tout fruit d'un déplorable effort,
> Un spectacle à mes yeux plus cruel que la mort.
> Allez: laissez aux Grecs achever leur ouvrage.   (1641–49)

Clytemnestre, unconvinced, tries to follow Iphigénie; but again the camp intervenes:

> Mais on se jette en foule au-devant de mes pas.   (1668)

It is at this point that Arcas arrives to describe the scene at the altar.

There will be two such descriptions, one by Arcas and the second by Ulysse, recounting the two phases of the denouement. In both, the camp will be prominent. The first presents the initial struggle between Achille and the soldiers:

> Il a brisé des Grecs les trop faibles barrières.
>
> . . . .
>
> On se menace, on court, l'air gémit, le fer brille.   (1702–5)

The second relates the continuation of that struggle:

> Déjà de tout le camp la discorde maîtresse
> Avait sur tous les yeux mis son bandeau fatal,

Et donné du combat le funeste signal.
De ce spectacle affreux votre fille alarmée
Voyait pour elle Achille, et contre elle l'armée;
Mais, quoique seul pour elle, Achille furieux
Épouvantait l'armée, et partageait les dieux.
Déjà de traits en l'air s'élevait un nuage;
Déjà coulait le sang, prémices du carnage.   (1734-42)

Those who would "save Iphigénie" have thus been reduced to the single Achille, those who would "sacrifice Iphigénie" have been augmented to include the whole of the Greek army. The unequal conflict is interrupted by Calchas, who recognizes and identifies the other Iphigénie. Nor does Racine fail to narrate the response of the camp to that identification:

Ainsi parle Calchas. Tout le camp immobile
L'écoute avec frayeur, et regarde Ériphile.   (1761-62)

Mais puisque Troie enfin est le prix de sa mort,
L'armée à haute voix se déclare contre elle,
Et prononce à Calchas sa sentence mortelle.   (1768-70)

Ériphile carries out the sentence herself, the camp (and the gods) are satisfied, the winds rise, and—replacing the immobility of frustration by the complete mobility of satisfaction—"tout s'empresse, tout part."

The indispensable role of the "camp," the "soldiers," the "Greeks" in the plot of *Iphigénie* becomes, for Racine, the occasion for a carefully conceived and meticulously pursued development in the area of "thought" or probability. Proceeding as the dramatist must proceed, he prepares for the end from the beginning, interspersing facts and hints and reports about the camp with the other, major developments of the play. These all have an order and each has a time, since the camp must be brought to readiness for action at those precise moments when first Ériphile, then Achille, then Calchas need to act with it or against it. Its mere existence, with a kind of character, serves as a constant background for the decisions of the protagonist and other principal personages; its state of knowledge, at any given point, provides particular directions for the advancing action. The latter capacity is the more important for it, since its main function is in the domain of probability rather than in that of necessity.

In a large number of the passages devoted to the camp that I have cited, the particular formula "tout le camp" was used. Racine uses the traditional poetic means of attaching a fixed form of expression to a particular object or "person," thereby at once fixing the identity of the object and establishing a basis for visualization, for comprehension, and for an emotional response from the audience. The insistent repetition of a single formula is an economical device for indicating the continued presence of a single object; far from suggesting poverty of language (or the limitations of a "classical" vocabulary), it shows poetic diction at its best—when the word becomes the clear and unambiguous representative of the thing and endows it with the proper emotional context. Indeed, the device is not a linguistic one at all; for what is at issue here is not the repeated use of a given word or phrase, but the persistence in the poem (with all the right attendant circumstances) of the object represented by the word.

There is, in *Iphigénie,* another such case of an unfailing use of the same word for an important object, and that is the case of the word "autel." Again, the problem was not one of diction or language; Racine had rather the task of putting into his play an indispensable object and of associating with it, for the audience, a particular set of meanings and emotions. His solution of the problem constitutes another poetic and artistic triumph for Racine, this time in the special areas of "thought" and of diction. No character is involved; only a set of circumstances and a place, represented always by the same word. In a sense, through his handling of the concept of "autel" Racine adds another dimension to his plot. We may think of it this way: if there is a movement in time from the first summoning of Iphigénie to the ultimate consummation of the sacrifice (of "Iphigénie"), there is also a movement in space from distant Mycenae to the altar at which the sacrifice takes place. If the action may be stated as a conflict between those who would "sacrifice Iphigénie" and those who would "save Iphigénie," it may also be stated as a contention between those who would "bring Iphigénie to the altar" and those who would "keep Iphigénie from the altar." The second statement adds the dimension of space to that of time; it provides a kind of geographical focus for the plot, a *terminus ad quem* for the various kinds of motion involved in the action.

One of Racine's genial inventions with regard to the altar is his discovery that he might use it both as the place of the sacrifice and the place of the marriage; hence the possibility of an ambiguity, of a *double entendre,* that enabled him to exploit fully Agamemnon's capacity for dissimulation. (In the same way, he found that he could use "cérémonie" to refer, ambiguously, to the marriage and the sacrifice; see line 897.) For one group of personages, the altar remains always the site of the sacrifice; for another, but only for a while, the site of the marriage. Thus the wish to "bring Iphigénie to the altar" becomes more complex as it divides into two goals, "bring Iphigénie to the altar to be sacrificed" and "bring Iphigénie to the altar to be married"; an additional danger to the safety of the protagonist is thus introduced, one that adds another element of suspense for the audience. For only the audience knows, at all times, of the double meaning and the double intention. Racine, in a carefully planned dramatic strategy, separates the audience's knowledge from that of the interested persons: once again, the ignorance : knowledge ratio is operative in the creation and the development of probability within the play and suspense for the spectator.

We should distinguish between two uses of "autel" in *Iphigénie,* one generic (and usually in the plural), found in references to the "altars of the gods," the other specific, designating the altar of Diana at Aulis, where the sacrifice will take place. The latter is the one that interests us. It is named in the oracle itself, quoted by Agamemnon in the first scene:

«Si dans un sacrifice auguste et solennel
            Une fille du sang d'Hélène
        De Diane en ces lieux n'ensanglante l'autel.»   (58–60)

Agamemnon thinks of this altar in geographical terms, even
when he does not name it specifically; thus he says to Arcas:

        Si ma fille une fois met le pied dans l'Aulide,
        Elle est morte. Calchas, qui l'attend en ces lieux,
        Fera taire nos pleurs, fera parler les dieux,   (134–36)

and later to Ulysse:

        Mais malgré tous mes soins, si son heureux destin
        La retient dans Argos, ou l'arrête en chemin ...   (331–32)

Both speeches come at a moment when his tactic is to "keep
Iphigénie from the altar." When the tactic fails and Iphigénie
arrives, his intention is reformulated in terms of the altar:

        Laissez-moi de l'autel écarter une mère.   (394)

It is the same altar of the sacrifice—victim unknown—that is mentioned in Iphigénie's ingenuous question:

        Verra-t-on à l'autel votre heureuse famille?   (577)

Agamemnon's first ambiguous and deceptive use of the term
comes in the scene in which he orders Clytemnestre to remain
at a distance. He begins by saying:

        Vous pouvez à l'autel envoyer votre fille;
        Je l'attends ... ,   (782–83)

a parallel formula to his "Vous y serez, ma fille." When he asks
Clytemnestre to stay away, she is amazed:

        Qu'après l'avoir d'Argos amenée en Aulide,
        Je refuse à l'autel de lui servir de guide?   (797–98)

She, too, has a sense of the focal value of the altar. Having received the order, she can only ask:

> D'où vient que d'un soin si cruel
> L'injuste Agamemnon m'écarte de l'autel ? (819-20)

Achille, too, thinks of the altar as the place of his marriage:

> Votre père à l'autel vous destine un époux, (852)

as does Iphigénie:

> Montrez que je vais suivre au pied de nos autels
> Un roi ... (871-72)

To this point, the persons favoring the marriage of Iphigénie to Achille have worked to bring her to the wedding altar—or, in some cases, to be there themselves. But at the beginning of III, 5, they are undeceived; Arcas, after making the double-edged statement,

> Madame, tout est prêt pour la cérémonie.
> Le Roi près de l'autel attend Iphigénie, (897-98)

finally clarifies the situation:

> Il l'attend à l'autel pour la sacrifier. (912)

Clytemnestre now understands:

> Je ne m'étonne plus de cet ordre cruel
> Qui m'avait interdit l'approche de l'autel, (923-24)

and she assigns to the altar its proper function:

> Ira-t-elle, des dieux implorant la justice,
> Embrasser leurs autels parés pour son supplice ? (937-38)

From now on, all the persons concerned with the fate of Iphigénie will see the altar as a sacrificial altar. A general change in the situation, in the direction of the plot, has removed the ambiguity.

First to do so is Achille, in the scene in which he remonstrates with Iphigénie:

> Me montrer votre cœur fumant sur un autel. (976)

> Vous iriez à l'autel me chercher vainement. (984)

Next is Clytemnestre, prevented from approaching the altar by Agamemnon's guards:

> Il me fait de l'autel refuser le passage.
> Des gardes, que lui-même a pris soin de placer,
> Nous ont de toutes parts défendu de passer.   (1050-52)

This represents a kind of countermovement: keep Clytemnestre— or anybody else who might interfere—away from the altar. Next Ériphile, who alludes in a general way to the altars of the gods (1132), but who has in mind specifically the altar of the sacrifice. Clytemnestre describes Agamemnon's impatience—

> Le barbare à l'autel se plaint de sa paresse—   (1150)

in terms that he himself takes up immediately:

> Ne peut-elle à l'autel marcher que sur vos pas?   (1160)

Since he does not know that Clytemnestre has been informed by Arcas of the true nature of the "ceremony," he again makes the ambiguous allusion:

> Calchas est prêt, Madame, et l'autel est paré.   (1164)

Before she exposes him, Clytemnestre (with bitter irony) takes up the same deceptive usage:

> Venez remercier un père qui vous aime,
> Et qui veut à l'autel vous conduire lui-même.   (1169-70)

Finally, Agamemnon admits his guilty connivance:

> Un oracle cruel
> Veut qu'ici votre sang coule sur un autel.   (1223-24)

At the critical point in his relationship with Agamemnon, when he declares that he means to oppose the sacrifice, Achille shows his understanding of the deception:

> On dit que sous mon nom à l'autel appelée,
> Je ne l'y conduisais que pour être immolée;
> Et que d'un faux hymen nous abusant tous deux,
> Vous vouliez me charger d'un emploi si honteux.   (1329-32)

Later, when he thinks of Iphigénie's submissiveness, Agamemnon thinks of it as related to the altar:

> Ma fille, de l'autel cherchant à s'échapper,
> Gémit-elle du coup dont je la veux frapper? (1443–44)

In Act V, since much of the action takes place at the altar and is reported in "la tente d'Agamemnon," we will see the final movements "toward" or "away," then the scene at the altar itself. Achille, in scene 2, says to Iphigénie:

> Vous allez à l'autel, et moi, j'y cours, Madame.
> Si de sang et de morts le ciel est affamé,
> Jamais de plus de sang ses autels n'ont fumé. (1602–4)

Iphigénie's last words in the play are these:

> Eurybate, à l'autel conduisez la victime. (1666)

The first report of the denouement, that of Arcas, localizes the setting: "Achille est à l'autel" (1703); the second, that of Ulysse, repeats the phrase for Ériphile: "Elle était à l'autel" (1763). And Ériphile's final action, satisfying the oracle, is described as centering upon the altar:

> Furieuse, elle vole, et sur l'autel prochain
> Prend le sacré couteau, le plonge dans son sein. (1775–76)

Agamemnon, Ulysse, Calchas, the camp, and Achille; the Iphigénie who was to be saved and the Iphigénie who was to be sacrificed, have all converged upon the altar; the sacrifice has taken place, the gods and the camp have been satisfied, and Troy becomes a possibility.

It would seem, then, that Racine's artistry in *Iphigénie* manifests itself largely in all the intricate devices that are needed for the realization of a complex and complicated plot. What he does with the character of Agamemnon may serve as a sample of the excellence he achieves in relating and subordinating character to action. What he does with the person of Ériphile demonstrates his solution of a difficult problem in adapting character and probability to the needs of the plot. His handling of the camp

—"tout le camp"—shows the subtle and effective creation of a probability that was needed for the working out of the denouement, and the fixing of that probability through a single phrase. Thought and diction reach a high point of effectiveness in the role attributed to the altar, which at the same time adds a suspenseful dimension to the general movement—or the movements —of the plot. Other examples might be studied. The total effect is one of a plot that is exciting without being melodramatic (since every action has a basis in character and is firmly founded on internal probabilities) and that elicits from the spectator vigorous emotional responses appropriate to the situation and to the various personages. The one failing of the tragedy is a fundamental one, affecting the very concept of the action: the emotions aroused are insufficiently concentrated in the protagonist and tend either to relate to a general situation or to be dispersed among a number of highly interesting and colorful personages.

Phèdre

Phèdre, Racine's last tragedy of classical inspiration, was both produced and published in 1677. Three years had elapsed since the appearance of *Iphigénie,* thus bringing to a conclusion the annual rhythm of the preceding works, and Racine had apparently devoted himself through the intervening years to the perfecting of his most completely achieved drama.

Looking back over the tragedies that had come before *Phèdre,* we may reduce Racine's main problems and difficulties in the writing of tragedy to two: the construction of a central action that would organize successfully all the materials of the play, and the creation of a protagonist who would at once be a true focal point of that action and the dominant source of the spectator's emotion. The earliest plays had shown great hesitation and uncertainty with respect to both problems; in later ones, he had solved one or the other to an eminent degree. But in none, I think, had he achieved simultaneously his goals for both action and protagonist. Where the action had seemed to be satisfactorily compounded, the emotion had sometimes remained divided among several main personages, it had at other times failed to become a truly tragic emotion. Where the protagonist had seemed to possess the necessary qualities and to produce the desired effect, his general effectiveness had been impaired or limited by the lack of a properly dramatic action. Only in *Phèdre* will Racine combine the lessons learned about both action and protagonist into a brilliantly successful synthesis.

The plot of *Phèdre* is related to antecedent works about Phaedra

and Hippolytus only through certain details of the traditional
story—the story of a woman in love with her husband's son.
For the rest, it is an original and independent plot, devised by
Racine in accordance with principles developed throughout his
career as a writer of tragedy. First of these is the principle of
the "interiority" or the "intimacy" of the central action, a principle of his art that led him to place the really important events
of the plot within the soul of his protagonist rather than in external episodes. Since he was writing drama, of course, there
needed to be an externalization of those events; but the real
movement and progression of the plot was to consist, ideally, in
a change from one state of soul to another state of soul, through
intermediate steps and in a probable order. In *Phèdre* that movement is simple and clearly defined: from an initial state in which
Phèdre, because of her sense of guilt, wishes to die, to a final
state in which her guilt reaches unbearable proportions and she
must die.

Using a device that he had practiced and perfected through the
years, Racine makes concise formulations of this plot. When
Théramène speaks of Phèdre as

> Une femme mourante et qui cherche à mourir,   (44)

he states the situation with respect to both guilt and death at the
beginning of the action. When Phèdre, in her first scene with
Œnone, says that as a result of any revelation

> Je n'en mourrai pas moins, j'en mourrai plus coupable,
>
>   (242)

she predicts the total evolution of the action. Her final speech
(V, 7), linking her death with her guilt, integrates the denouement with everything that had preceded. There are numerous
other formulations, carefully spaced throughout the play. Œnone
describes Phèdre's state at the beginning:

> La reine touche presque à son terme fatal.
> En vain à l'observer jour et nuit je m'attache:

> Elle meurt dans mes bras d'un mal qu'elle me cache.
>
> (144-46)

Phèdre herself early speaks of her impending death,

> Soleil, je te viens voir pour la dernière fois, (172)

and Œnone reproaches her for so doing:

> Vous verrai-je toujours, renonçant à la vie,
> Faire de votre mort les funestes apprêts? (174-75)

Phèdre speaks of her shame:

> Œnone, la rougeur me couvre le visage:
> Je te laisse trop voir mes honteuses douleurs. (182-83)

Also in I, 3, Œnone describes Phèdre's attempts at suicide through enfeeblement—a preparation, at the outset, for her successful suicide at the end. Guilt, again, in Phèdre's statement,

> J'en ai trop prolongé la coupable durée, (217)

followed by another vision of the course of her action:

> Grâces au ciel, mes mains ne sont point criminelles.
> Plût aux dieux que mon cœur fût innocent comme elles!
>
> (221-22)

At that point where her hands are as guilty as her heart, she will have to die, and the denouement will occur.

If the general movement of the action is from guilt and a wish to die at the beginning to augmented guilt and a necessity to die at the end, then the main business of the plot will consist in the successive augmentation and intensification of Phèdre's guilt. This Racine achieves through two distinct developments: through a gradual spread, to one person after another, of the knowledge of her criminal passion, and through the actual committing of the act that makes her really more guilty. Long before the beginning of the present action, Phèdre had come to love Hippolyte, and this passion had from the start been accompanied by a strong feeling of guilt; love and guilt thus belong to the antecedents of the play, which opens with them. But both had existed, at that time, as passions known only to Phèdre; her love had been communicated to nobody, hence only she had been aware of her guilt. She has preferred death itself to the revelation of her love:

> Je meurs, pour ne point faire un aveu si funeste.   (226)

> Tu frémiras d'horreur si je romps le silence.   (238)

Yet (for reasons that I shall examine later) her silence is broken, and her confession to Œnone makes the old nurse the first to have knowledge of Phèdre's passion. In spite of the fact that the faithful servant is, among all those who will ultimately know, the one least apt to use the knowledge against her, Phèdre resists making the admission, and once it is made, she is reconciled to it only because of her intention to die immediately:

> Je voulais en mourant prendre soin de ma gloire,
> Et dérober au jour une flamme si noire:
> Je n'ai pu soutenir tes larmes, tes combats;
> Je t'ai tout avoué; je ne m'en repens pas,
> Pourvu que de ma mort respectant les approches,
> Tu ne m'affliges plus par d'injustes reproches.   (309-14)

In order for Phèdre to make the second confession—this one much more difficult for her and more important for the action of the play—she must be convinced that her husband, absent at the time of the first admission, is now dead, that her love for his son is thus now legitimate, and that the safety and the future of her children require a consultation with Hippolyte. In fact, we may judge that, in the total construction of the plot, the reported death of Thésée and the consequent political situation of Troezen and Athens are introduced, if not wholly at least in large part, in order to make the second confession possible. Moreover, the special character and the special activity of Œnone are necessary for the same purpose. If so much preparation and so much justification are necessary, it is again because of Phèdre's guilt: she could not declare her love to Hippolyte under any

other circumstances. Even so, she thinks still of her impending
death—

> Mon fils n'a plus de père, et le jour n'est pas loin
> Qui de ma mort encor doit le rendre témoin—   (587–88)

she makes the confession only with great reluctance, and it takes
the form (not entirely wilfully) of a weakness, a lapsus, an unwitting revelation. And always, it is accompanied by her own
guilty self-condemnation:

> J'aime. Ne pense pas qu'au moment que je t'aime,
> Innocente à mes yeux, je m'approuve moi-même;
> Ni que du fol amour qui trouble ma raison
> Ma lâche complaisance ait nourri le poison.
> Objet infortuné des vengeances célestes,
> Je m'abhorre encore plus que tu ne me détestes.   (673–78)

> Que dis-je? Cet aveu que je te viens de faire,
> Cet aveu si honteux, le crois-tu volontaire?   (693–94)

Once again, the confession is followed by an aggravated sense of
shame, of which she speaks to Œnone at the beginning of Act III:

> Cache-moi bien plutôt: je n'ai que trop parlé.
> Mes fureurs au dehors ont osé se répandre.
> J'ai dit ce que jamais on ne devait entendre.   (740–42)

It is important to note that, for Phèdre, an increase in her guilt
can come about only through its "publication"; since it had long
since reached a maximum as an internal state, her knowledge
that other interested persons now know will constitute a new
source of suffering for her. So in the case of her declaration to
Hippolyte:

> Il n'est plus temps. Il sait mes ardeurs insensées.
> De l'austère pudeur les bornes sont passées.
> J'ai déclaré ma honte aux yeux de mon vainqueur.

> (765–67)

So in her apostrophe to Venus in the following scene:

> O toi, qui vois la honte où je suis descendue,
> Implacable Vénus, suis-je assez confondue?   (813-14)

The news that Thésée is still alive and about to return not only changes Phèdre's situation, it also intensifies her remorse:

> J'ai fait l'indigne aveu d'un amour qui l'outrage.   (833)

Once more, she gives a succinct estimate of her present situation in a developing action:

> Sur mes justes remords tes pleurs ont prévalu.
> Je mourais ce matin digne d'être pleurée;
> J'ai suivi tes conseils, je meurs déshonorée.   (836-38)

Guilt and death are here once more linked, with an indication that guilt has grown through its avowal. In her next speech, Phèdre gives an even clearer appraisal:

> Je sais mes perfidies,
> Œnone, et ne suis point de ces femmes hardies
> Qui goûtant dans le crime une tranquille paix,
> Ont su se faire un front qui ne rougit jamais.
> Je connais mes fureurs, je les rappelle toutes.
> Il me semble déjà que ces murs, que ces voûtes
> Vont prendre la parole, et prêts à m'accuser,
> Attendent mon époux pour le désabuser.
> Mourons. De tant d'horreurs qu'un trépas me délivre.
> . . . .
> Je ne crains que le nom que je laisse après moi.
> . . . .
> Je tremble qu'un discours, hélas! trop véritable,
> Un jour ne leur reproche une mère coupable.   (849-66)

If Phèdre has moved closer to her death through the revelations to Œnone and Hippolyte, the second more damaging than the first, her next and last act should be a confession to Thésée himself, since he is, of all, the most interested party. His knowledge of her guilt would imply the maximum degree of her shame. In IV, 4, Phèdre comes to Thésée in order to make such a confession, and her initial speeches show that she is about to conform to her principle that she could not "opprimer et noircir l'innocence" (893). Thus she first says to Thésée:

> Respectez votre sang, j'ose vous en prier.
> Sauvez-moi de l'horreur de l'entendre crier;
> Ne me préparez point la douleur éternelle
> De l'avoir fait répandre à la main paternelle. (1171–74)

The imminence of her confession, and the reasons for it, are disclosed after the interview is over:

> Je cédais au remords dont j'étais tourmentée.
> Qui sait même où m'allait porter ce repentir?
> Peut-être à m'accuser j'aurais pu consentir;
> Peut-être, si la voix ne m'eût été coupée,
> L'affreuse vérité me serait échappée. (1198–1202)

But at the last minute Phèdre remains silent, shocked by the discovery that Hippolyte loves Aricie; her jealousy impedes her impulse to justice and honesty.

Before Thésée will finally come to full knowledge of Phèdre's love, two other personages will learn about it—both of them, we are to suppose, through Hippolyte. In the case of Aricie, the situation is made completely clear in the first scene of Act V, where Hippolyte defends his reticence with respect to his father and begs Aricie to share it. She yields to his wishes, although in her conversation with Thésée (V, 3) she makes hints and suggestions quite similar to those of Hippolyte at two earlier points (III, 5, and IV, 2). As a matter of fact, there is a whole series of partial disclosures to Thésée before Phèdre's final admission: the three by Hippolyte and Aricie, having as their function to make Thésée doubt (ultimately) the rightness of his decision; the report, by Panope, of Phèdre's banishment of Œnone and Œnone's suicide; finally, the sketchy notations of Théramène in his final *récit*:

> J'ai vu des mortels périr le plus aimable,
> Et j'ose dire encor, Seigneur, le moins coupable.   (1493-94)

The latter include the citation of Hippolyte's last words:

> «Le ciel, dit-il, m'arrache une innocente vie.
>
> . . . .
>
> Cher ami, si mon père un jour désabusé
> Plaint le malheur d'un fils faussement accusé ...»
>
> (1561-64)

We may guess that Théramène has divined Phèdre's guilt, not only through these last words of Hippolyte, but also through earlier statements; although we have no positive knowledge to that effect. At any rate, awareness of her guilt by Aricie and Théramène does not directly affect Phèdre's state of soul, and we have no reactions on her part to it. This awareness serves rather to prepare Thésée for the ultimate clarification.

When that clarification comes (V, 7), it is made by Phèdre quickly and directly. Her exculpation of Hippolyte is an economical way of indicating her own guilt:

> Il faut à votre fils rendre son innocence.
> Il n'était point coupable.   (1618-19)

That guilt is once more associated with her death in her last, long speech of confession:

> Mais je laissais gémir la vertu soupçonnée.
> J'ai voulu, devant vous exposant mes remords,
> Par un chemin plus lent descendre chez les morts.
>
> (1634-36)

All the personages of the tragedy now know of Phèdre's guilty love, silence has given way to speech, complete ignorance to complete knowledge, and the action, in so far as it involves an increase of Phèdre's guilt through its progressive "publication," has been concluded. That action has been conducted in a steady fashion throughout the tragedy, following an order that moves not only from less interested to more interested persons (from Œnone to Hippolyte to Thésée), but also from less to more violent sentiments of remorse on the part of the protagonist.

As I have already pointed out, however, Phèdre's guilt is double or doubly increased; on the one hand, it is increased "internally" as, with each successive revelation, her shame becomes more massive; on the other hand, it is increased "externally" as she becomes guilty of Hippolyte's death. Even so, guilt from an external source is the same passion, and in *Phèdre* both lines of the main action are made to serve a single state of soul. The "interiority" of the action is thus assured. For Racine, the problem of bringing about the external act and of making Phèdre ultimately responsible for it was a difficult and a delicate one. Phèdre could not do the deed herself, for that would be as much outside her character and her capacities for action as it would be revolting to the audience. Nor could she, again because of the nobility of her moral character, make the kind of direct accusation that would lead to Hippolyte's death. Hence the indirect accusation through Œnone, with Phèdre's acquiescence if not at her bidding. Yet she must, in the last analysis, be morally responsible for it if she is to feel the proper measure of guilt. This is brought about through the *confession manquée:* at that point in the action where Phèdre might have saved Hippolyte's life through a timely self-accusation, she fails to do so because another passion, jealousy, is brought into play. She may thus feel fully responsible for his death without having actually caused it.

The line of guilt through the external act is just as carefully pursued in the play as the line of knowledge, although it is less considerable and less completely developed. I have already quoted Phèdre's words in which she juxtaposes the guilt of the hand to the guilt of the heart:

> Grâces au ciel, mes mains ne sont point criminelles.
> Plût aux dieux que mon cœur fût innocent comme elles!
>
> (221–22)

These words come as a reply to Œnone's question:

> Vos mains n'ont point trempé dans le sang innocent? (220)

It is Œnone who, as she urges Phèdre to agree to the false accusation, points out that Hippolyte's death might be one of the consequences; in so doing, she repeats her words:

> Je parlerai. Thésée, aigri par mes avis,
> Bornera sa vengeance à l'exil de son fils.
> Un père en punissant, Madame, est toujours père:
> Un supplice léger suffit à sa colère.
> Mais le sang innocent dût-il être versé,
> Que ne demande point votre honneur menacé? (899–904)

Knowing this, Phèdre already assumes some moral responsibility when she agrees to have Œnone make the accusation. But the victim, even before Œnone speaks against him, feels secure in his innocence:

> Mais l'innocence enfin n'a rien à redouter.   (996)

Thésée's response is more violent than Œnone had anticipated, and he calls upon Neptune to avenge him:

> J'abandonne ce traître à toute ta colère;
> Étouffe dans son sang ses désirs effrontés.   (1074–75)

The innocent blood will therefore be shed unless some intervention causes Thésée to recall his vow: Phèdre's *confession manquée* is intended to provide that intervention. She begins by begging Thésée,

> S'il en est temps encore, épargnez votre race,
> Respectez votre sang, j'ose vous en prier,   (1170–71)

and as she does so she recognizes her own responsibility:

> Ne me préparez point la douleur éternelle
> De l'avoir fait répandre à la main paternelle.   (1173–74)

Thésée replies that he has put Hippolyte's life in the hands of the gods:

Non, Madame, en mon sang ma main n'a point trempé;
. . . .
Une immortelle main de sa perte est chargée. (1175-77)

Phèdre's jealousy keeps her from revealing Hippolyte's innocence; but it does not prevent her from realizing (IV, 6) the
extent to which she is still guilty and responsible. The scene with
Œnone brings her to a discovery of the state to which she has
come:

Mes homicides mains, promptes à me venger,
Dans le sang innocent brûlent de se plonger. (1271-72)

Shocked by Œnone's completely amoral attitudes, she recapitu-
lates what has happened and the steps by which she has been
brought to her present guilt:

Au jour que je fuyais c'est toi qui m'as rendue.
Tes prières m'ont fait oublier mon devoir.
J'évitais Hippolyte, et tu me l'as fait voir.
De quoi te chargeais-tu? Pourquoi ta bouche impie
A-t-elle, en l'accusant, osé noircir sa vie?
Il en mourra peut-être, et d'un père insensé
Le sacrilège vœu peut-être est exaucé. (1310-16)

But it is now too late—or still too early—for her to clear Hippolyte. As Aricie points out to him at the beginning of Act V,
only he can save himself:

Mais du moins en partant assurez votre vie.
Défendez votre honneur d'un reproche honteux,
Et forcez votre père à révoquer ses vœux. (1334-36)

Yet he believes that he may be saved by flight and, still respect-
ing his father's honor, forbids Aricie to communicate to Thésée
what she knows about Phèdre. She obeys—not, however, without
urging Thésée to spare Hippolyte:

Cessez: repentez-vous de vos vœux homicides:
Craignez, Seigneur, craignez que le ciel rigoureux
Ne vous haïsse assez pour exaucer vos vœux. (1434-36)

Her insinuations, to which are added Panope's reports, cause
Thésée to regret his request and he asks Neptune, but too late,
to delay his compliance:

> Ne précipite point tes funestes bienfaits,
> Neptune; j'aime mieux n'être exaucé jamais.   (1483-84)

Hippolyte dies, as the result of multiple causes in which Phèdre
holds a major share of responsibility. That fact is recognized by
Thésée in their final scene:

> Hé bien! vous triomphez, et mon fils est sans vie.
>
> . . . .
>
> Mais, Madame, il est mort, prenez votre victime:
> Jouissez de sa perte, injuste ou légitime.   (1594-98)

Phèdre herself admits her love for Hippolyte directly, her role in
his death only indirectly; but she admits it none the less as she
speaks of her remorse:

> Elle s'en est punie, et fuyant mon courroux,
> A cherché dans les flots un supplice trop doux.
> Le fer aurait déjà tranché ma destinée;
> Mais je laissais gémir la vertu soupçonnée.
> J'ai voulu, devant vous exposant mes remords,
> Par un chemin plus lent descendre chez les morts.
> (1631-36)

The guilt of her hands, fully realized only when Hippolyte is
dead, is added to the guilt of her heart that has grown with each
successive revelation.

In *Phèdre,* then, Racine achieves a simple plot firmly centered
about his protagonist, involving a clear movement from the beginning to the end. The movement is dual; but both of its parts
pertain to a single passion in the heroine, which they augment
progressively and bring to a critical point. Since this is the case—
since external episode and material act contribute to an internal
development—Racine is able to apply better than ever before in

his tragedies that principle of "interiority" which had been one of his main concerns throughout his career as a dramatist.

The second principle informing the development of the plot in *Phèdre* is that of the subordination of all secondary actions and episodes to the main action. Again, the problem had absorbed Racine in all his plays. Sometimes, he had found it necessary to invent elaborate secondary actions, either in order to fill out a plot that otherwise might have been too meager or in order to provide the kinds of probability needed to implement the main action. As we have seen, when they were not handled with complete sureness, such materials tended at times to become dominant and to obscure the major lines of the intrigue, at other times to make secondary personages the rivals of the protagonist for the attention and the sympathy of the spectator. Even in certain of his greatest tragedies (*Andromaque,* for example), the process had resulted in the weakening and the dispersion of the total effect. In *Phèdre,* we may judge that there is really no "secondary action" at all; for such auxiliary persons and episodes as exist are completely integrated into the main action, which could not exist without them.

We may consider, as the best example, the personage of Aricie and the events related to the love of Hippolyte and Aricie. These are built into the plot primarily to serve one purpose: to make possible Phèdre's jealousy, which leads to the *confession manquée,* which leads to the death of Hippolyte. Without her jealousy and its consequences the guilty act becomes impossible, and one of the essential parts of the action is lost. This purpose may seem to be single and simple enough; yet its achievement required a fairly elaborate combination and concatenation of dramatic elements. First, the character of Hippolyte and his reputation for chastity needed to be firmly established, and this Racine does as early as the opening scene with Théramène. (This kind of sure and fully adequate blocking out of a character, in the initial stages of a play, was one of Racine's constant excellences.) Next, the woman whom the chaste Hippolyte actually loved, Aricie, had to be placed in such circumstances that there could be no suspicion of their love; hence the history of Aricie's family and the interdict placed upon her by Thésée. Finally and most important, Phèdre needed to be provided—among her numerous traits of character—with the capacity for jealousy that would manifest itself at the critical moment. It was to this capacity that Racine devoted the greatest attention.

The very first time that Phèdre is mentioned in the tragedy, it is in terms of a rival and the possibility of jealousy:

> Phèdre depuis longtemps ne craint plus de rivale.   (26)

Hippolyte is of course referring to Thésée's amorous past and to the many women who had occupied it; the rival whom Phèdre might fear would be another such woman. But the fact that Phèdre had had to fear rivals in the past is important; and Hippolyte's words take on a strong dramatic irony as the "rival" turns out to be his own beloved. Moreover, without any particular reference to jealousy, Phèdre's tendency to violent emotional reactions, to flaring passion, becomes apparent as she describes to Œnone the progress of her love for Hippolyte. There can be no question of active jealousy with respect to Hippolyte as long as Phèdre believes him chaste, and his response to her declaration of love elicits from her a variety of other emotions, but no jealousy. She is sanguine on that score:

> Je ne me verrai point préférer de rivale.   (790)

Indeed, in her soliloquy of III, 2, she calls upon Venus to make the conquest of Hippolyte: "Qu'il aime..." (823). Her crisis of jealousy will come suddenly when Thésée tells her of Hippolyte's love for Aricie. Her first response is one of astonishment: "Quoi, Seigneur?" (1188); her second one, in the monologue that follows, is a full expression of her jealousy and an admission of the way in which it has impeded her avowal to Thésée:

> Hippolyte est sensible, et ne sent rien pour moi!
> Aricie a son cœur! Aricie a sa foi!

Ah, Dieux! Lorsqu'à mes vœux l'ingrat inexorable
S'armait d'un œil si fier, d'un front si redoutable,
Je pensais qu'à l'amour son cœur toujours fermé
Fût contre tout mon sexe également armé.
Une autre cependant a fléchi son audace;
Devant ses yeux cruels une autre a trouvé grâce.
Peut-être a-t-il un cœur facile à s'attendrir.
Je suis le seul objet qu'il ne saurait souffrir;
Et je me chargerais du soin de le défendre?   (1203–13)

The third response, in the scene with Œnone (IV, 6), begins with the simple formula:

Œnone, qui l'eût cru? j'avais une rivale,   (1218)

then goes on to a complete retailing of the multiple feelings—all of them jealous—that had burst upon her with Thésée's news. But, as for so many other elements in this same scene, the more Phèdre reflects upon her passion and pushes it to its most extreme consequences, the more she realizes how opposed it is to her normal morality:

Dans mes jaloux transports je le veux implorer.
Que fais-je? Où ma raison se va-t-elle égarer?
Moi jalouse! et Thésée est celui que j'implore?
Mon époux est vivant, et moi je brûle encore!   (1263–66)

We should note that there is no mention, in Phèdre's final confession, of this jealousy and of its results; by now all sources and forms of her guilt have combined into one, the overriding passion that produces her death.

We should note also that, having invented and exploited the various elements that contribute to Phèdre's jealousy, Racine puts them to additional uses in the organization of his plot. Hippolyte is able, when he presents his defense to Thésée (IV, 2), to allege his chastity as a proof of his innocence; and when he tells of his love for Aricie, he explains his hesitation on the basis of Thésée's interdict. Besides, the interdict serves as the basis for a *quid pro quo* on the part of Thésée, who takes Hippolyte's admission of his "véritable offense" as an "artifice grossier" (1121, 1127). Aricie, in turn, becomes useful in several ways; she helps, through her insinuations, to arouse Thésée's doubts about the rightness of his curse, she is the object of the rendezvous "aux portes de Trézène" (1392) that leads Hippolyte to his death, and she becomes, at the very end, the person who may serve as the beneficiary of Thésée's repentance.

The whole of the Hippolyte-Aricie line in *Phèdre* is thus auxiliary rather than secondary; I mean by this that it at no time becomes for the spectator the center of a separate and independent interest, that it at all times is instrumental to the accomplishment of the main action. There are, indeed, no secondary actions in the play. Such fairly extensive developments as the absence, reported death, and return of Thésée, the activity, disgrace, and death of Œnone, the political maneuverings at the time of the reported death, are all firmly integrated into the structure of the central plot and have no separate existence or separate interest outside it. We therefore have the impression (perhaps for the first time in Racine's tragedies) that everything "belongs" to the principal action, that all persons and events serve its purposes and help it to move in an orderly fashion to a necessary conclusion. There is here no sense that supernumerary elements are introduced in order to round out a sparse action, that external episodes are multiplied in order to give dramatic substance to an internal crisis, or that the protagonist suffers from an excessive attention to other personages.

Racine's third principle of plot construction in *Phèdre* is, again, one that he had recognized as essential from the very beginning and one with which he had been throughout successful, the principle of the meticulous provision and the full realization of probabilities for every event in the action. In *Phèdre,* the problem was more difficult than elsewhere in at least one instance, the preparation for the supernatural death of Hippolyte, and the success of Racine's solution is thus all the more notable. Racine had at all times been wary of any major episode, and especially of any denouement, for which the probabilities did not correspond to his audience's conceptions of natural probability. He organized his plots in such a way that the denouements, although unexpected and endowed with a proper degree of suspense, did not depend upon supernatural intervention, upon the *deus ex machina*. In *Phèdre,* however, the exigencies of the action were such that he could not use natural probabilities for the death of Hippolyte. Clearly, *Phèdre* herself could not kill Hippolyte, just as she could not make the false accusation to Thésée; her general moral nobility was such that both actions would have been out of character. Moreover, such an act would have lost her the sympathy of the audience and would have interrupted that slow progression in Phèdre's sense of her guilt that was needed to bring about the denouement. Nor could Thésée commit the murder; his character both as man and as father would prevent— his hands must no more be bloody than Phèdre's—and such a deed by him would, once again, render impossible the progressive timing of condemnation, doubt, and ultimate forgiveness. An accidental death (as anywhere in poetry) would be completely out of the question.

Such reasons as these must have led to Racine's unusual decision to entrust Hippolyte's death to the gods. In order to do so, he had not only to create such internal artistic probabilities as might justify the supernatural death itself, but also to establish the general probability for events of the kind. Had the supernatural death remained an isolated act in a context in which all other acts corresponded to an audience's expectations for natural probability, it would have been difficult to accept. The problem was to surround it with a proper context of supernatural expectations. Racine proceeded to make these a basic part of the tragedy. Several of the major personages have close parentage with the gods and are fairly immediately descended from them. Phèdre's mother was Pasiphaé, daughter of the Sun:

Noble et brillant auteur d'une triste famille,
Toi, dont ma mère osait se vanter d'être fille,

. . . .

Soleil ...   (169–72)

Her father, Minos, was the son of Jupiter and Europa. Aricie,
her rival, is descended, through Pallas and Erechtheus, from the
Earth. Thésée and Hippolyte, though of less divine origins, belong to a family whose founders were among the first of the
Greek kings. Racine insists on these elements that place his action
in the earliest mythological times and that make his personages a
subject of awe and amazement; so Théramène in his search for
Thésée:

J'ai demandé Thésée aux peuples de ces bords
Où l'on voit l'Achéron se perdre chez les morts;
J'ai visité l'Élide, et laissant le Ténare,
Passé jusqu'à la mer qui vit tomber Icare.   (11–14)

So the identification of Phèdre as "La fille de Minos et de Pasiphaé" (36). So Hippolyte as he recalls the narrative of his father's
deeds:

Quand tu me dépeignais ce héros intrépide
Consolant les mortels de l'absence d'Alcide,
Les monstres étouffés et les brigands punis,
Procruste, Cercyon, et Scirron, et Sinnis,
Et les os dispersés du géant d'Épidaure,
Et la Crète fumant du sang du Minotaure.   (77–82)

The walls of Athens are "Les superbes remparts que Minerve a
bâtis" (360), the report of Thésée's death by Ismène includes
marvelous details:

On dit même, et ce bruit est partout répandu,
Qu'avec Pirithoüs aux enfers descendu,
Il a vu le Cocyte et les rivages sombres,
Et s'est montré vivant aux infernales ombres.   (383–86)

Traits of this kind, concentrated at the beginning of the play and multiplied throughout, introduce an atmosphere in which the extraordinary is ordinary, the marvelous commonplace; and in this way they create a poetic probability for the occurrence of similar events within the action.

Especially in the case of Thésée, a firm association with the world of gods, heroes, monsters, and mythology is of primary importance; for it is he who brings about the supernatural death. We have already seen some of the factors; there are many others. Thus Hippolyte falls short of his father's accomplishments:

> Qu'un long amas d'honneurs rend Thésée excusable,
> Qu'aucuns monstres par moi domptés jusqu'aujourd'hui
> Ne m'ont acquis le droit de faillir comme lui.   (98–100)

He speaks of Thésée as "L'ami, le compagnon, le successeur d'Alcide" (470), and Phèdre repeats the story of her husband's death:

> Puisque Thésée a vu les sombres bords,
> En vain vous espérez qu'un dieu vous le renvoie;
> Et l'avare Achéron ne lâche point sa proie.   (624–26)

She speaks of the conquest of the Minotaur and of the fabulous events that had preceded her marriage to Thésée (643–61). Hippolyte repeats his self-reproaches in the same terms, after Thésée's return:

> Vous n'aviez pas encore atteint l'âge où je touche,
> Déjà plus d'un tyran, plus d'un monstre farouche
> Avait de votre bras senti la pesanteur;
> Déjà, de l'insolence heureux persécuteur,
> Vous aviez des deux mers assuré les rivages.
> Le libre voyageur ne craignait plus d'outrages;
> Hercule, respirant sur le bruit de vos coups,
> Déjà de son travail se reposait sur vous.   (937–44)

Thésée's own account of his recent adventures (957–70) is of a nature to fill the spectator with wonder and with a sense of mystery, especially in such features as "Lieux profonds, et voisins de l'empire des ombres" (966).

It is Thésée who informs us of the pact between himself and Neptune:

> Et toi, Neptune, et toi, si jadis mon courage
> D'infâmes assassins nettoya ton rivage,
> Souviens-toi que pour prix de mes efforts heureux,
> Tu promis d'exaucer le premier de mes vœux.
> Dans les longues rigueurs d'une prison cruelle
> Je n'ai point imploré ta puissance immortelle.
> Avare du secours que j'attends de tes soins,
> Mes vœux t'ont réservé pour de plus grands besoins:
> Je t'implore aujourd'hui.   (1065–73)

This single indication, for all its vigor, might be insufficient to impress an audience in the theater; Racine takes pains to repeat and amplify it. Thus Thésée insists in his brief monologue (IV, 3):

> Neptune, par le fleuve aux dieux mêmes terrible,
> M'a donné sa parole, et va l'exécuter.   (1158–59)

He makes a similar statement to Phèdre immediately afterward:

> Une immortelle main de sa perte est chargée.
> Neptune me la doit, et vous serez vengée.

> PHÈDRE

> Neptune vous la doit! Quoi? vos vœux irrités ...
>   (1177–79)

And again:

> Espérons de Neptune une prompte justice.
> Je vais moi-même encore au pied de ses autels
> Le presser d'accomplir ses serments immortels.   (1190–92)

Phèdre recognizes the likelihood that his wish will be granted by Neptune:

> Il en mourra peut-être, et d'un père insensé
> Le sacrilège vœu peut-être est exaucé. (1315-16)

In addition to these particular details about the relationship of Thésée and Neptune, coming fairly close to the granting of the wish, Racine includes a general statement about them early in the play; with proper dramatic irony, it is Hippolyte who utters the words, and to Phèdre:

> Neptune le protège, et ce dieu tutélaire
> Ne sera pas en vain imploré par mon père. (621-22)

This is in keeping with Racine's practice of establishing a general probability before passing on to specific applications.

Besides the supernatural of the gods, in *Phèdre* the poet needed to create a probability for the supernatural of monsters— again to render Hippolyte's death acceptable to his audience. An extended development is provided in this connection. We have already seen a few of the examples of the monsters associated with Thésée (80, 99, 938); there are many others. Phèdre refers to the Minotaur as "le monstre de la Crète" (649); Hippolyte expresses his wish to emulate his father—

> Souffrez, si quelque monstre a pu vous échapper,
> Que j'apporte à vos pieds sa dépouille honorable—
> (948-49)

and Thésée refers twice to the monsters in his latest adventure:

> J'ai vu Pirithoüs, triste objet de mes larmes,
> Livré par ce barbare à des monstres cruels
> Qu'il nourrissait du sang des malheureux mortels.
> (962-64)

> A ses monstres lui-même a servi de pâture. (970)

The recency and the immediacy of these is of special importance for the audience's belief, and Hippolyte's long-time wish to con-

quer a monster gives verisimilitude to his last act. But there exist
also, in *Phèdre*, monsters of a different kind; these are the moral
monsters, and they fall into two categories. First are the persons who, because of their unnatural loves, fall outside the normal limits of human action and morality. Phèdre's mother,
Pasiphaé, is one of these, although the term is not actually used:

> Dans quels égarements l'amour jeta ma mère!   (250)

(Racine's audience would associate immediately with these
words the image of Pasiphaé possessed by the white bull.)
Phèdre applies the term twice to herself after having confessed her love for Hippolyte:

> Digne fils du héros qui t'a donné le jour,
> Délivre l'univers d'un monstre qui t'irrite.
> La veuve de Thésée ose aimer Hippolyte!
> Crois-moi, ce monstre affreux ne doit point t'échapper.
>
> (700–703)

Aricie applies it, but only by innuendo, to Phèdre as she attempts to defend Hippolyte:

> Vos invincibles mains
> Ont de monstres sans nombre affranchi les humains:
> Mais tout n'est pas détruit, et vous en laissez vivre
> Un ...   (1443–46)

Second are the persons (Hippolyte and Œnone) who are characterized as "monsters" by those who disapprove of their conduct, with only a suggestion of its unnatural character. Of this
order is Phèdre's judgment of Hippolyte,

> Je le vois comme un monstre effroyable à mes yeux,
>
> (884)

Thésée's invective directed at his son,

> Monstre, qu'a trop longtemps épargné le tonnerre,
> Reste impur des brigands dont j'ai purgé la terre,
>
> (1045–46)

and Phèdre's outraged characterization of Œnone:

> Va-t'en, monstre exécrable. (1317)

Through such uses as these last, largely metaphorical, the term "monster" becomes generalized; it takes on, for the audience, a moral as well as a material significance; and it renders acceptable, to a degree that would not otherwise be possible, the appearance of the real monster in Théramène's narrative.

In a sense, many of the materials relevant to the gods and to monsters are introduced into the tragedy for the sole purpose of endowing with credibility the events related in the *récit* of Théramène. But it should not be thought that that narrative is compounded exclusively of supernatural elements. Indeed, one of the essential bases for its credibility is the constant intermixture of elements that proceed from natural and from supernatural probabilities; and the natural ones become "poetic" through just as careful and as consecutive a preparation as that given the others. We may see the *récit* as made up of several kinds of components: supernatural beings and circumstances, rendered credible by the kinds of preparation that we have seen; natural beings and actions, rendered poetically credible through the normal processes of establishing probability; and descriptive details which, as they make both types of events visually convincing, add a third sort of general credibility. Without taking into account the descriptive details, we may see how successive parts of the *récit* depend upon passages and developments antecedent to it in the play:

> A peine nous sortions des portes de Trézène, (1498)

> Aux portes de Trézène, et parmi ces tombeaux, (1392)

> Il était sur son char ... (1499)

> Avouez-le, tout change; et depuis quelques jours
> On vous voit moins souvent, orgueilleux et sauvage,
> Tantôt faire voler un char sur le rivage. (128–30)

Quand pourrai-je, au travers d'une noble poussière,
Suivre de l'œil un char fuyant dans la carrière? (177–78)

Mon arc, mes javelots, mon char, tout m'importune. (549)

Sa main sur ses chevaux laissait flotter les rênes.
Ses superbes coursiers, qu'on voyait autrefois
Pleins d'une ardeur si noble obéir à sa voix. (1502–4)

Tantôt, savant dans l'art par Neptune inventé,
Rendre docile au frein un coursier indompté. (131–32)

Et mes coursiers oisifs ont oublié ma voix. (552)

Parmi des flots d'écume, un monstre furieux. (1516)

Le ciel avec horreur voit ce monstre sauvage. (1522)
[cf. the lines already cited on monsters]

Dans le temple voisin chacun cherche un asile. (1526)

Est un temple sacré formidable aux parjures. (1394)

Hippolyte lui seul, digne fils d'un héros. (1527)

Digne fils du héros qui t'a donné le jour. (700)

Arrête ses coursiers, saisit ses javelots. (1528)
[cf. 549 above]

Ne pourrai-je, en fuyant un indigne repos,
D'un sang plus glorieux teindre mes javelots? (935–36)

La frayeur les emporte, et sourds à cette fois,
Ils ne connaissent plus ni le frein ni la voix. (1535–36)
[cf. 132, 552 above]

On dit qu'on a vu même, en ce désordre affreux,
Un dieu qui d'aiguillons pressait leur flanc poudreux.   (1539-40)
   [cf. the references to Neptune's intervention]

Ils s'arrêtent, non loin de ces tombeaux antiques
Où des rois ses aïeux sont les froides reliques.   (1553-54)

     ... et parmi ces tombeaux
   Des princes de ma race antiques sépultures.   (1392-93)

For the spectator who needs to believe, the recalling of so
many formulas and phrases, images and references, that had
been used earlier in the play at striking junctures, gives the impression of the return of what is known; and in a poem, what
once is known is forever credible. Racine seems to work backward from his most difficult episode, as far as probability is
concerned, preparing and establishing its credibility in numerous
antecedent passages. The supernatural, in this respect, is in no
way different from the natural.

The tragedy of *Phèdre*, then, obtains its qualities of plot
from an extremely simple plan of organization, which is "Racinian" and "classical" in the sense that the basic movement is
a change from one state of soul to another within the protagonist. In order that the clarity and simplicity of plan may be
preserved, all personages and episodes are subordinated to the
needs of the central plot; there are no subplots or secondary
lines of action. And in order that the whole of the action, including the marvelous and supernatural parts, may be accepted
by the audience as credible, great care is taken to erect within
the play a tight system of poetic probabilities. From the clarity
and definiteness of the plot and from the general credibility
results an emotional effect appropriate to the events, surer and
more concentrated than had been the effects of most of the preceding tragedies precisely because of the absence of factors that
might weaken and dilute it.

The particular quality of the effect—the specific emotion awakened and developed in the audience—does not, however, result from excellences of structure; it derives rather from the nature of the events that constitute the plot and from the character of the protagonist around whom the plot is built. In *Phèdre,* the problem of character and deeds was a difficult one for Racine. If one starts from guilt and ends with increased guilt, if increased guilt results from the false accusation and the death of an innocent and honorable man and from the widespread knowledge of what had been a private shame, how is one to obtain and maintain the sympathy of an audience for the personage in whom the guilt is centered? How is one to prevent the arousal of moral indignation and revulsion, and awaken instead sentiments of understanding and pity? How, in a word, is one to assure the presence of a truly tragic emotion? From the devices introduced to solve it, we may be fairly certain that Racine conceived of his artistic problem in some such terms; and from the success of those devices, we may judge that his final conception of the plot and the character was a properly tragic one.

First of these devices was, I think, the exclusion from the plot itself of Phèdre's love for Hippolyte. I mean by this that the whole history of her love for her stepson and the passion itself, which might have turned a spectator against her, are separated from the action proper and made to precede it. Not that her love does not enter into the action; for it is the basis of the guilt with which we start. But the beginnings and the development of her passion, the efforts she had made to combat it, belong to a time preceding the action of this play and in a sense constitute a separate action. We shall be told about them at the proper time within the play; but that is far different, and far less damaging for the character of Phèdre, than if they were enacted before us and integrated into the plot. For Phèdre will relate these facts, first to Œnone and then to Hippolyte, in retrospect; they will be accompanied by the moral judgment that she now makes upon them; they will be seen in the light of her own disapproval of herself and of her passion. The long speech of revelation to Œnone, beginning with "Mon mal vient de plus loin" (269), is punctuated with formulas of self-disavowal:

> Par des vœux assidus je crus les détourner. (279)

> Contre moi-même enfin j'osai me révolter. (291)

> J'ai conçu pour mon crime une juste terreur;
> J'ai pris la vie en haine, et ma flamme en horreur.
> (307–8)

Similarly, the confession to Hippolyte carries with it passages of related intent:

> J'aime. Ne pense pas qu'au moment que je t'aime,
> Innocente à mes yeux, je m'approuve moi-même;
> Ni que du fol amour qui trouble ma raison
> Ma lâche complaisance ait nourri le poison.
> Objet infortuné des vengeances célestes,
> Je m'abhorre encor plus que tu ne me détestes. (673–78)

> Que dis-je? Cet aveu que je te viens de faire,
> Cet aveu si honteux, le crois-tu volontaire? (693–94)

The long hesitations that precede each of these declarations, the semi-involuntary character of each, add to the atmosphere of guilt that surrounds them.

As a consequence, our first impression of Phèdre's character, one of her high moral dignity and her correct standard, comes to us as the opposite of the circumstances and the passion that she now suffers. The passion may be the work of destiny or of the gods, a thing borne against her will; but the resistance to the passion is a matter of her will, an affirmation of her moral superiority to it. That same impression of Phèdre's high moral character will be corroborated throughout the play; on each occasion where she is required to give a judgment or act in accordance with moral principles, that character will be manifested. In I, 5, she yields to Œnone's arguments because they emphasize her duty to her son. In III, 3, when she learns that Thésée is alive, she recognizes the enormity of her crime and expresses her wish to die; when Œnone proposes the false accusation, her reply is one of shocked righteousness:

> Moi, que j'ose opprimer et noircir l'innocence?   (893)

The following scene brings her face to face with Thésée, and although she has agreed to the accusation, her own words might well be—should be—interpreted as words of self-condemnation:

> Je ne mérite plus ces doux empressements.
> Vous êtes offensé. La fortune jalouse
> N'a pas en votre absence épargné votre épouse.
> Indigne de vous plaire et de vous approcher,
> Je ne dois désormais songer qu'à me cacher.   (916–20)

It is only later, when Œnone has "interpreted" these words, that Thésée turns them against Hippolyte. We have already seen how, in IV, 4, she comes to Thésée with the purpose of exculpating Hippolyte, how her jealousy prevents her from so doing, and how (in the following scene with Œnone) she discovers the extent to which she has operated in contradiction to her moral principles. This is the scene (IV, 6) in which Phèdre comes to a full realization of the moral degeneration represented by her acts:

> Mes homicides mains, promptes à me venger,
> Dans le sang innocent brûlent de se plonger.
> Misérable! et je vis? et je soutiens la vue
> De ce sacré soleil dont je suis descendue?
> . . . .
> Où me cacher? Fuyons dans la nuit infernale.
> . . . .
> Ah! combien frémira son ombre épouvantée,

> Lorsqu'il verra sa fille à ses yeux présentée,
> Contrainte d'avouer tant de forfaits divers,
> Et des crimes peut-être inconnus aux enfers!　　　(1271–84)

Yet she herself has not degenerated, and these words testify to the persistence of her moral standard. So does the speech in which she rejects Œnone and sends her to her death:

> Je ne t'écoute plus. Va-t'en, monstre exécrable:
> Va, laisse-moi le soin de mon sort déplorable.
> Puisse le juste ciel dignement te payer!
> Et puisse ton supplice à jamais effrayer
> Tous ceux qui comme toi, par de lâches adresses,
> Des princes malheureux nourrissent les faiblesses,
> Les poussent au penchant où leur cœur est enclin,
> Et leur osent du crime aplanir le chemin.　　　(1317–24)

Phèdre's moral standard finally asserts itself fully in the confession to Thésée (V, 7), where she assumes the guilt that had been wrongly placed upon Hippolyte and where her self-inflicted death serves as punishment for all her wrongdoing.

Racine thus endows his heroine with the kind of moral character, of high moral dignity, that she needs if she is to obtain the sympathy of an audience and awaken the kinds of emotions proper to a tragic heroine. Yet she does commit the crimes that lead to her death and she does (as in the last scenes that I have cited) admit moral responsibility for the events that increase her guilt and for the death of Hippolyte. Her morality is thus not perfect—or, at least, she permits sufficient deviations from her principles to put her into a posture of crime and guilt. In order to ascribe wrongdoing to a morally worthy person, Racine uses two devices of plot construction: he reduces Phèdre to a state of physical and spiritual enfeeblement where she is no longer mistress of her reason and her actions, and he invents the personage and the activity of Œnone.

The present circumstances are not the only ones in which Phèdre has lost control of her reason. As she describes to Œnone

the progress of her love, she speaks of "ma raison égarée" (282).
Now, however, her state of debilitation is both mental and
physical; she is "une femme mourante" in a very literal sense,
and this is apparent when she first appears on the stage:

> Je ne me soutiens plus: ma force m'abandonne.   (154)

> Où laissé-je égarer mes vœux et mon esprit?
> Je l'ai perdu: les dieux m'en ont ravi l'usage.   (180–81)

Œnone gives a partial explanation:

> Les ombres par trois fois ont obscurci les cieux
> Depuis que le sommeil n'est entré dans vos yeux,
> Et le jour a trois fois chassé la nuit obscure
> Depuis que votre corps languit sans nourriture.   (191–94)

She pleads with her mistress to put an end to this slow suicide—

> Mais ne différez point: chaque moment vous tue.
> Réparez promptement votre force abattue—   (213–14)

and she recognizes Phèdre's present state of inanition:

> Quoiqu'il vous reste à peine une faible lumière ...   (229)

Phèdre herself is aware of her weakness, and in terms of it she
makes her first concession to Œnone's counsels:

> Hé bien! à tes conseils je me laisse entraîner.
> Vivons, si vers la vie on peut me ramener,
> Et si l'amour d'un fils en ce moment funeste
> De mes faibles esprits peut ranimer le reste.   (363–66)

From this point on there will be a series of events—those
involved in Phèdre's guilt—in which Phèdre will rely upon
Œnone to sustain her spirits or will hand over to Œnone the
initiative for action. Thus at the beginning of her interview
with Hippolyte:

> J'oublie, en le voyant, ce que je viens lui dire.

ŒNONE

Souvenez-vous d'un fils qui n'espère qu'en vous.   (582–83)

At the end of the interview, Œnone puts a stop to her rash actions:

Que faites-vous, Madame? Justes dieux!
Mais on vient. Evitez des témoins odieux;
Venez, rentrez, fuyez une honte certaine.   (711–13)

Théramène, speaking of "Phèdre ... qu'on entraîne" (714), permits us to visualize and appreciate the situation. In the third act, after having again admitted her feebleness—

Moi régner! Moi ranger un état sous ma loi,
Quand ma faible raison ne règne plus sur moi!
Lorsque j'ai de mes sens abandonné l'empire!—   (759–61)

she assigns to Œnone her first mission, that of persuading Hippolyte to a political compromise:

Pour le fléchir enfin tente tous les moyens:
Tes discours trouveront plus d'accès que les miens.
Presse, pleure, gémis; plains-lui Phèdre mourante;
Ne rougis point de prendre une voix suppliante.
Je t'avoûrai de tout; je n'espère qu'en toi.   (807–11)

When Œnone returns to report that Thésée is alive, Phèdre's first impulse is to desist from any further action and to go on with her determination to die; but Œnone's arguments are irresistible to her in her perplexed and troubled state, and she agrees to the false accusation:

Fais ce que tu voudras, je m'abandonne à toi.
Dans le trouble où je suis, je ne puis rien pour moi.

(911–12)

It is in the light of this agreement that she speaks to Thésée the ambiguous words already cited.

Twice in the course of the succeeding action, as the play draws toward its end, Phèdre makes brief summaries of the ways in which Œnone, profiting from her mistress' surrender of her will, has taken the initiative for the action. The first of these is in the speech of reproach to Œnone (IV, 6):

> Qu'entends-je? Quels conseils ose-t-on me donner?
> Ainsi donc jusqu'au bout tu veux m'empoisonner,
> Malheureuse? Voilà comme tu m'as perdue.
> Au jour que je fuyais c'est toi qui m'as rendue.
> Tes prières m'ont fait oublier mon devoir.
> J'évitais Hippolyte, et tu me l'as fait voir.
> De quoi te chargeais-tu? Pourquoi ta bouche impie
> A-t-elle, en l'accusant, osé noircir sa vie?   (1307–14)

The second is a part of her final confession to Thésée:

> Le ciel mit dans mon sein une flamme funeste;
> La détestable Œnone a conduit tout le reste.
> Elle a craint qu'Hippolyte, instruit de ma fureur,
> Ne découvrît un feu qui lui faisait horreur.
> La perfide, abusant de ma faiblesse extrême,
> S'est hâtée à vos yeux de l'accuser lui-même.   (1625–30)

These are not only summations of the kind that Racine had frequently used to render his action perspicuous to his audience; since they are made by the protagonist herself, they indicate her estimate of the respective responsibilities and they constitute her judgment of the degree to which her weakness, her physical and spiritual feebleness, was a factor in the increase of her guilt.

The character of Œnone is a necessary counterpart to two of Phèdre's characteristics: her permanent moral nobility and her temporary weakness. The character is constructed, therefore, in terms of a complete lack of moral scruple and of a permanent capacity for vigorous action. Œnone's third trait—and it is the most effective one for linking the two personages—is her unfailing devotion to Phèdre. Combined, these traits make it possible for her to exercize over her mistress an influence of which nobody else was capable, to persuade her to actions that she would not normally take, and herself to commit acts in absolute disregard for any moral code. She may thus serve Racine as a third device for accomplishing the action of his tragedy without making its protagonist odious—hence without destroying the possibility of a proper tragic effect.

Œnone's devotion to Phèdre is apparent from their first dialogue (I, 3), in which the repeated marks of her solicitude are followed by this statement:

> Cruelle, quand ma foi vous a-t-elle déçue?
> Songez-vous qu'en naissant mes bras vous ont reçue?
> Mon pays, mes enfants, pour vous j'ai tout quitté.
> Réserviez-vous ce prix à ma fidélité?   (233–36)

Her next speech shows the degree to which her devotion is a passion:

> Et que me direz-vous qui ne cède, grands dieux!
> A l'horreur de vous voir expirer à mes yeux?   (239–40)

After her first counsels—and Phèdre's first reproaches—she states her motivation:

> Hélas! de vos malheurs innocente ou coupable,
> De quoi pour vous sauver n'étais-je point capable?
>   (773–74)

When she suggests the false accusation, it is again in terms of the alternative possibility:

> Vous me verriez plus prompte affronter mille morts.
> Mais puisque je vous perds sans ce triste remède,
> Votre vie est pour moi d'un prix à qui tout cède.   (896–98)

This faithfulness, this utter subjection to the interests of Phèdre, makes Œnone acceptable to Phèdre, who on various occasions calls her "chère Œnone" (cf. 153, 1214); it also makes her acceptable to the audience. Even at the very end her apostrophe to the gods, "Ah, Dieux! pour la servir j'ai tout fait, tout quitté"

(1327), followed by her recognition of her guilt ("Je l'ai bien mérité"), retains for her a modicum of tolerance on the part of the spectator. We feel that hers is a kind of unthinking and unquestioning affection, and that the image of Phèdre's possible death, above all else, leads her to extreme amoral decisions.

Moreover, there is a progression in these decisions and in her suggestions to Phèdre that makes her, at the outset, totally admirable. Phèdre wishes to die, her old nurse and servant wishes her to live; "Vivez donc," "Vivez" (209, 210, 349), constitutes the refrain of her earliest pleadings. We can hardly blame her for that. She accompanies these early suggestions with a tone of moral righteousness that is entirely in her favor. Thus her reaction to Phèdre's announcement of her love for Hippolyte:

> Juste ciel! tout mon sang dans mes veines se glace.
> Ô désespoir! ô crime! ô déplorable race!
> Voyage infortuné! Rivage malheureux,
> Fallait-il approcher de tes bords dangereux?   (265–68)

Phèdre yields to the first prayer:

> Vivons, si vers la vie on peut me ramener.   (364)

The acceptance involves also a response to Œnone's second prayer, that Phèdre (now that Thésée is reported dead) should enter into an agreement with Hippolyte to protect her son's and her own political interests (337 ff.). Although Œnone now speaks of the "legitimacy" of Phèdre's love, she does not hint that Phèdre might attempt to satisfy it; hence the prayer, once again, seems proper. It is in the light of the same suggestion that Phèdre is persuaded to confer with Hippolyte (583), and as she later admits or pretends, her maternal concern is the basis for the conference:

> Tremblante pour un fils que je n'osais trahir,
> Je te venais prier de ne le point haïr.   (695–96)

Conference turns to confession, and after Hippolyte has displayed his rejection of Phèdre, Œnone proposes two alternative lines of action; Phèdre may either reign—

> Ne vaudrait-il pas mieux, digne sang de Minos,
> Dans de plus nobles soins chercher votre repos,
> Contre un ingrat qui plaît recourir à la fuite,
> Régner, et de l'état embrasser la conduite?— (755–58)

or she may flee (763). In both these proposals, Œnone seems to adopt a moral position superior to that of Phèdre. The proposals are perfectly honorable and would seem to serve Phèdre's best interests.

On at least two subsequent occasions, Œnone gives evidence of the possession of some moral scruple. Her announcement of Thésée's return is preceded by an admonishment to her mistress—

> Il faut d'un vain amour étouffer la pensée,
> Madame. Rappelez votre vertu passée— (825–26)

and she pretends to some hesitation about accusing Hippolyte:

> Tremblante comme vous, j'en sens quelque remords.
> (895)

But by this time she has already fully displayed the kind of disregard for moral considerations that will lead her to her subsequent actions. The rapidity with which she is able to condone Phèdre's love, once Thésée is thought dead, may serve as a sign; her horror of a few minutes before is now reversed:

> Vivez, vous n'avez plus de reproche à vous faire:
> Votre flamme devient une flamme ordinaire.
> Thésée en expirant vient de rompre les nœuds
> Qui faisaient tout le crime et l'horreur de vos feux.
> Hippolyte pour vous devient moins redoutable;
> Et vous pouvez le voir sans vous rendre coupable. (349–54)

Another sign is the way she turns against Hippolyte, nourishing her mistress' resentment and incidentally her passion; this is in the scene (III, 1) following Hippolyte's rejection of Phèdre:

> Mais si jamais l'offense irrita vos esprits,
> Pouvez-vous d'un superbe oublier les mépris?
> Avec quels yeux cruels sa rigueur obstinée
> Vous laissait à ses pieds peu s'en faut prosternée!
> Que son farouche orgueil le rendait odieux!
> Que Phèdre en ce moment n'avait-elle mes yeux!   (775-80)

The extent of the reversal may be appreciated if we compare with lines 825-26 (quoted above) the words she speaks to justify the false accusation:

> ... et pour sauver notre honneur combattu,
> Il faut immoler tout, et même la vertu.   (907-8)

"Notre honneur" indicates how vividly she identifies herself with her mistress.

Up to the point where she proposes the false accusation, then, Œnone is the object of a double development; Racine makes her acceptable to the audience by emphasizing her positive qualities, especially her devotion to Phèdre, while he prepares for her later actions by suggesting a real lack of moral scruple. At the same time, he is able to establish for her a capacity for forceful argument, for adapting herself to the feelings of her mistress and for anticipating and forming those feelings. The enfeebled Phèdre cannot resist these arguments. Not, that is, until they become so "monstrous" as to shock Phèdre into a reawakened sense of right and justice. Œnone's first truly immoral act is to propose the false accusation of Hippolyte; Phèdre accepts. Next, she herself makes the accusation to Thésée. We are present only at the second part of the revelation, but Thésée summarizes the first for us (1001-13). Œnone continues and completes her story before us in such a way that we reach the proper degree of hatred and horror for her; it is especially through the overt lie—

J'ai vu lever le bras, j'ai couru la sauver.
Moi seule à votre amour j'ai su la conserver—   (1019–20)

that we arrive at these attitudes. Yet Œnone saves herself, to a
degree, through her final reticence and her incapacity to build
upon and embroider the lie. When Thésée seeks to probe into
the details, she resorts to ambiguity,

> Seigneur, souvenez-vous des plaintes de la reine.
> Un amour criminel causa toute sa haine,   (1029–30)

and when he proceeds in his questioning, she takes refuge in
flight:

> Je vous ai dit, Seigneur, tout ce qui s'est passé.
> C'est trop laisser la reine à sa douleur mortelle;
> Souffrez que je vous quitte et me range auprès d'elle.
> (1032–34)

The net effect of the scene is to direct toward Œnone the moral
indignation that we should feel against Phèdre (this is one way
of preserving our sympathy for Phèdre) and at the same time
to retain some minimal regard for Œnone so that she does not
become wholly odious. After all, she has one more function to
perform in the play.

That final act is her advice to Phèdre (in IV, 6) to regard her
love for Hippolyte as normal, natural, and in no wise reprehensible. She gives this advice because, once again, she fears for
Phèdre's life and strives to allay her suffering; her motivation
does not change. She gives it in a single speech:

> Hé! repoussez, Madame, une injuste terreur.
> Regardez d'un autre œil une excusable erreur.
> Vous aimez. On ne peut vaincre sa destinée.
> Par un charme fatal vous fûtes entraînée.
> Est-ce donc un prodige inouï parmi nous?
> L'amour n'a-t-il encor triomphé que de vous?
> La faiblesse aux humains n'est que trop naturelle.
> Mortelle, subissez le sort d'une mortelle.

Vous vous plaignez d'un joug imposé dès longtemps:
Les dieux même, les dieux de l'Olympe habitants,
Qui d'un bruit si terrible épouvantent les crimes,
Ont brûlé quelquefois de feux illégitimes.   (1295-1306)

This time the suggestion is "monstrous," both as judged by
Phèdre's moral standard and as reflected against the audience's
code (itself determined by Phèdre and by the other personages
within the play). Œnone's devotion and despair have driven
her too far; Phèdre turns against her; after admitting her
wrong, she has only to end her own life.

The personage of Œnone is thus instrumental in every respect; the character is tailored to the needs of a difficult and
delicate situation. Her traits are assembled in such a way that
she may exercise upon Phèdre the necessary influence at each
point, and each of her acts either pushes Phèdre to an action
required by the progress of the plot (but which Phèdre would
be unwilling to undertake on her own) or it takes the place of
an action by the heroine. When she has finished what she has
to do in the tragedy, she disappears; but even her death is made
useful to the plot, since as it is reported by Panope to Thésée it
becomes one of the bases for his increasing suspicion that he may
have committed an error of judgment.

Just as the character of Œnone is very thoroughly—and yet
very economically—developed in terms of its usefulness to the
plot and in terms of effects upon the audience, so the characters
of the other personages are conceived as auxiliary to Phèdre's
action and to the spectator's response to that action. In the case
of Hippolyte, one might demonstrate at length (for example)
how his youthful disparagement of his father's amorousness led
first to his own chastity, second to his feeling of guilt about his
love for Aricie, third to his horror at the enormity of Phèdre's
confession. For Thésée, one might show how his experience
as a lover causes him both to believe Œnone's accusations and
to refuse to believe Hippolyte's disclaimers, and how the fresh-
ness of his recent adventures (in the service of Pirithoüs' love)

makes him all the more sensitive to the spreading of "love's poison" in his own household. But such demonstrations are unnecessary; Racine's handling of plot as a whole and of the details of character and action makes all the interrelationships completely apparent. So, indeed, are the subordinations, and one has in *Phèdre*—for the only time, I think, in all of Racine's tragedies—the clear conviction that the main plot and the protagonist dominate all other factors in the work. The emotional impact is correspondingly strong.

In several earlier plays we have seen how such a centralization of the action permitted Racine to extend even into the area of language the use of unifying and ordering devices. *Phèdre* confirms the observation. As a single example, we may look at the special ways in which Racine endows the word "jour"—commonplace enough in any lexicon—with private meanings that belong only to this plot. As spoken by others, it may seem to have the ordinary meaning of "the light of day"; but since for Phèdre herself it means life and honor, the reader attaches these supplementary meanings as well to other appearances. The contexts help him to do so. Thus Théramène's early description of Phèdre as "Une femme mourante et qui cherche à mourir" is followed by these lines:

> Phèdre, atteinte d'un mal qu'elle s'obstine à taire,
> Lasse enfin d'elle-même et du jour qui l'éclaire,
> Peut-elle contre vous former quelques desseins? (45–47)

Already there is a vague association with "mourir." When Œnone announces that Phèdre is about to appear, she does so by saying, "Elle veut voir le jour" (149), and Phèdre's first speech includes the line,

> Mes yeux sont éblouis du jour que je revois. (155)

Œnone reproaches her:

> Vous vouliez vous montrer et revoir la lumière.
> Vous la voyez, Madame, et prête à vous cacher,
> Vous haïssez le jour que vous veniez chercher? (166–68)

It is then that Phèdre apostrophizes her grandfather, the Sun:

> Noble et brillant auteur d'une triste famille,
> Toi, dont ma mère osait se vanter d'être fille,
> Qui peut-être rougis du trouble où tu me vois,
> Soleil, je te viens voir pour la dernière fois.   (169–72)

This rapid succession of passages, at a point in the play where no truth about Phèdre is known as yet, gives an intimation of several important aspects of the plot; "seeing the light of day" represents, for Phèdre, a kind of brief return to life, yet because of her guilt (the undefined "trouble") her presence in the day constitutes a blemish upon it. When, through death, she will be removed from the light, the blemish will disappear with her.

Œnone speaks in related terms when she says to Phèdre,

> Quoiqu'il vous reste à peine une faible lumière,
> Mon âme chez les morts descendra la première,   (229–30)

and Phèdre expands upon the notion of her guilt later in the same scene:

> Je voulais en mourant prendre soin de ma gloire,
> Et dérober au jour une flamme si noire.   (309–10)

In IV, 6, under the impact of her jealousy, Phèdre again relates day, light, and death,

> Et moi, triste rebut de la nature entière,
> Je me cachais au jour, je fuyais la lumière;
> La mort est le seul dieu que j'osais implorer,   (1241–43)

just as she later opposes night to day:

> Où me cacher? Fuyons dans la nuit infernale.   (1277)

Her speech of vituperation to Œnone contains the same image:

> Au jour que je fuyais c'est toi qui m'as rendue.   (1310)

Finally, after she has admitted her guilt to Thésée and is about to expire, she brings the whole image to its necessary conclusion:

Et la mort, à mes yeux dérobant la clarté,
Rend au jour, qu'ils souillaient, toute sa pureté. (1643-44)

Passing from day to night, from life to death, she removes her guilt from the world. The admirable quality of these lines lies not in the sound (in poetic analysis, matters of sound are always secondary) but in what we might call their multivalence. They conclude the plot, since they announce Phèdre's death as the ultimate consequence of her guilt; they do so in terms of that reference to the "jour" which has been constant in Phèdre's mind throughout and which has served as one of the ways of identifying her guilt; and they bring to a sudden fulfillment all the feelings that the audience has everywhere associated with Phèdre, her increasing guilt and her obligatory death. At the same time, we should note that the voluntary nature of her death and the full acknowledgment of her guilt (present in these lines) elicit from the audience something that is close to a pardon; in any case, they clinch that sense of sympathy, of admiration for her moral stature, and of pity that have constituted from the beginning the central emotion aroused by her character, her circumstances, and her actions.

With respect to the general emotional effect of *Phèdre,* it is both very powerful and very sharply defined. Very powerful, I believe, because very sharply defined. As we have seen in the course of this discussion, the emotion centers clearly about the protagonist—who, in this regard, has no "rivals." We do, of course, have strong feelings of sympathy and of pity for Hippolyte, lesser feelings of the same order for Aricie. But the character of Hippolyte is not such as to cause a vigorous sentiment on our part, and his death is rather the source of a resentment against Thésée, Œnone, and Phèdre than of a deep sorrow over him. This is because of the way in which the action is contrived and conducted. Aricie is even more subordinate. We

could have, for these two, no such surge of affection or disapproval as we experience, for example, toward Oreste and
Hermione. Thésée stirs in us a mixed reaction; we feel sorry
for the husband wronged (although surely his career as a
lover mitigates our commiseration), we feel sorry for the father
who finds himself finally responsible for his son's death. But
mostly we blame the father for his readiness to see himself in
his son, we are impatient with his willingness to act on the
basis of a servant's lies and his unwillingness to heed the intimations of his son and his son's beloved, we condemn him for
his haste in taking the most extreme and the most violent revenge possible. He deserves his suffering, at least in part, and
he does not seriously detract from the emotion that grows up,
through the course of the play, around Phèdre and her misfortune.

That emotion is a truly tragic emotion and—as is the case in
every great tragedy—a very special and particular one. It is not
merely pity for a noble woman who, in her struggle against a
passion that she regards as ignoble, through weakness and
despair hands over her destiny to an unworthy servant. It is not
only such pity augmented by the sense of her responsibility for
the gradual growth of her guilt and by the voluntary nature of
her death. It comprises as well a sensitivity to her weakness in
the face of the forces opposed to her, an appreciation of her
moral superiority, an admiration for her wish (at one point in
the play) to set things right and her ultimate success (even
though it is now too late) in doing so. We do not blame her
for her love; but we blame her for thinking that that love
might be fulfilled—

> Et l'espoir, malgré moi, s'est glissé dans mon cœur—   (768)

and especially for allowing that love to turn to jealousy and for
permitting jealousy to overcome justice. In a way, and because
of her centrality in the plot, all the emotions that we attach to

the other personages become a part of the emotion that we attach to her.

The clarity and the richness of that emotion, hence its vigor, result, I am sure, from the way in which the play as a whole is constructed. Racine at last succeeds in his *gageure* to produce a plot whose main line was completely simple, yet sufficiently complicated to support a considerable action, and whose protagonist would serve as the true focal point of the action. He accomplishes his wish to establish a proper hierarchy among the personages of the play, with the protagonist at the top, and to endow each personage with precisely the character necessary for his role in the action. Whereas, in many earlier plays, he had created fully achieved and convincing characters, now in *Phèdre* he manages to strike a proportion among such characters that prevents any other personage from challenging the primacy of the protagonist. The character of Phèdre herself is a model of restraint, subtlety, and expertness in the adaptation of the protagonist to the plot; the character of Œnone may serve as an example of a brillant use of a secondary personage and a brillant conception of her character. As he works through the action, Racine gives a meticulous yet not overobvious care to the development of all the probabilities that he needs to implement it, whether natural or supernatural. All these elements find expression in a language that is as simple as the plot itself, as clear as the relationships among its parts, and intimately appropriate to the characters of the persons who speak it and to the emotions that they feel.

X

Esther

A PERIOD of twelve years elapsed between the *première* of *Phèdre* and Racine's next tragedy, *Esther,* first performed at Saint-Cyr on January 26, 1689, and published a few months later. When he returned to the theater after these years of absence, it was to treat (as he would again in his last tragedy) a subject of biblical inspiration.

Although the specific theme of Esther's appeal to Assuérus to save the Jews was not imposed upon Racine by Madame de Maintenon, who asked him to write a play for performance by the young ladies of Saint-Cyr, many of the features of the work result from the nature of the request. In his Preface, Racine indicates the limiting factors included in the commission: "... faire, sur quelque sujet de piété et de morale, une espèce de poème où le chant fût mêlé avec le récit, le tout lié par une action qui rendît la chose plus vive et moins capable d'ennuyer." According to Madame de Caylus in her *Souvenirs,* Madame de Maintenon had asked Racine to write "quelque espèce de poème moral ou historique dont l'amour fût entièrement banni, et dans lequel il ne crût pas que sa réputation fût intéressée, puisqu'il demeurerait enseveli dans Saint-Cyr, ajoutant qu'il n'importait pas que cet ouvrage fût contre les règles, pourvu qu'il contribuât aux vues qu'elle avait de divertir les demoiselles de Saint-Cyr en les instruisant" (ed. Émile Raunié [Paris, 1886], p. 142). The conditions thus imposed have their importance; for once, Racine does not work absolutely in terms of his intuitions about the structure of his poem. For both its action and the execution of its detail, he is guided and restrained by external considerations.

With respect to the action, the statements quoted indicate, on the positive side, that it must concern morality, piety, and possibly history, and that it must serve to link all elements of the play; on the negative side, that it must not treat of love. The subject of Esther ideally fitted all these requirements; based on scriptural history, and excluding love as its central passion, it was of a nature to edify through its pious sentiments and its moral conclusions. We shall have to discover whether or not it served "to link all elements of the play." With respect to the realization of the plot, Racine mingled song with story through the introduction of the chorus, both as participant in certain of the scenes and as commentator (with no actors present) upon the progress of the action both past and future.

Apropos of his assignment to write a poem "où le chant fût mêlé avec le récit," Racine remarks in the Preface that it corresponded to a project that he had frequently considered, "de lier, comme dans les anciennes tragédies grecques, le chœur et le chant avec l'action, et d'employer à chanter les louanges du vrai Dieu cette partie du chœur que les païens employaient à chanter les louanges de leurs fausses divinités." In the realization of this plan, he employed a number of devices to effect the "linking." The chorus is made up of young girls under the protection of Esther, and she explains their presence in the hostile palace:

> Cependant mon amour pour notre nation
> A rempli ce palais de filles de Sion,
> Jeunes et tendres fleurs, par le sort agitées,
> Sous un ciel étranger comme moi transplantées.
> Dans un lieu séparé de profanes témoins,
> Je mets à les former mon étude et mes soins.
>
> . . . .
>
> Mais à tous les Persans je cache leurs familles. (101–11)

Their first appearance is in response to an invitation from Esther:

Il faut les appeler. Venez, venez, mes filles,
Compagnes autrefois de ma captivité,
De l'antique Jacob jeune postérité.   (112–14)

Subsequently the chorus is listed as appearing in thirteen of the
twenty-two scenes into which the play is divided; but the nature
and the extent of its intervention varies greatly from scene to
scene.

In I, 2, after a brief prayer by Élise for the safety and prosperity
of the girls, Esther asks them to sing

... quelqu'un de ces cantiques
Où vos voix si souvent se mêlant à mes pleurs
De la triste Sion célèbrent les malheurs.   (129–31)

The chant that follows, sung partly by a single Jewess, partly by
the whole chorus, treats two related themes: the present misfortunes of Zion, compared with her former glories, and the
sorrow of her exiled people. In the next scene (I, 3), the chorus
is present but silent except for one line spoken by one of the
girls after Mardochée has announced the impending fate of the
Jews (183). During Esther's prayer in I, 4, the chorus at the back
of the stage neither speaks nor sings. But the final scene of the
act is devoted entirely to individual and choral song, a kind of
lamentation over the situation of Israel, now menaced with
extermination, combined with a prayer to a just God for his
succor. The handling of the chorus in this first act establishes a
pattern for the rest of the play: occasional contributions to the
dialogue of the actors, much silent presence, and a closing scene
of song and prayer. So in Act II the chorus appears only in two
scenes, in II, 7, where four of the girls carry Esther's train but
utter no sound (Esther addresses them at one point), and in II,
8, where Élise and the chorus declaim and sing together. (Élise,
after her first conversation with Esther, really becomes another
one of the "jeunes filles" in the chorus and has no separate role
in the action.) Their subject in the final scene is triple. First,
quickly, they state the opposition between Esther and Aman,

which they liken to a battle between God and man. Next, they attribute Assuérus' softening in the preceding scene to God's action. Finally, contrasting the lot of the pious with that of the impious, they state their preference for the peace of the innocent.

Of the nine scenes of Act III, the chorus is listed as being present in seven. In the part of scene 3 that is spoken, one or another of the girls identifies Aman as he enters the hall for the feast, characterizing him as the oppressor of Israel; then, after Élise has invited all to sing for the guests (they have been summoned for this purpose), they chant the praises of just kings and urge Assuérus not to commit the contemplated injustice. During the next five scenes the chorus stands by, presumably in the garden, and watches the proceedings without participating in them (except for the brief prayer in line 1141). But the final scene of the play (III, 9) is again occupied by a lengthy choral composition in which the chorus thanks God for having saved the Jews, derives moral conclusions from what has happened, and urges Zion to rejoice in her liberty. The closing strophes celebrate the glory of God.

I think we may say that, if these various activities and pronouncements of the chorus are "linked" with the action, they in no way affect it or change its progress. They are linked through the physical presence of the chorus during many of the scenes, through the expression by the chorus of the successive states of feeling of the people of Israel, through certain commentaries on the characters or the intentions of active personages. Another kind of connection is found in the admonishments made by the young girls to given persons to act in given ways; example, their appeal to Assuérus (III, 3) to disdain wicked counsel and to spare the blood of the innocent. But the connection is apparent rather than real, for in no case does the person involved act as a consequence of what the chorus says; Assuérus sets aside Aman's advice, but it is because Aman is exposed by Esther, and he spares the Jews because of Esther's appeal. The chorus' words never become effective argument, they never are made into the kind of "thought" that creates or increases probabilities for action. On the whole, activity of the chorus is parallel to the main action or derivative from it—rather than contributory to it. It may, of course, serve other rhetorical ends by contributing to the piety and the morality of both actors and audience, ends of instruction by permitting the young ladies of Saint-Cyr to recite and sing together. But these are not poetic considerations. Racine's attempt to expand and strengthen his dramatic art by using a chorus in this particular way was, we must conclude, wholly unsuccessful.

The necessity of providing space and time for a chorus may, indeed, have influenced Racine's total conception of the action in *Esther*. This is the first of his plays in three acts, and it is considerably shorter than the five-act tragedies. When one subtracts from its total volume the scenes assigned to the chorus (some four hundred lines in all, or a little less than a third of the aggregate), the space remaining can suffice only for an action of very moderate dimensions. Perhaps the problem should be stated inversely; it may be that because of the modest scope of his action as he conceived it, Racine decided to write a shorter play and to devote a goodly part of it to choral song and recitation. In any case, the plot is brief and uncomplicated, as the following summary statement will indicate:

Act I. In the opening scene, Esther relates to Élise how she became Assuérus' queen through Mardochée's counsels, how Mardochée had helped to save Assuérus' life, and how Israel still remains in captivity. In scene 3, Mardochée informs Esther and Élise of Aman's authorization, obtained from Assuérus, to kill all the Jews, and he enjoins Esther, even at the peril of her life, to intercede in their behalf. Scene 4 presents Esther's prayer to God for his help in her undertaking.

Act II. Aman, the enemy of the Jews, and Hydaspe, one of Assuérus' officers, speak of the king's disturbing dream, of his present reading of Persia's history, of Aman's resentment against Mardochée as the basis of the plan to kill off the Jews. Scene 2 permits the change of persons; in scene 3 Assuérus discusses with

Asaph, another officer, his failure to recompense Mardochée for
having revealed the plot against him, and in the next scene he
calls for Aman to advise him. Through a *quid pro quo* in scene
5, Aman recommends exaggerated honors for an anonymous
person, thinking that he himself is involved; but he is chagrined
to learn that he must help pay these honors to Mardochée. Assuérus, alone (scene 6), comments on his decision and repeats
his determination to kill the Jews. It is in scene 7 that Esther
risks her life by appearing before Assuérus without invitation;
but Assuérus, because of his affection for her, pardons her and
accepts her invitation to dine with her this day, acceding also to
her request to invite Aman.

Act III. Aman tells his wife, Zarès, of his humiliation through
the honoring of Mardochée, and she, fearing further disgrace,
urges that they flee the court. In scene 2, Hydaspe summons
Aman to the feast, reassuring him with the report that the sages,
consulted about Assuérus' dream, have warned of an attempt
upon Esther's life by a foreigner; this must necessarily be a Jew.
At the feast, Assuérus offers to grant any wish of Esther's (scene
4), and she asks as single boon that the Jews be pardoned, revealing her ancestry. Assuérus forbids Aman to speak and listens to
Esther's defense and history of the Jews, to her denunciation of
Aman and his plans, and to her praise of Mardochée. Assuérus
leaves, ordering Mardochée to be summoned. During his absence
(scene 5), Aman begs Esther to intercede for him, and Assuérus,
returning (scene 6), finds him at her feet. The king orders Aman
to be killed immediately. In scene 7, Assuérus gives Aman's
wealth to Mardochée, revokes his order concerning the Jews, and
orders that the Jews be restored to a position of honor. Aman's
death is reported in scene 8, and Assuérus leaves to see to the
execution of his orders.

One of the possible hypotheses with respect to this action is
that Esther is its protagonist and that what she does constitutes
the central plot of the tragedy. If this is the case, then that plot
reduces to the simplest terms: Esther accepts the mission to inter-

vene for the Jews, even at the risk of her life; she risks her life
by presenting herself before Assuérus; she makes the appeal and
is successful. It might even be possible, I suggest, to think of the
whole action in terms of one major episode, consisting in Esther's
appeal to Assuérus on behalf of her people. According to such
a supposition, the other two episodes that I have indicated would
merely be preparations for the final one; they would provide the
motivation and the occasion, respectively, for a culminating act
that would be the whole end and essence of the drama. Esther's
main traits of character can be explained in terms of such an
action. Principal among them is her devotion to her people, its
tradition, its ideals, and its cause. Her unselfishness, her complete
unconcern for glory, position, and finery, her sacrifice of her person to the needs of political circumstance, even her faith in God,
are a part of this devotion. She has no will except the will of her
people, expressed through Mardochée. The only other trait that
she need have (her beauty is a natural accident and not a matter
of character) is that kind of softness and grace, the outward expression of her virtue, that will make it possible for her to dominate Assuérus. The king himself recognizes this aspect of her
character:

> Je ne trouve qu'en vous je ne sais quelle grâce
> Qui me charme toujours et jamais ne me lasse.
> De l'aimable vertu doux et puissants attraits!   (669–71)

So, also, is Assuérus' character composed in terms of this simple
action. If he is to yield to Esther's prayer to save the Jews, he
must have (in addition to the admiration for Esther already
noted) a strong sense of justice, a capacity to recognize moral
right and moral wrong, and the flexibility of spirit that will
enable him to pass from one position to its opposite once he has
discovered the truth. All these qualities are assigned to him before
their application in III, 4–8.

   If indeed the action be of this kind, made up of a single act
rather than a composite of episodes and acts, it represents an ex-

periment by Racine with a new kind of plot, one which he had
never attempted before. In all his previous tragedies, Racine had
worked with the "grand plot," the plot whose accomplishment
demanded not only the successive but the progressive realization
of a series of acts before the denouement (the act that solved all
the remaining difficulties) could be properly achieved. Now, in
Esther, he tries his hand at the plot composed of a single episode.
(I borrow the distinction from Elder Olson's *Tragedy and the
Theory of Drama.*) Previously, his problems of composition had
centered upon the necessity of constructing the large plot in such
a way that it might occupy with due proportion the full scope
of the drama and that its protagonist might be the true focal point
of the action and of the audience's emotion. In the new play,
the problem is different but not entirely new; for in some of the
earlier works, his preoccupation had been with "filling out" a
meager plot, and this will be essentially his concern in *Esther.*
But whereas the earlier solutions had been found in the invention of episodes related, in one way or another, to the main plot,
he is now obliged—since the multiplication of episodes would
alter the basic nature of his plot—to seek other devices. He finds
them, I think, in two kinds of developments: in the creation of
a parallel (but not auxiliary) action whose effect is largely exemplary and hortatory, and in the display of character for purposes of moral edification.

The parallel action is dual; it might even be considered two
actions. It involves the ascending movement in Mardochée's fortunes and the descending movement in Aman's fortunes. When
the play opens, Mardochée's affairs are at the lowest possible state;
Aman describes him as a "vil esclave" in rags before the palace
door:

> Du palais cependant il assiège la porte:
>
> . . . .
>
> Je l'ai trouvé couvert d'une affreuse poussière,
> Revêtu de lambeaux, tout pâle.   (433–39)

Asaph restates this condition:

> Assis le plus souvent aux portes du palais,
> Sans se plaindre de vous, ni de sa destinée,
> Il y traîne, Seigneur, sa vie infortunée.   (560-62)

Hydaspe calls him "Un si faible ennemi" (423). The "lambeaux" and "poussière" that Aman mentions are the haircloth and ashes worn by Mardochée to symbolize his grief over Israel—

> ... ce cilice affreux,
> Et cette cendre enfin qui couvre vos cheveux—   (159-60)

for he is doomed to die along with the rest of his people (164). Yet this position is deserved neither in terms of his past actions nor of his character. For as Esther early points out, Mardochée has been responsible for saving the life of Assuérus:

> Déjà même, déjà par ses secrets avis
> J'ai découvert au roi les sanglantes pratiques
> Que formaient contre lui deux ingrats domestiques.
>   (98-100)

For this act he has had, as Hydaspe relates, no recompense:

> Le roi promit alors de le récompenser.
> Le roi, depuis ce temps, paraît n'y plus penser.   (447-48)

Esther provides the epithet that characterizes him most succinctly; he is the "sage Mardochée" (44). He is governed above all by a sense of duty to his people, to which everything else must be sacrificed; this is apparent in his speech to Esther (I, 3):

> Quoi? Lorsque vous voyez périr votre patrie,
> Pour quelque chose, Esther, vous comptez votre vie!
> Dieu parle, et d'un mortel vous craignez le courroux!
> Que dis-je? Votre vie, Esther, est-elle à vous?
> N'est-elle pas au sang dont vous êtes issue?
> N'est-elle pas à Dieu dont vous l'avez reçue?
> Et qui sait, lorsqu'au trône il conduisit vos pas,
> Si pour sauver son peuple il ne vous gardait pas? (205-12)

As he continues in the same speech, it is apparent that for Mardochée God and Israel are inextricably linked; his faith is commensurate with his sense of duty, and he believes firmly in God's powers:

> Et quel besoin son bras a-t-il de nos secours?
> Que peuvent contre lui tous les rois de la terre?
> En vain ils s'uniraient pour lui faire la guerre:
> Pour dissiper leur ligue il n'a qu'à se montrer;
> Il parle, et dans la poudre il les fait tous rentrer.
> Au seul son de sa voix la mer fuit, le ciel tremble;
> Il voit comme un néant tout l'univers ensemble;
> Et les faibles mortels, vains jouets du trépas,
> Sont tous devant ses yeux comme s'ils n'étaient pas.
>
> (220–28)

The other traits attributed to him (largely by his enemies) are merely manifestations of this central faith; if he is proud (429, 1126), it is because he refuses to bow before wickedness and impiety; if he is audacious (441), it is because of his consciousness of the rightness of his beliefs and of his courage to defend them.

It might be pointed out that, merely through the representation of his character, Mardochée serves one of the rhetorical purposes of the play. He is the example of the just man. He has all the qualities of patriotism and piety that are needed for one who is devoted wholly to his people and his God. People and God are in a sense indistinguishable, and Mardochée's wisdom consists in his complete subordination of all other concerns to their service and in the discovery of the best means for serving them. If now to this character, which in itself is exemplary, be added an action that will show how virtue and justice are in the end rewarded, the whole personage may be of moral utility in the play, even independently of the central action.

Mardochée's first chance of an improvement in his position comes with the recalling to Assuérus, by his historians, of how his life was saved by an unknown benefactor; this leads him to inquire:

Mais ce sujet zélé qui, d'un œil si subtil,
Sut de leur noir complot développer le fil,

. . . .

Quel honneur pour sa foi, quel prix a-t-il reçu? (535–39)

When Assuérus learns that the benefactor has gone unrewarded, he reproaches himself with his neglect and determines to provide a recompense. Meanwhile, the epithets that he uses add to the impression of Mardochée's character; Assuérus speaks of his "vrai zèle" (549), of his "intérêt fidèle" (550), of his "mérite" (551, 588), "vertu" (563, 617), and "foi" (588). Several times, he insists on the fact that Mardochée has asked no return, has allowed himself to be forgotten. Even the discovery that Mardochée is a Jew does not change Assuérus' determination:

Mais, puisqu'il m'a sauvé, quel qu'il soit, il n'importe.

(573)

Thus he asks Aman's advice on the form of the recompense:

... que doit faire un prince magnanime
Qui veut combler d'honneurs un sujet qu'il estime?

(585–86)

The honor is proposed by Aman, who thinks that he will be the recipient: crowned, bedecked, and magnificently mounted, the subject is to be led through the streets of Suze by the next in greatness after Assuérus himself. Assuérus orders the ceremony (618), Aman is obliged to carry through on his proposals (844 ff.). The ceremony moves Mardochée from a position of obscurity to one of renown—from rags to borrowed riches—and it provides an external reward for neglected merit.

But Mardochée's essential position is still what it was: he is exiled with his people and condemned to die. Hydaspe reassures Aman on this score:

Laissez-le s'applaudir d'un triomphe frivole.
Croit-il d'Assuérus éviter la rigueur?

. . . .

On a payé le zèle, on punira le crime. (913–16)

Moreover, there is an even more imminent possibility of Mardochée's death. On Hydaspe's advice (523–24), Aman has erected a
gibbet before his door (1131) and intends to execute his enemy
immediately. This time, if his situation is to be improved, a
particular act on his behalf will not suffice; the general danger
facing the Jews must be averted, and Aman must be deprived
of his power to harm Mardochée. The solution of the parallel
action comes to depend both upon the solution of the main action and upon the movement affecting the other personage involved in the "dual" development; it will form a part of the general denouement. The first step in this direction is made by
Esther when she reveals to Assuérus that Mardochée was her
foster father, that Aman's hatred for him had been responsible
for the whole campaign against the Jews, and that Aman now
plans to kill him (1121 ff.). Assuérus calls Mardochée in order to
hear his case (1140). As a result of his reflections and of the intervening events, Assuérus gives him Aman's rank and properties:

> Viens briller près de moi dans le rang qui t'est dû.
> Je te donne d'Aman les biens et la puissance.   (1179–80)

We should note that Assuérus considers this as an act of justice;
he gives to a just man what he had justly merited, taking it from
an unjust man:

> Possède justement son injuste opulence.   (1181)

Finally, Mardochée profits from the general pardon accorded all
the Jews.

The fortunes of Aman follow an exactly opposite direction.
Racine emphasizes the opposition at every point, but especially
at the beginning and at the end. When Mardochée's status is at
its lowest, Aman's is the highest possible. Hydaspe exclaims upon
this:

> Hé! qui jamais du ciel eut des regards plus doux?
> Vous voyez l'univers prosterné devant vous.   (415–16)

The "fortunate" Aman ("l'heureux Aman" [411]) enumerates the
elements of his glory:

Je gouverne l'empire où je fus acheté.
Mes richesses des rois égalent l'opulence.
Environné d'enfants, soutiens de ma puissance,
Il ne manque à mon front que le bandeau royal.   (452–55)

He speaks of "le rang où je suis élevé" (488), thinks of himself as second only to Assuérus,

Enfin de votre empire après vous le premier,   (607)

a judgment with which his wife agrees:

Vous êtes après lui le premier de l'empire.   (864)

He has the power to destroy the Jews (480, 505), his wealth will be increased by the acquisition of theirs (508), his credit with the king is of the highest (579). If Mardochée sits before the palace door in ashes and haircloth, Aman's presence there is of an opposite order:

ASSUÉRUS

Regarde à cette porte.
Vois s'il s'offre à tes yeux quelque grand de ma cour.

HYDASPE

Aman a votre porte a devancé le jour.   (574–76)

Yet his character is not such as to justify this good fortune and this high station. He is not only the "impie" (313)—a judgment that could be made only by those of another religion—but he is a man whose essential passions are hatred and pride. Hence his violent feelings toward Mardochée:

Lui, fièrement assis, et la tête immobile,
Traite tous ces honneurs d'impiété servile,
Présente à mes regards un front séditieux,
Et ne daignerait pas au moins baisser les yeux.   (429–32)

And again:

De cet amas d'honneurs la douceur passagère
Fait sur mon cœur à peine une atteinte légère;
Mais Mardochée, assis aux portes du palais,

> Dans ce cœur malheureux enfonce mille traits;
> Et toute ma grandeur me devient insipide,
> Tandis que le soleil éclaire ce perfide. (457–62)

Hence, too, his wish for revenge both upon the man and upon his people (466, 470). In a way, the character is all of a piece: whereas Mardochée is completely unselfish and devotes his life to his people and to God, Aman is completely selfish and is concerned only with petty, personal matters. He represents (for those who draw morals from the personages and the action) all that is basely human. Thus Élise is able to make the following juxtaposition:

> D'Esther, d'Aman, qui le doit emporter?
> Est-ce Dieu, sont-ce les hommes
> Dont les œuvres vont éclater? (714–16)

Aman's wife reads clearly her husband's impulses and motivations; of the honoring of Mardochée she says:

> Ce zèle que pour lui vous fîtes éclater,
> Ce soin d'immoler tout à son pouvoir suprême,
> Entre nous, avaient-ils d'autre objet que vous-même?
> (875–77)

This is a correct analysis, as Aman's own words (591–92) acknowledge.

Even more so than in the case of Mardochée, Aman's life and works are taken as an object lesson for the spectator. The chorus points the lesson on several occasions. Having referred to him specifically as the "impie" (313, 754), they then generalize by singing of the "gloire de l'impie" and the "bonheur du méchant" in a lengthy choral development (II, 8). When the girls see him appear at Esther's table (III, 3), they recognize his character in his face—

> L'orgueil et le dédain sont peints sur son visage.
> . . . .
> On lit dans ses regards sa fureur et sa rage— (939–40)

and they foresee the "fare" that he will be fed:

> Le sang de l'orphelin,
>
> .   .   .   .
>
> les pleurs des misérables.   (952)

They also allude to him, indirectly but nevertheless clearly, later
in the same scene, using such abstractions as "la calomnie," "la
vengeance," "la fraude," "le perfide imposteur," "le riche im-
périeux," "le conseil barbare et mensonger." Each of these terms
is made a part of a moral *sententia,* and the abstractions derived
from the particular serve in their own right the rhetorical purposes of the play.

The chorus also predicts, in the first act, Aman's fate at the
hands of God—

> Il renverse l'audacieux—   (348)

just as Mardochée had foretold: "Il peut confondre Aman" (235).
The two statements epitomize the "descending" movement in
Aman's affairs through the course of the play. Assuérus' order to
Aman for the honoring of Mardochée,

> Ordonne son triomphe, et marche devant lui,   (620)

marks the first step in this movement. This first humiliation (for
which he himself is entirely responsible) seems to be offset by
the fact that he alone, of all the court, is invited to Esther's feast.
That, at least, is the interpretation of the two events by Zarès,
who sees no serious alteration of Aman's status:

> Seul entre tous les grands par la reine invité,
> Ressentez donc aussi cette félicité.
> Si le mal vous aigrit, que le bienfait vous touche.
>
> .   .   .   .
>
> Il est des contretemps qu'il faut qu'un sage essuie.
> Souvent avec prudence un outrage enduré
> Aux honneurs les plus hauts a servi de degré.   (834–43)

Aman, however, sees only the affront (838) and notes—what would be extremely important for him—the reaction of the people to his disgrace:

> Et tout le peuple même avec dérision,
> Observant la rougeur qui couvrait mon visage,
> De ma chute certaine en tirait le présage. (851–53)

Zarès recognizes that this act of hatred on the part of the people is merely an expression of its general attitude—

> Enfin la cour nous hait, le peuple nous déteste— (881)

and she finally admits her fear that more trouble may lie ahead (887 ff.); she proposes to Aman that they flee (taking their wealth with them) while there is still time.

The rest of Aman's "fall" is quickly achieved in the remaining scenes of the play. In the same series of revelations that includes her own and Mardochée's identities, Esther informs Assuérus that Aman is really his enemy,

> Un ministre ennemi de votre propre gloire, (1088)

and she fixes upon Aman the responsibility for the condemnation of the Jews. Her last argument, and the one that arouses Assuérus' anger, is the indication that Aman has planned to execute Mardochée on his own authority (1131). As far as Aman is concerned, his second "affront" comes when Assuérus, at Esther's request, forbids him to speak, his third when Esther refuses to hear his appeal. Assuérus finds him clasping Esther's knees in supplication (1168) and orders his death; immediately afterward, Aman's wealth is given to Mardochée; his death on the gibbet that he had prepared for Mardochée and the destruction of his body by the enraged crowd, are reported as the last events in his career.

Although the directions of the two careers are opposite, with Mardochée moving from low to high station and Aman from high to low—the one from death to life and the other from life

to death—Racine puts them to the same use in the general conception of his play. Both men are exemplars, in their characters
as well as in their actions. Their characters represent two kinds
of men, the pious and the disinterested as against the impious
and the selfish; and the chorus and other personages state clearly
how such characters merit praise and blame, respectively. From
them the young ladies of Saint-Cyr—and presumably any subsequent spectators—might derive conclusions about what constitutes good and bad moral disposition, and they might develop
their own attitudes accordingly. The actions of Mardochée and
Aman, resulting from their characters, show the necessary consequences of moral goodness and badness; the lessons from activity
are as manifest as those from character. As the two lines move
and cross, it becomes evident that neither would have its full effectiveness without the existence of the other; hence the symmetry, which is of a rhetorical rather than a poetic nature, is required for purposes of the demonstration. Mardochée's goodness
is enhanced by Aman's wickedness, the failure of Aman's life is
more conspicuous through the success of Mardochée's. And clear
moral apothegms, usually pronounced by the chorus, inform the
spectator of the conclusion that he is to reach.

For the total structure of *Esther,* the important problem is the
relationship of this dual parallel action to the main plot. Racine
wished to have "le tout lié par une action"; he succeeded, with
these two men, in the sense that both are important for Esther's
single act of saving her people. To Aman may be attributed the
original jeopardy of the Jews, since he had aroused Assuérus
against them and obtained the fatal order. Mardochée both is responsible for Esther's initiative and provides her with her best
argument: a Jew has been instrumental in saving Assuérus' life.
Aman's link, however, is through an act that preceded the beginning of the present action, and it is thus similar to many other
acts—the exile of the Jews, Vashti's disgrace, the choice of Esther
as queen—that "belong" in the sense that they are antecedent and
even causal, but they do not contribute, as probable elements, to

the accomplishment of the action itself. The case is much the same for Mardochée, although his initial act really sets the plot in motion. Yet essentially the single episode of the appeal to Assuérus is Esther's own doing. Aman's fall and Mardochée's rise are concomitant with it, not factors in it; appeal and pardon could have happened without involving the final step in the career of each of the two men (except that, in so far as he was a Jew, Mardochée would have benefited from the general reprieve). For purposes of this plot, Aman did not need to lose everything and then die, Mardochée did not need to inherit everything that Aman had lost.

The links are thus tenuous if not specious. To say this is to remove from the plot other lengthy and proportionately considerable sections of the play. I have already (without even mentioning the Prologue, clearly an hors-d'œuvre) stripped away from the plot almost all those parts of the play assigned to the chorus and to Élise. If now we propose a similar elimination of most of the scenes or portions of scenes devoted to the characters and actions of Mardochée and Aman, very little indeed will remain—only, in fact, the materials pertaining to Esther's successful appeal to Assuérus. In a way, both the chorus and the parallel action of Aman and Mardochée serve similar purposes in the work, only vaguely related to its plot; their end is a common rhetorical end, since it is through them that moral lessons are derived, that edification is provided, that the "sujet de piété et de morale" leads to the desired instruction. Presumably the other end of entertainment—possibly although not necessarily a more poetic end—is served by the plot itself.

Here I should like to raise another question whose answer, were it affirmative, might be further damaging to the poetic achievement of Racine in *Esther:* Is not much of the play that does relate to Esther's appeal, indeed to her whole activity and character, itself rhetorical in nature? Some of the statements by the chorus would seem to lead to this conclusion, for they insist upon the "representative" function of the queen; that is, she stands for goodness and right just as Aman stands for evil and wrong:

> D'Esther, d'Aman, qui le doit emporter?
> Est-ce Dieu, sont-ce les hommes
> Dont les œuvres vont éclater?   (714–16)

At the end of the action, when the chorus is concluding, it speaks first (in abstract terms) of the fall of the wicked and the impious; then, in response to the question, "Quelle main salutaire a chassé le nuage?" (1222), it attributes to Esther's beauty and virtue the turn in the affairs of the Jews. Again, this is a kind of abstraction, for (in spite of the direct reference) the turn has been brought about by innocence, zeal, love of God, working in Esther as their instrument:

> Elle a parlé. Le ciel a fait le reste.   (1227)

> La nature et le ciel à l'envi l'ont ornée.   (1229)

> Jamais tant de beauté fut-elle couronnée?   (1231)

> Jamais tant de vertu fut-elle couronnée?   (1233)

This representative quality becomes even more apparent when we look at Esther's character and her action. I do not mean to suggest that she becomes an allegorical personage; for *Esther* is not allegory and its heroine has a particular character. But she has a particular character in an unusual way. On the one hand, many of her traits are simplified almost to the point of abstraction; her innocence, her zeal, her love of God, have no personal touch, no idiosyncratic aspect that would make them hers alone. They are innocence, zeal, love of God in an elemental and undifferentiated form. Compare Phèdre's love and guilt or Hermione's jealousy and wrath: these are passions which, in the mere naming, take on a highly special and individual color. Because Esther's passions are fundamentally so "typical," the chorus may use them and the audience may interpret them as these passions in an exemplary state; the moral lessons result. On the other hand, her traits are given her not so that she may pursue and achieve any private aims but so that she may save and liberate her people. Consequently—and in terms of their utility—they always manifest themselves in an impersonal rather than a personal way. Much of what Esther has to say in the drama subordinates her self to her people. Mardochée, indeed, has given her this mission:

> Et sur mes faibles mains fondant leur délivrance,
> Il me fit d'un empire accepter l'espérance. (51–52)

She reproaches herself with any condition that differentiates her from her people (83–88), seeks only to forget herself (107–10). In such a monologue as the prayer of I, 4, she not only repudiates all the vainglory of the world, but she accepts her responsibility as intermediary between the Jews and God:

> Tu sais combien je hais leurs fêtes criminelles,
> Et que je mets au rang des profanations
> Leur table, leurs festins et leurs libations;
> Que même cette pompe où je suis condamnée,
> Ce bandeau, dont il faut que je paraisse ornée
> Dans ces jours solennels à l'orgueil dédiés,
> Seule et dans le secret je le foule à mes pieds;
> Qu'à ces vains ornements je préfère la cendre,
> Et n'ai de goût qu'aux pleurs que tu me vois répandre.
> J'attendais le moment marqué dans ton arrêt,
> Pour oser de ton peuple embrasser l'intérêt.
> Ce moment est venu: ma prompte obéissance
> Va d'un roi redoutable affronter la présence.
> C'est pour toi que je marche. (274–87)

When she makes her appeal to Assuérus, it is only secondarily for "ma propre vie"; it is primarily for "les tristes jours d'un peuple infortuné" (1029–30), and her appeal consists in a lengthy history and eulogy of her race (1045 ff., 1104 ff.).

What is curious about her action is that it is with difficulty dis-

tinguishable from Mardochée's action—such is the degree to
which it is unselfish and impersonal (as is his action). I do not
think it useful for purposes of analysis to propose, as has sometimes been proposed, that both Esther and Mardochée act under
the impulsion of God and that God is the real protagonist of the
play. This avoids all the real issues in the interpretation of the
play and solves none of the problems; and it is essentially false.
Esther is the protagonist and it is she who acts; but the will under
which she acts is as much Mardochée's as her own—perhaps more
so—and through Mardochée, perhaps, the will of her people. If
Esther's principal act is the appeal to Assuérus and the two preparatory acts her acceptance of the mission and her uninvited
appearance before the king, all these have as a single goal the
saving of her people. The saving of her own life is incidental. The
same is the case for Mardochée: he charges Esther with the mission—and this is his only action relevant to the central plot—in
order to save the Jews, for whom he serves as spokesman; his own
life is never a consideration. He is an intermediary, at one remove
farther from Assuérus, but at one remove closer to his people.

Esther's character is designed to permit the accomplishment of
this totally altruistic deed. Her only "particular" traits (as distinguished from the simplified abstract virtues) are precisely ones
that will lead to the subordination of self. She has no love for
her husband; she respects and honors him as a master. She is
devoted to Mardochée and grateful to him for his protection. Her
timidity is a counterpart of her modesty, and both may be replaced by courage and boldness when the occasion demands. She
wishes neither wealth nor glory for herself, and only freedom for
her people. Her "amour pour notre nation" (101), in the face
of the nation's desperate circumstances, stimulates her penchant
to sadness, to meditation, and to prayer. Once Mardochée has
told her what to do, she accepts in terms that indicate her basic
selflessness:

> Contente de périr, s'il faut que je périsse,
> J'irai pour mon pays m'offrir en sacrifice.   (245–46)

These traits do not make for a vigorous or dominating personality; nor does she need such a personality. The vigor required will come from Mardochée, and Assuérus will be dominated by his own love for Esther, by his admiration for her beauty, her charm, and her innocence.

My answer to the question about the rhetorical nature of Esther's role is thus only partially affirmative. To a degree, and in so far as she demonstrates that virtue, piety, and love of one's people may produce extraordinary effects, Esther is an example; she teaches a lesson. Like the chorus, she becomes the mouthpiece for certain proverbs that generalize from her own character and situation:

> Dieu tient le cœur des rois entre ses mains puissantes;
> Il fait que tout prospère aux âmes innocentes,
> Tandis qu'en ses projets l'orgueilleux est trompé.   (67–69)

> L'Éternel est son nom. Le monde est son ouvrage;
> Il entend les soupirs de l'humble qu'on outrage,
> Juge tous les mortels avec d'égales lois,
> Et du haut de son trône interroge les rois.
> Des plus fermes états la chute épouvantable,
> Quand il veut, n'est qu'un jeu de sa main redoutable.
>
>   (1052–57)

Such proverbs have their own, independent didactic value. Like Mardochée and Aman, Esther displays the consequences for action of a certain kind of character; her initial circumstances and their resolution are almost identical with those of Mardochée, hence the opposite of Aman's. Yet these features of the role are not the only ones. There is a proper poetic action, albeit reduced to a single major episode, and it is properly prepared through the necessities of character and the probabilities of situation and argument.

What distinguishes *Esther* from all Racine's earlier plays is the fact that, in the effort to expand a slim plot to a full-scale drama (and a three-act one at that), he turned for the first time to the use of rhetorical rather than poetic devices. It is as if a modern writer, with sufficient materials at hand for a short story, were to attempt to make of them a complete novel, and to do so by exploiting social, political, or religious ideas as addenda to his fictional base. Racine's addenda were moral and edifying. Historically, they were so because that is what his patroness had demanded of him; but this is of no direct concern in the analysis or the evaluation of the work. We need rather to recognize that through the creation of the chorus and through the development of the "parallel" action of Mardochée and Aman, even through the deviation of Esther's role toward ends of exemplification, the "plot of a single episode" is reduced to secondary status in the play. Instead of being enriched and amplified (as had sometimes been true before), the plot tends to be lost in the mass of instructional accompaniments. Proverbs and hymns of praise, commentaries that point a moral, characters and actions of an exemplary nature, a denouement in which poetic justice is fully achieved, all these withdraw our attention from the plot as plot. To a degree, they dissipate and cloud any suspense we might feel with respect to the outcome of the action, just as they dilute our feelings for the heroine and her plight. Unless we are edified, we remain unmoved; if we resist the moral conclusions, the poem as such is essentially without effect.

XI

Athalie

LIKE *Esther,* Racine's last tragedy was written for performance by the young ladies of Saint-Cyr, who presented it for the first time on January 5, 1691, two years after their *première* of *Esther.* Its publication came a few months later. Like its predecessor, too, *Athalie* was based on a biblical rather than a classical theme.

We may say, right off, that although *Athalie* was written under the same circumstances as *Esther,* and presumably to comply with a similar request, Racine managed to avoid or correct most of the errors that had damaged the dramatic effectiveness of *Esther.* The rhetorical elements are drastically reduced, even though they are not completely eliminated. This is apparent in the role of the chorus, which Racine retained—again because of the nature of his assignment—but which he used in a somewhat different way. The chorus makes four major appearances, at the end of each of the first four acts; in addition, it is present at some time during each of the acts, and throughout the fifth, although it neither speaks nor sings. In the closing scenes of Acts I–IV, through recitation or choral song, it celebrates the greatness and the goodness of God (I), it praises Joas and inveighs against Athalie (II), it deplores the state of Israel and expresses its hope in God (III), it calls upon God for aid in the present peril (IV). Besides, in III, 7, it participates with Joad in the moment of prophetic ecstasy. All these sections are identical, in content and in function, with the parallel scenes assigned to the chorus in *Esther.* They constitute commentaries on the action (but generalized and made abstract), they are pious for the sake of piety, their intention is basically rhetorical.

It should be pointed out, however, that these rhetorical passages are proportionately much less considerable than were their counterparts in *Esther*. *Athalie* on the whole is a much longer play, half again as long as *Esther,* yet the total number of lines given the chorus is much smaller (about two hundred and fifty as against four hundred). As a result, we do not feel that a major share of presence and activity is accorded the chorus; the rhetorical purpose is less patent and dominant. Moreover, since there is here no "parallel" action of obviously didactic intent, no exemplification of virtue and vice through a Mardochée or an Aman, the chorus is not called upon to derive moral lessons of a secondary nature. Its commentary, in so far as it makes one, refers only to the major actors in the drama, Joas and Athalie, and seems to belong more directly to the plot itself.

There is another way in which the rhetorical passages in *Athalie* appear to be less detached and independent than they were in *Esther*. Racine tries to make the "praise of God" an integral part of his play, rather than an edifying hors-d'œuvre. When Joad pronounces *sententiae* such as the following, it is in order that they may help him to persuade his interlocutor (in this case Abner) to a desired action:

> Celui qui met un frein à la fureur des flots
> Sait aussi des méchants arrêter les complots.   (61–62)

> La foi qui n'agit point, est-ce une foi sincère?   (71)

His intention becomes perfectly clear as he concludes the speech:

> Voici comme ce Dieu vous répond par ma bouche:
> «Du zèle de ma loi que sert de vous parer?
> Par de stériles vœux pensez-vous m'honorer?
> Quel fruit me revient-il de tous vos sacrifices?
> Ai-je besoin du sang des boucs et des génisses?
> Le sang de vos rois crie, et n'est point écouté.

> Rompez, rompez tout pacte avec l'impiété;
> Du milieu de mon peuple exterminez les crimes,
> Et vous viendrez alors m'immoler vos victimes.»   (84–92)

Whereas these lines may serve to give a lesson in piety and devotion to the spectator, the circumstances under which they are spoken make of them a particular argument in Joad's rhetoric directed at Abner. They become that peculiar kind of poetical rhetoric which, being internally useful to establish probabilities for action, serves as a part of the causation in the plot. The same is true of Joas' recitation to Athalie of the lessons he has learned (II, 7); it is not meant to "persuade" Athalie, but rather to inform her about Joas' character and to augment her anger against the priests of the temple.

There are possible exceptions to this integration of the rhetorical element into the plot. Aside from the choral songs, which are clearly independent, the most dubious case is that of Joad's prophecy in III, 7. During a conversation with the girls of the chorus, Joad addresses God and affirms his confidence in God's help. Then the divine spirit moves him:

> Mais d'où vient que mon cœur frémit d'un saint effroi?
> Est-ce l'Esprit divin qui s'empare de moi?
> C'est lui-même. Il m'échauffe. Il parle. Mes yeux s'ouvrent,
> Et les siècles obscurs devant moi se découvrent.   (1129–32)

Accompanied by the chorus and by the priests' music, Joad foretells the fall of the Temple, the new Jerusalem, and the coming of the Savior. He speaks to the heavens and uses the words of the prophets. Nobody present is directly apostrophized, and in any case nobody present could be involved, even remotely, in the actions predicted. The prophecy is made for the benefit of the spectator, primarily to show the presence of God in Joad and in the action that is taking place, only secondarily to link that action with Christ and the Christian devotion of the audience. The prophecy is rhetorical. I say this because, asking if what is said in it could by any means alter or direct the course of the action—

through persons present and listening—I find the answer negative. The chorus and the priests, Azarias and Josabet, are already
predisposed through their characters to act in favor of Joas and
against Athalie; they do not need the stimulus of Joad's enthusiasm, nor is there any indication later that they act in accordance with it.

"The presence of God in Joad and in the action that is taking
place": this is one of the most curious of the rhetorical aspects
of *Athalie*. Just as he had been extremely wary, in his handling
of pagan subjects, about the intervention of the gods in his actions, so Racine is circumspect in his use of God as a dramatic
agent in his biblical tragedies. Among the former, only in *Phèdre*
is there anything approaching a supernatural basis for an action
integral to the plot, and this is made probable (as we have seen)
through an extremely complex and long-range preparation.
Among the latter, the visiting of the divine spirit upon Joad is, I
think, the nearest thing to a participation of God in the play.
For the rest, both in *Esther* and in *Athalie* God is "present" only
in the sense that a certain number of personages in each play
have, as a part of their characters, a faith in God; that they act
in accordance with that faith; and that both plots involve crises in
the fate and in the faith of the Jewish people. But God does not
act; and even in the case that I have cited from *Athalie,* the episode is derivative from the plot rather than contributory to it. It is
really not a part of the action, but it belongs instead to the
rhetoric of the drama. As a dramatist highly sensitive to the obligation of founding every act upon the necessities of character and
the probabilities of circumstance, and as one who understood the
impossibility of doing so if supernatural forces were introduced,
Racine avoided the *deus ex machina*—and even the *Deus ex
machina*—in both his pagan and his Christian tragedies. He did
not make the mistake of taxing the spectator's credulity (as Corneille had done in *Polyeucte*) by the introduction of actions or
episodes dependent upon divine agency.

In *Athalie,* God is present in the ways that I have described.

He exists as a kind of "coloring" of the central problem and of the characters of the main personages. He is directly present at the moment of Joad's prophecy, indirectly present in the motivations of various personages, in the speeches that they make to others, constantly dominant in the utterances of the chorus. But that is all. It is as improper to speak of God as the protagonist or as the central personage of *Athalie* as it is to assign to God the same functions in *Esther*. The agency, in both biblical tragedies, is strictly human.

Who, then, is the protagonist? For we must once more ask the same question about *Athalie* that we asked about many of the earlier plays. Racine, in his Preface, makes a clear statement of his own conception, explaining at the same time why he chose the title that he did: "Elle a pour sujet Joas reconnu et mis sur le trône, et j'aurais dû, dans les règles, l'intituler *Joas*. Mais la plupart du monde n'en ayant entendu parler que sous le nom d'*Athalie*, je n'ai pas jugé à propos de la leur présenter sous un autre titre, puisque d'ailleurs Athalie y joue un personnage si considérable, et que c'est sa mort qui termine la pièce." The reasoning in the second part is not very convincing. For a poet does not readily allow popular usage to determine the title of his work; and other persons in this tragedy "play important parts" and have their careers terminated—one way or another—in the denouement. I am not sure that we should conclude from these statements that there was an ambivalence in Racine's mind with respect to the hero of his tragedy, for there seem to be very good reasons for considering Joas really the protagonist. But we may at least suppose that the audiences of the day, who chose the definitive title, had some basis for their choice in the way in which the play is organized.

Athalie has, indeed, many claims to the predominant position that contemporary audiences apparently assigned her. Her main function in the plot is to constitute a threat to the persistence of the Jewish faith, to the temple in which it is practiced, and to the "descendant of David" who presumably will insure its continuation. This is essentially a negative role; but in order that it may be accomplished, three things will be required: a past history for Athalie that will account for her present position and her future actions, a character that may serve as the basis for her extraordinary acts, and a series of decisions that will bring her multiple "threat" to realization. To all of these Racine gives his usual expert care, profiting from his experience in the handling of complex situations and vigorous personalities. Athalie's history is told completely and on several occasions. It is summarized in the first scene of Act I, in a way to emphasize the present threat:

> Huit ans déjà passés, une impie étrangère
> Du sceptre de David usurpe tous les droits,
> Se baigne impunément dans le sang de nos rois,
> Des enfants de son fils détestable homicide,
> Et même contre Dieu lève son bras perfide.   (72–76)

At the end of the same scene we are told that she had killed, among other kings, "ce roi fils de David":

> Athalie étouffa l'enfant même au berceau.   (141)

Through Josabet's eyes we see, in the second scene, the carnage in which the child had been one of the victims (241–46), along with an image of the "implacable Athalie." She herself gives the two longest versions, the first in II, 5, where she recalls not only more recent political events but also her mother's death, the second in II, 7, where she summarizes the horrible sights she has witnessed. There are other references to the same events, such as Athalie's recognition of Joas:

> Je reconnais l'endroit où je le fis frapper.   (1770)

These serve to make of the past a vivid part of the present, and to establish Athalie's capacity for inhuman action.

In fact, much of what we know of Athalie's character is the result of a deduction from past action rather than a product of

If Mathan had said, "Ce n'est plus cette reine éclairée," it was by
way of recognizing a change in her:

> Ami, depuis deux jours je ne la connais plus.
>
> .   .   .   .
>
> La peur d'un vain remords trouble cette grande âme:
> Elle flotte, elle hésite; en un mot, elle est femme.
>
> .   .   .   .
>
> J'ai trouvé son courroux chancelant, incertain,
> Et déjà remettant sa vengeance à demain.   (870–86)

Nabal uses the word "confusion" to describe this state—

> D'où naît dans ses conseils cette confusion?—   (862)

whereas Athalie tends to insist on the synonym, "trouble":

> Non, je ne puis: tu vois mon trouble et ma faiblesse.   (435)

> Voilà quel trouble ici m'oblige à m'arrêter.   (541)

> Quel prodige nouveau me trouble et m'embarrasse?   (651)

Thus indecision has taken the place of decision, hesitation that of
forthrightness, doubt that of certainty (see also 460, 511).

There is, moreover, an effort throughout the play to make this
extraordinary state the result of a special visitation of God's will
upon the unhappy queen. It is Joad, God's high priest, who begs
this favor of the divinity:

> Livre en mes faibles mains ses puissants ennemis;
> Confonds dans ses conseils une reine cruelle.
> Daige, daigne, mon Dieu, sur Mathan et sur elle
> Répandre cet esprit d'imprudence et d'erreur,
> De la chute des rois funeste avant-coureur!   (2

After a certain time, he notes that his prayer is being gra

> Déjà ce Dieu vengeur commence à la troubler.

direct statements. There are few of the latter. Athalie herself, in a speech already cited, characterizes through their opposites her courage, her heartlessness, her lack of pity:

> Et moi, reine sans cœur, fille sans amitié,
> Esclave d'une lâche et frivole pitié,
> Je n'aurais pas du moins à cette aveugle rage
> Rendu meurtre pour meurtre, outrage pour outrage,
> Et de votre David traité tous les neveux
> Comme on traitait d'Achab les restes malheureux?
>
> (717–22)

Mathan speaks of her manly qualities of vigor, intelligence, and fearlessness:

> Ce n'est plus cette reine éclairée, intrépide,
> Élevée au-dessus de son sexe timide,
> Qui d'abord accablait ses ennemis surpris
> Et d'un instant perdu connaissait tout le prix.
>
> (871–74)

Such epithets as "audacious" (13), "jealous" (31), "wicked" (36), "proud" (51), "furious" (54) are applied to her by Abner; Joad calls her "impious" (72), "perfidious" (76), "lawless" (171). Josabet uses the summary phrase, "l'implacable Athalie" (244). All these judgments by herself and others, added to the witnesses of her past actions, form a picture of a woman without heart, without scruple, violent and vigorous, who pursues her goals in a direct and relentless manner.

Yet this complete and well-defined character, this permanent set of dispositions, was apparently not sufficient for the accomplishment of the actions that Racine needed to give Athalie. His personages insist, at various points, that she is not now her normal self, that new and unexpected motives and tendencies seem to be shaping her action. Abner is the first to call attention to this special state:

> Enfin, depuis deux jours la superbe Athalie
> Dans un sombre chagrin paraît ensevelie.
>
> (51–52)

Both Joad and Abner interpret the latter's unexpected liberation as a result of God's intervention, Joad through his question,

> Par quel miracle a-t-on obtenu votre grâce?   (1575)

Abner through his reply,

> Dieu dans ce cœur cruel sait seul ce qui se passe.   (1576)

Once she has been trapped and defeated, Athalie recognizes that God's action has caused her downfall:

> Impitoyable Dieu, toi seul as tout conduit.
> C'est toi qui, me flattant d'une vengeance aisée,
> M'as vingt fois en un jour à moi-même opposée,
> Tantôt pour un enfant excitant mes remords,
> Tantôt m'éblouissant de tes riches trésors
> Que j'ai craint de livrer aux flammes, au pillage.
>
> (1774–79)

We may entertain, with respect to God's "confounding" of Athalie, two distinct hypotheses. The first of these is that Racine meant, through this device, to add to the rhetorical effectiveness of the work, to augment the glorification of God by showing how the prayers of the faithful are granted and how the impious are punished. I think that this is not the case; for if it were, we might expect the chorus (mainly charged with the rhetorical function) to utilize so notable a proof. Moreover, the prayers of the faithful are granted in a much more striking way in the crowning of Joas and the destruction of the enemy than in Athalie's crisis of confusion. The second hypothesis is that, because of the actions required of Athalie, Racine was obliged to provide her with dispositions that were not only absent from her permanent character, but that sometimes ran counter to it. The reasons for her extraordinary state would thus be poetic rather than rhetorical, and a fourth factor for the accomplishment of her role would be added.

The problem for Racine in the construction of Athalie's role was to bring her, first, from the *stasis* involved in being a permanent but still potential threat to people, temple, and king, to the activity in which that potential might be realized; then, to divide that activity into a set of successive acts, properly spaced so that the supporters of Joas might take the necessary counteractions and, in so doing, achieve their purposes with respect to Joas. For the first of these, Athalie's characteristics of vigor, directness, and will power were completely sufficient. She needed only, on any pretext, order the destruction of the temple (as Assuérus had ordered the destruction of the Jews) in order to bring her threat to actualization. But this would not make a play, at best it would make an episode. And moreover, it would not correspond to the form of the action that was central in Racine's conception; his goal was not to bring about the destruction of the temple and all it stood for (and contained) but rather to remove the threat to the temple, assure the liberation of the people, and effect the crowning of the king. Athalie's action must be unsuccessful, and it must be unsuccessful because her opponents were able to take effective countermeasures—for which they needed, at each juncture, sufficient time. The solution lay in the breaking-up of Athalie's action into segments, and in the provision of "extraordinary" dispositions that would make each part of her action possible.

We may see the segments of Athalie's action as constituted by the following separate acts: First, and before the beginning of the plot, the dream. The dream has two components, the vision of Jézabel's death and her warning to Athalie, and the vision of the child bringing about Athalie's own death. Together they are the source of her "trouble," awakening at once her fear of "le cruel Dieu des Juifs" (498) and her apprehension of her own death at the hands of the child. The dream precedes the plot and is not a part of it; it is one of the "givens" of the play for which we need have no prior probability. But it creates probabilities for several subsequent acts. Because of her fear of God, Athalie is moved to enter the temple:

Que ne peut la frayeur sur l'esprit des mortels?
Dans le temple des Juifs un instinct m'a poussée,
Et d'apaiser leur Dieu j'ai conçu la pensée;
J'ai cru que des présents calmeraient son courroux,
Que ce Dieu, quel qu'il soit, en deviendrait plus doux.

(526–30)

Her first act within the plot is thus a result of her dream and an expression of her extraordinary state. So is the second; for within the temple, at the altar, she sees the child who had appeared in her dream:

J'ai vu ce même enfant dont je suis menacée,
Tel qu'un songe effrayant l'a peint à ma pensée. (535–36)

This in turn leads to her determination to see the boy again and to examine him more closely—a determination in which she is aided by Mathan, opposed by Abner. Her "regular" character also contributes to the decision, for she is angered at Joad for having driven her from the altar and would not brook a further insult:

Mais je sens que bientôt ma douceur est à bout. (598)

She thus issues two orders, one to Abner to have the boy brought in, the other to Mathan to have her soldiers armed; these are decisive and unhesitating acts.

Athalie's conversation with Joas splits into two halves, and it is at the end of the first that her unexpected reaction to him takes place:

Quel prodige nouveau me trouble et m'embarrasse?
La douceur de sa voix, son enfance, sa grâce,
Font insensiblement à mon inimitié
Succéder ... Je serais sensible à la pitié? (651–54)

The last line is to be juxtaposed to her more typical mockery of "une lâche et frivole pitié" (718). The other half, revealing Joad's and Josabet's teachings about her, leads her from this momentary tenderness (expressed again in the invitation to the child to come to her palace) to an upsurge of hatred for Joas and the line of David. Between Act II and Act III, and encouraged by Mathan, Athalie makes another decision; her words are quoted by Mathan in III, 3:

> «Les feux vont s'allumer, et le fer est tout prêt;
> Rien ne peut de leur temple empêcher le ravage,
> Si je n'ai de leur foi cet enfant pour otage.»   (898–900)

But Mathan, sent to fetch Éliacin, is obliged to leave without him. Athalie's ways of revenge are related in the following act: Athalie's army has been sent against the temple, Abner has been imprisoned. In the final act, while her armies surround and attack the temple, Athalie reverses her decision with respect to Abner; instead of having him killed, she releases him and sends him to the temple with a double mission: to bring back Éliacin, and to fetch the treasure which is reputed to be hidden there. Abner thus becomes Athalie's second emissary, following Mathan and making the same demand but adding the insistence upon the treasure. It is to be noted that Abner, as he quotes Athalie's words, says that they were spoken "d'un air égaré" (1577).

Athalie enters the temple a second time when Joad, preparing an ambush for her, has the doors opened to her; she immediately demands child and treasure (1715). When she discovers what single "treasure" is being held there, she orders her soldiers to seize him. This is the old angry and decisive Athalie. But Joad's armed priests prevent her revenge, she recognizes Éliacin as Joas (admitting the confusion that had led her to hesitate with respect to the destruction of the temple), and she is sent off to be killed by Joad's supporters. Her death is reported in the last scene of the play (1809–12).

This is, for any personage in a drama, a fairly complex role and a large number of acts. Although she appears only twice, once uninvited and once upon Joad's "invitation," she makes a large number of decisions, sends two messengers to make her demands, sets her armies upon the temple, attempts to take by force what has been refused her. She is constantly present as a factor in the developing plot. But she is not the center of that plot. Instead, the whole of her action is secondary; it is always subordinated to the action surrounding Joas and his interests. Each of her acts becomes the occasion for an act on the part of Joad and his priests, and it is the aggregate of the latter, as they lead progressively to the revealing and crowning of Joas, that constitutes the central plot. Athalie's action is fragmented and divided, spaced through hesitation and confusion, in order to permit the development and the progression of these other acts. Thus her dream of two days earlier—Abner establishes the time sequence "depuis deux jours" and "hier" (51, 53)—leads to her present state, which prompts Abner to warn Joad of impending difficulties:

> Je tremble qu'Athalie, à ne vous rien cacher,
> Vous-même de l'autel vous faisant arracher,
> N'achève enfin sur vous ses vengeances funestes,
> Et d'un respect forcé ne dépouille les restes. (21–24)

On the basis of this warning, Joad convokes Abner to another meeting in the temple later in the day:

> ... quand l'astre du jour
> Aura sur l'horizon fait le tiers de son tour,
> Lorsque la troisième heure aux prières rappelle,
> Retrouvez-vous au temple avec ce même zèle. (153–56)

Explaining to Josabet that "les temps sont accomplis," he indicates the action that he means to take:

> Montrons ce jeune roi que vos mains ont sauvé. (173)

Joas will be revealed to the priests and Levites as the descendant of their kings (180).

Athalie's first visit to the temple, involving her expulsion by Joad, her vision of Joas and the determination to see him again, and the long questioning of the boy, produces another step by Joad. Having overheard the interrogation, Joad repeats his summons of Abner to the temple at the fixed hour; he also orders a sacrifice in order to cleanse the temple of Athalie's presence:

> Rentrons, et qu'un sang pur, par mes mains épanché,
> Lave jusques au marbre où ses pas ont touché.   (749–50)

Both steps are preparations for the events of the final act. Mathan's appearance in Act III, again violating the sanctity of the temple, is indirectly another presence of Athalie; for he comes to demand Joas on her behalf. In the course of his conversation with Josabet, Mathan suggests his hypothesis about Éliacin—

JOSABET

> Quel bruit?

MATHAN

> Que cet enfant vient d'illustre origine;
> Qu'à quelque grand projet votre époux le destine—
>
> (999–1000)

which, being so dangerously close to the truth, serves to alert the opposing party. Josabet tells Joad about it, judging that "L'orage se déclare" (1044), and Joad (setting aside all his wife's objections) announces his intentions with respect to Joas. Joas will be crowned and revealed in advance of the announced hour in order to forestall Mathan:

> Montrons Éliacin; et, loin de le cacher,
> Que du bandeau royal sa tête soit ornée.
> Je veux même avancer l'heure déterminée,
> Avant que de Mathan le complot soit formé.   (1094–97)

Joas has already ordered the temple to be closed (1098); he now commands that the crown be prepared (1177) and that the Levites take the arms that have been reserved for the purpose (1179 ff.).

In Act IV, after some of these orders have been carried out,

Athalie sends her troops to surround the temple and imprisons Abner. These acts have as their effect to increase further the peril to Joas and his cause. Joad counters the first of them by disposing his own armed men about the temple and by leading Joas into the sanctuary for the coronation (1445 ff.). In V, 2, Abner appears again, bringing with him Athalie's message and in a sense her presence. Abner is enlisted in the defense of the boy (whose identity is partially disclosed to him) and in the project for the trapping of Athalie; Joad gives final orders to Ismaël for the ambush, to Josabet and the chorus for the revelation of Joas, and to one of the priests for the publication of his crowning. All these events will be timed to correspond to the arrival of Athalie, which occurs in scene 5, and all are accomplished when she does appear. In a sense, the action is now complete; the defeat of Athalie's troops and her own death merely serve to assure the security of king, people, and temple—to remove the threat that had existed for a long time in the past and that had become acute at the beginning of the play.

Athalie's role, then, is conceived as a sequence of acts each one of which brings Joas closer to his coronation, the temple to its security, the Jewish people to its liberation. In order that she may so act, she will need not only the traits of her permanent character but also certain temporary departures from it, and these are provided by Racine in the form of the dream and her ensuing confusion. Such is the reason for her "trouble" and "faiblesse," rather than any intervention of God to confound her counsels.

Just as Athalie's role is auxiliary to the plot affecting Joas, so Mathan's role is ancillary to Athalie's. He stands, at a second remove, as an instrument for making Athalie's "threat" both active and efficacious. We early learn, through Abner, of Mathan's influence on Athalie and of his wish to destroy the temple and seize its treasure:

> Mathan, d'ailleurs, Mathan, ce prêtre sacrilège,
> Plus méchant qu'Athalie, à toute heure l'assiège. (35–36)

He himself later confirms his activity to influence Athalie's decisions:

> J'avais tantôt rempli d'amertume et de fiel
> Son cœur, déjà saisi des menaces du ciel.
> Elle-même, à mes soins confiant sa vengeance ...   (877–79)

Through the course of the play, Mathan profits by this position—as counselor of evil—to suggest or to reinforce given lines of action on the part of the queen. He has, in the past, appealed to her lust for gold by telling her of the treasure in the temple (48); now, after Athalie has seen Joas and Zacharie, he urges that she seize them both (550) and argues against Abner's arguments for not doing so. He is the first to warn Athalie that

> Quelque monstre naissant dans ce temple s'élève,   (603)

a warning which produces the order to arm Athalie's Tyrian soldiers (616). He expands his fiction in a way to bring Athalie's prompt demand for the child:

> Ces mots ont fait monter la rougeur sur son front.
> Jamais mensonge heureux n'eut un effet si prompt.
>   «Est-ce à moi de languir dans cette incertitude?
> Sortons, a-t-elle dit, sortons d'inquiétude.»   (893–96)

Result: Mathan is sent to get Éliacin from Josabet, and their peril is made even clearer to the Jews. The whole of III, 4, is devoted to Mathan's conversation with Josabet, producing only resistance and reaction. Joad drives him from the temple (1034), and we see no more of him. But it is Mathan again, we learn, who presses Athalie to attack the temple—

> Mathan près d'Athalie, étincelant de rage,
> Demande le signal et presse le carnage—   (1631–32)

and Abner's account of this act precipitates Joad's defense. As the Jews triumph, Mathan is killed.

Since he is to participate with Athalie in a common action,

Mathan must have a character very similar to hers. He is, if anything, more wicked—"plus méchant qu'Athalie" (36). Abner de-
picts him as an apostate and impious, a persecutor of virtue, an
angry and dishonest man (37 ff.). In his arguments for seizing
Éliacin and Zacharie, Mathan shows himself to be unfeeling and
bloodthirsty, and his principles of action correspond to Athalie's
traditional practice:

> Est-ce aux rois à garder cette lente justice?
> Leur sûreté souvent dépend d'un prompt supplice.
> N'allons point les gêner d'un soin embarrassant;
> Dès qu'on leur est suspect, on n'est plus innocent. (567–70)

As he recounts his past history to Nabal, he exposes his capacity
for flattery and intrigue, his genius for expediency—

> De mesure et de poids je changeais à leur gré— (938)

and for lying, and his pitilessness. He defines his motives as
"l'amour des grandeurs, la soif de commander" (925), and these
are accomplished on the one hand through his prudence and
wiliness, on the other hand through his wrath. But Mathan, too,
has his weaknesses, and they are useful in the same way as
Athalie's in preventing immediate and effective action against
the temple. It will be remembered that Joad's malediction, his
prayer for "cet esprit d'imprudence et d'erreur" (293), had fallen
both on Athalie and on Mathan. The most striking example of
"error" is Mathan's departure from the temple without Joas,
whom he had been sent to fetch; the moment is brief but telling:

> MATHAN (*Il se trouble*)
> Avant la fin du jour ... on verra qui de nous ...
> Doit ... Mais sortons, Nabal.
>
> NABAL
>   Où vous égarez-vous?
> De vos sens étonnés quel désordre s'empare?
> Voilà votre chemin. (1041–44)

Whether or not this "trouble" is the result of Joad's prayer (or of
the chorus' appeal at the beginning of the act, "Mathan! O Dieu
du ciel, puisses-tu le confondre!"), at any rate it is very close to
Athalie's manifestation of the same state; and Racine points up
the resemblance through his choice of vocabulary, not only in
the "trouble" (visible only in the printed text) but in the "égarez"
(Abner will refer to Athalie's "air égaré" [1577]), in the "sens
étonnés" (Agar had spoken of Athalie's "sens agités" [434], and
Zacharie had said that "Surtout Éliacin paraissait l'étonner"
[414]), and in the "désordre" (Athalie herself had characterized
the "désordre" of her mind at the time of the dream [507]). This
is an effective device of diction for insisting upon the parallelism
of the two states. If there is "imprudence" in Mathan's conduct,
it is manifest on two occasions. Whereas it was useful for him to
invent the story about Éliacin for purposes of persuading Athalie
to action, there is no good reason why he should communicate
to Josabet his theory of the child's illustrious origin (999); this
merely serves to alert the Jews further—which is, indeed, why
Racine introduces it. Again, Mathan's whole strategy with respect to the destruction of the temple is "imprudent." This is a
goal which he seeks for his own ends, to avenge himself on the
God of Israel and, by so doing, to eliminate his remorse over his
apostasy (955 ff.). But if he wished to destroy the temple, he
should not have aroused Athalie's hopes that a treasure was hidden there, since this served as a deterrent to her:

> Tantôt m'éblouissant de tes riches trésors
> Que j'ai craint de livrer aux flammes, au pillage;
>
> (1778–79)

nor should he, in his haste and his rage (1631), have counseled
Athalie in such a way that both she and her soldiers might fall
into the trap prepared for them.

Together, Athalie and Mathan constitute a massive opposition
to the fortunes of Joas and to the intentions and the plans of his
proponents. That is their function in the play. In order to fulfill

it, they must have both vigorous and wicked characters; but the vigor must be tempered, lest they accomplish their purposes too quickly and too directly, and the wickedness must be less than absolute, lest they be regarded by the audience as utter villains and hence lose their dramatic effectiveness. Racine therefore provides Athalie with mitigating passions: love for Jézabel and horror at her death, fear for her own life, the sudden tenderness for Éliacin. Mathan evinces remorse over his desertion of the God of Israel and a residual fear of divine retribution. "Wickedness," of course, is defined in terms of the moral universe established for the play, in which the "sympathetic" personages delimit (as they exemplify) virtue and define the vice that they attribute to their "antipathetic" opposites. In this way the sympathies and the antipathies of the spectator are aroused and developed.

Against the opponents, the proponents. The case for Joas and the action in his favor will necessarily, as *Athalie* is constructed, be more extensive and more fully realized; for this is the action to which the other is contributory, the end for which the other furnishes certain needed means. Besides, this is the one which must direct throughout the essential emotion of the spectator, and in such a way that it will override the emotions attached to Athalie and Mathan. The positive, constructive action is divided primarily among three proponents of Joas—Joad, Abner, and Josabet—although in unequal proportions and in the order of importance indicated. Joad is undoubtedly the prime mover of the action leading to the coronation of Joas, the saving of the temple, and the freeing of the Jews. We may see his action as consisting in the answering of the doubts expressed by Abner and Josabet (he himself has none); in the discovery to Joas of his identity and his responsibilities and the discovery of Joas to all the others; and in the physical acts needed to defend the temple and to capture and punish his opponents.

Joad's character is what it has to be under these circumstances. It is complex and it is vigorous. Not complex in any modern sense, but made up of a large number of characteristics. Chief of these is his unfailing faith in God, expressed earnestly and fervently each time that he appears on the stage. This faith is at once his most notable trait and his best argument. Racine has it serve both purposes in Joad's first long speech to Abner:

> Celui qui met un frein à la fureur des flots
> Sait aussi des méchants arrêter les complots.
> Soumis avec respect à sa volonté sainte,
> Je crains Dieu, cher Abner, et n'ai point d'autre crainte.
>
> (61–64)

The speeches following reaffirm Joad's belief:

> Et quel temps fut jamais si fertile en miracles?
> Quand Dieu par plus d'effets montra-t-il son pouvoir?
>
> (104–5)

> Aux promesses du ciel pourquoi renoncez-vous?   (137)

In the same way, he makes repeated affirmations to Josabet:

> Quoi! déjà votre foi s'affaiblit et s'étonne?   (187)

> Et comptez-vous pour rien Dieu qui combat pour nous?
> Dieu, qui de l'orphelin protège l'innocence
> Et fait dans la faiblesse éclater sa puissance?   (226–28)

> Mais Dieu veut qu'on espère en son soin paternel.   (266)

Several qualities of these speeches should be noted. Through their repetition of an unshakable faith, superior to the hesitations and the doubts of the others, they contribute to Joad a kind of grandeur that makes him equal in stature to Athalie. Moreover, whereas they might seem (as I have said before) to exist above all for rhetorical purposes—to move and persuade an audience—their primary function is that of characterization. They indicate, as they express his belief, the dominant trait of the believer, the one that will be largely determinant of his actions in the play. Finally, they incorporate a virtue which is the direct opposite of the vice, impiety, that informs the characters of Athalie and Mathan.

Other virtues come to complement Joad's piety. His confidence in God makes him inflexible and intractable, since he is sure that his positions are the right ones and that they will be successful; his enemies are the first to recognize these attitudes (cf. 904 ff.). This means that once he has made a decision he will stand by it, and that his enemies as well as his friends will expect from him a decisive and unilinear action. He is courageous and fearless. He does not hesitate to drive Athalie from the temple (404-6), in a mood vividly described by Zacharie:

> Mon père.... Ah! quel courroux animait ses regards!
> Moïse à Pharaon parut moins formidable. (402-3)

He displays a similar violent anger in the scene with Mathan (III, 5), who is expelled from the temple in these terms:

> Sors donc de devant moi, monstre d'impiété.
> De toutes tes horreurs, va, comble la mesure.
> Dieu s'apprête à te joindre à la race parjure,
> Abiron et Dathan, Doëg, Achitophel.
> Les chiens, à qui son bras à livré Jézabel,
> Attendant que sur toi sa fureur se déploie,
> Déjà sont à ta porte et demandent leur proie. (1034-40)

Wrath and violence are thus just as much a part of his character as they are of Athalie's, and serve to give him a comparable vividness on the stage. He also has that quality of action, surprising in a man of God, which had usually been Athalie's prerogative and which now places Joad in the category of the ancient prophets. He separates himself from the "ministres saints" who, in Josabet's words, can only weep and pray (223); all the qualities of a soldier and general are manifest in his direction of the successful defense of the temple and the capture and execution of Athalie.

Such characteristics are of course required by Joad's role in the play. Having to stand against Athalie and her military power, he must have strengths of a different kind; and since he must win against her, his talents must on the whole be superior to hers. Athalie's "confusion" is one of the ways of weakening her position; Joad's faith, with all his concomitant virtues, has as its result to strengthen his position. Just as Mathan acts as an auxiliary to Athalie (although with results sometimes opposite to those desired), so Joad is seconded by Abner and by Josabet. But their functions are different from that of Mathan—they do not merely help the accomplishment of Joad's action in favor of Joas—and different from each other. Abner's sympathies and allegiances must be, if not undecided, at least unclear during much of the play. Were he always and unambiguously on the side of Joad, he could not fill the need for a person who might intermediate between the two camps and who might at once further the "delaying" and the "splitting" of the one action and the acceleration of the other. Racine made a multiple use of Abner, once he had determined how the officer was to be fitted into the plot. Josabet, however, rather than a necessary element for the furthering of the action, becomes a personage largely useful for the control of the audience's feelings.

Abner's first appearance (in I, 1) itself serves various ends. As he warns Joad of impending danger (21–24), he sets in motion the whole series of acts that result in the completion of Joad's goals. As he deplores the state of Israel and expresses his doubts about God's present willingness to help the Jews—doubts that reflect those of the Jewish people—he provides the occasion for Joad's fervent affirmation of his own faith and for his lengthy argument in support of God's continuing favor. As he expresses his devotion to the line of David, he prepares for his future adherence to Joas' cause. It is on the basis of the latter expression that Joad invites Abner to return to the temple later in the day (153). In the same scene, the prime ingredients of Abner's character are presented: his devotion to the God and the traditions of Israel (1–12), accompanied by a strong aversion for the "shameful" and "blasphemous" worshipers of Baal (18–20); his devotion to the Jewish people itself, as exemplified by the kings descended from David (129 ff.); the concomitant hatred for Athalie and Mathan (13, 35); his sympathy with the current discouragement of the Jews,

> Hé! que puis-je au milieu de ce peuple abattu?
> Benjamin est sans force, et Juda sans vertu;   (93-94)

his capacity for a fervent and courageous intervention should the occasion arise (146). Josabet as she speaks of "le brave Abner," Joad as he says that they can be confident of Abner's loyalty (199, 201), confirm this quality of his character, while Joad's narrative of the general's effective defense of his king (77-82) prepares for Abner's later military successes.

When next Abner appears on the stage, it is as a member of Athalie's suite, as a commander of her armies whose aid she requires in the present situation. She pays this tribute to his character—unaware of the equivocal nature of her last statement:

> Je sais que, dès l'enfance élevé dans les armes,
> Abner a le cœur noble, et qu'il rend à la fois
> Ce qu'il doit à son Dieu, ce qu'il doit à ses rois.   (456-58)

Even as he accompanies Athalie, however, Abner pleads the cause of Joad, declaring that the priest was merely doing his religious duty when he expelled her from the temple; and when Athalie orders the two children brought before her, he defends Éliacin against Mathan's extreme recommendations. At the close of the scene, he accepts his first mission as Athalie's messenger: to bring the children to her. This he does in scene 7, where he also attempts to give a benign interpretation to her dream (655 ff.) and where, at the end, he indicates that he has kept his promise to Josabet with respect to the boys' safety (738). Abner makes only one more important appearance on the stage, in V, 2; his presence in scenes 5-7 is merely as one of the new defenders of Joas crowned. The dialogue between him and Joad in scene 2, however, is crucial for Abner, for this is the point where he must decide whether he will turn against Athalie (and his own military obligations to her) and become Joad's ally. Released from imprisonment by Athalie in order that he may again act as her messenger and deliver her ultimatum, he begins by urging Joad to comply by giving up both treasure and child. Joad's testing of him leads to a reaffirmation of his stand; but it becomes evident that he speaks as he does out of loyalty to God and to David's descendants. When his arguments fail, he expresses these allegiances:

> Hé bien! trouvez-moi donc quelque arme, quelque épée;
> Et qu'aux portes du temple, où l'ennemi m'attend,
> Abner puisse du moins mourir en combattant.   (1644–46)

Joad, satisfied now, sends Abner back to Athalie with a countermessage, the one that will result in the trapping and the killing of the queen. Abner returns with her shortly thereafter, witnesses with her the presentation of the new king, and recognizes Joas as his master.

In a sense, Abner has no decision to make, no real conflict to resolve. We know what his basic loyalties are from the outset. But he needs to be convinced that the circumstances are such that a declaration in favor of Joad and against Athalie will be both useful and timely. His moral allegiance remains constant, his material position changes with the development of the total situation. He is to a degree representative of the whole attitude of the Jewish people; but he participates more fully in the action, and more effectively. His ambivalence through much of the play is required for purely utilitarian reasons; but the net effect of his activity is a strong support of Joad and Joas.

Josabet, as wife to the high priest and foster mother to the hidden king, displays no such ambiguities and hesitations. Aside from Joad, only she among the active persons in the play knows Éliacin's true identity, and only she is party from the beginning to Joad's decision that the time for the revelation has come. She has only one concern, Joas' safety, and just as she has saved his life once before, she would save it now at all costs:

Hélas! de quel péril je l'avais su tirer!

Dans quel péril encore est-il prêt de rentrer! (185–86)

This concern is the basis for her constant fear now that the critical moment has arrived—fear that Joad's friends and especially Abner will not be strong enough to help him (198 ff.), fear that the priests and Levites will not constitute a sufficiently powerful guard (209 ff.), fear that God may wish to visit upon Joas the anger previously displayed against the whole house of David (235 ff.); fear, at a later point, that Athalie will seize the child (421 ff.), fear that the temple will fall to Athalie's soldiers (1431 ff.) and that the newly crowned king will be captured—

Ma mère, auprès du roi, dans un trouble mortel,

L'œil tantôt sur ce prince et tantôt vers l'autel,

Muette, et succombant sous le poids des alarmes,

Aux yeux les plus cruels arracherait des larmes. (1549–52)

Yet this fear does not in any way affect the progress of the action. It leads Josabet to propose to Joad that he delay the coronation (1053 ff.); but he follows his own counsels rather than hers. It has the salutary effect of leading Josabet to withhold her answers to Mathan's questions (1013); but, in the last analysis, it is Joad's positive action rather than Josabet's reticence that solves the problem of Mathan's request. We can with difficulty see any direct effect of Josabet's presence upon the development of the plot.

Her usefulness to the play is, I think, of another kind. It is a usefulness that derives from the peculiar nature of Joas as protagonist and from his general position in the work. Normally, with Racine's protagonists (as with those of any expert dramatist), the emotional response of the audience to the hero or heroine is built in two ways: through the direct presence of the protagonist on the stage, and indirectly through the statements of others. With such a heroine as Phèdre, the major part of the response results from her presence, from her thoughts, her passions, and her actions as she herself expresses them; and this is

the case in most of the other tragedies that we have been analyz-
ing. But in *Athalie,* Joas is on the one hand seldom present before us, and on the other hand, when he is present, he must manifest only such passions as faith in God and in his people, only
such virtues as intelligence, discretion, and confidence. He can
show no fear, for in a sense that would disqualify him for the
mission with which he is about to be entrusted. If then the
audience is to feel some fear for Joas' safety, for his fate and his
fortune—and I think that this must be one of the ingredients of
feelings if the play is to be at all suspenseful—that fear must be
provided indirectly through another personage. Josabet's main
function is to incorporate and express that fear, to reiterate on
various occasions her judgment of the dangers surrounding the
boy, to dramatize those dangers through her own strong ap-
prehensions. I might even suggest (at the risk of seeming to over-
emphasize the mechanism of the drama) that she is to a degree
a counterpart to Abner: just as he represents the feelings and
the conscience of the Jewish people with respect to the existence and the revelation of their new king, so she represents the
attitude of the audience toward him, the essential nature of its
emotional identification with him. At any rate, she is one of the
most effective elements in the shaping of the audience's reaction.

Racine's basic conception for the structure of the action in
Athalie might be formulated thus: an action to be accomplished,
revolving about the coronation of Joas which would involve, simultaneously, the liberation of the Jewish people and the security
of its temple; a series of acts by a group of Joas' proponents, leading to the achievement of these goals; a series of acts by his opponents, tending to prevent their achievement or to accomplish
contrary ends: the destruction of the temple, complete domination over the Jews, and the seizing of Joas. In a word, two groups
of personages aligned on opposite sides of a central issue, struggling the one against the other for the attainment of opposite
ends. Both groups are fully and strongly developed, with the
striking qualities of Athalie and Mathan on the one side matched

by the vigor and the relief of Joad, Abner, and Josabet on the other. This pattern recalls, among Racine's other plays, that of *Iphigénie;* except that whereas in *Iphigénie* a clear opposition might be discerned between those who would "sacrifice Iphigénie" and those who would "save Iphigénie," in *Athalie* the opposition is by no means so distinct. Those who would "crown Joas" (with all the concomitants) are set against others who would find the satisfaction of their own passions—greed, lust for power, bloodthirstiness, fear—in the single destruction of the Jewish cause. The structure is less symmetrical, probably because Joas, unlike Iphigénie, is a representative of a whole complex of interests— religious, political, and military—rather than a hero in his own right.

"Hero" is hardly the word. For if there is any one great weakness in the concept of Joas as protagonist, it is in the unheroic quality of his character and his action—one might go so far as to say the "undramatic" quality. He is no hero in his character, not because, in any usual or vulgar sense, he is incapable of heroics but because he has neither the qualities nor the passions that would equip him for actions of any moral importance. He is a child; and almost by definition he is deprived of the maturity of judgment and the capacity for decision that are needed for full moral responsibility. His virtues, such as they are, are really the virtues of others. If he can reply sensibly and with moderation to an interrogatory, it is because he has been carefully schooled by Joad and Josabet. If he is devout, it is because he has been raised by those whose devotion was unquestionable. He is courageous:

> De nos princes hébreux il aura le courage,
> Et déjà son esprit a devancé son âge;   (175–76)

but this is no more than a reflection of Joad's courage and of the examples that have been held up to him. He has a kind of noble dignity and at the same time of sweet innocence—the qualities that strike Athalie when she first sees him:

Joas les touchera par sa noble pudeur,
Où semble de son sang reluire la splendeur.   (273–74)

The second of these is a function of his age; the first might well
be either a matter of appearance only or something that Joad
is too eager to discover in his protégé. None of these virtues, with
the possible exception of his courage, are of a kind that would
lead to positive and strong action; and his courage is used only
for acquiescence and acceptance.

For although Joas may be the center of the action in *Athalie,*
he himself acts very little. We have seen, in the study of the
actions of others, that for the most part he is acted upon rather
than acting. Their concern and their activity centers upon him
and his fortunes, he himself has practically nothing to do about
them. His appearances in the drama are limited to three, one of
which is fairly long. In the first, the questioning by Athalie, Joas
must give the kinds of answers that will obtain for him Athalie's
affection; but he must also show his firm adherence to Joad's
teachings and he must refuse Athalie's invitation to accompany
her. All these are necessary if the plot, as Racine conceives it, is
to be worked out. Joas does make a decision, and perhaps it is a
courageous one; it consists essentially, however, in an option for
his foster parents and their (and his) normal way of life, and
there is at no time any indication that he might have made the opposite choice. In the second appearance, extending through the
whole of Act IV, he learns his identity, accepts his responsibilities
as king as they are outlined to him, and he expresses his love and
his gratitude to those who have formed and protected his childhood. He is more spoken to than speaking throughout. His ac-
ceptances, involving again his decisions, are expressed in terse
formulas. Asked whether he is willing to pay his debt to God,
he replies:

Je me sens prêt, s'il veut, de lui donner ma vie.   (1274)

(We should note that Joad, as he asks the question, imposes the
answer:

Il est temps de montrer cette ardeur et ce zèle
Qu'au fond de votre cœur mes soins ont cultivés,
Et de payer à Dieu ce que vous lui devez.   (1270–72)

A child, especially in Joas' situation, could hardly respond otherwise.) Asked to state his ideas of a king's duties—

On vous a lu souvent l'histoire de nos rois.
Vous souvient-il, mon fils, quelles étroites lois
Doit s'imposer un roi digne du diadème?—   (1275–77)

he repeats the precepts that have been taught him. All this, much
like the interrogation by Athalie, is a catechism in which a child
repeats answers learned long in advance. Necessarily, for at his
age his ideas cannot be his own, cannot result from meditation
and choice. When Joad tells him who he is, his one reply is
"Joas? Moi?" (1294); there is no other comment or acceptance
until, in the next scene, Joad again provides the answer along
with the question:

Et vous, à cette loi, votre règle éternelle,
Roi, ne jurez-vous pas d'être toujours fidèle?

JOAS

Pourrais-je à cette loi ne me pas conformer?   (1381–83)

After Joad's long enumeration of the duties involved in his new
office, Joas makes his promise in more positive terms:

Je promets d'observer ce que la loi m'ordonne.   (1409)

Joas is present throughout the second part of the final act.
During scenes 4, 5, 6, and 8, he says nothing; he is the object
of discussion, of adoration, of the activity centering about him.
Only in scene 7 does he make one speech, of four lines, in which
he prays God that Athalie's malediction may be without effect.
This "presence," this form of minimal participation in what is
going on, is characteristic of Joas' whole role in the play. Everything (or almost everything) happens around him, practically

nothing happens because of him. This may be the reason why audiences of Racine's time thought of it as Athalie's play rather than Joas' and wished to call it by her name—the reason, also, why later critics have desperately sought a protagonist elsewhere than in the person of Joas, even in the person of God. For Joas is the most completely passive of all Racine's protagonists. That observation becomes abundantly clear if we compare him, for example, to Iphigénie. Iphigénie, too, is a personage upon whom the action of the tragedy centers and whose own action is relatively slight. While everybody in the play is preoccupied with her fate and acts for one or the other of the alternative solutions, she herself remains essentially in the position of a victim—acted upon but not acting. Yet her own participation is much more considerable than that of Joas. She needs to intercede for herself by pleading her own case, for her father by defending him against Achille's anger. She needs, above all, to accept her death and to go willingly to the altar to be sacrificed. For all these acts, she must have definite and strong traits of character—the ones that Racine gave her. Joas is gentle and neutral; and this is perfectly adequate, since he has nothing to do.

The juxtaposition of Joas' character to the characters of the other personages and of his inactivity to their activity results in an imbalance, a disproportion in the total structure of the play. Great violence of passion and all kinds of military power are set against him; great faith and the extraordinary strength ensuing from it are made to operate in his behalf. Two forces, two groups of strong and well-defined personages are opposed one to the other, but the subject of their contention plays practically no part in the winning of the cause. Hence the audience is struck by the vigor of the other characters—those of Joad, Abner, Athalie, Mathan—and by the paleness of the protagonist's. This makes it extremely difficult to develop any proper emotion with respect to Joas. We feel, I think, fairly clear and distinct sympathies or antipathies to the other persons, we remain largely indifferent to Joas. It may be, even, that our emotional response to the play reduces to a taking of sides, to a wish that the "wrong" side may lose and the "right" side may win. In a word, because of the confusion of the passions attributable to the failure of the protagonist, we may tend to feel in terms of the rhetorical aspect, of the problem, instead of participating fully and properly in the emotions associated with a dramatic plot.

Perhaps these weaknesses of *Athalie* are a necessary consequence of a flaw inherent in the subject itself. Perhaps it was not possible to make a proper protagonist of Joas, to build an effective dramatic action around him. For we are not to suppose that Racine had lost either his powers or his art since the time when he wrote *Phèdre*. There are too many clear indications in *Athalie* of the persistence of that art: most strikingly, in the swiftness and the deftness with which characters are developed and presented, in the complete integrality and distinctness of each character; but also in the sure preparation of probabilities, in the economical handling of the exposition of circumstances, in the sense of the construction of a scene or an act. These had been among the earliest excellences of Racine in his plays, and in the last of them all reappear at a high degree of development. But two things militated against their use with full dramatic effectiveness: the rhetorical intention and the inadequacy of the subject. It is curious to note that, faced with these difficulties, Racine turned to the type of solution that had characterized his earliest plays—and with some of the same results. As in *La Thébaïde,* he established two opposing groups of persons, contending for resolution of a central problem; here, as there, the groups dominate, the protagonist is doubtful or ineffectual. As in *Alexandre le Grand* (where there is also an opposition of two groups), he writes something that resembles a "poem of praise"; but here the praise is lost, in large measure, at least as far as the protagonist is concerned; for any admiration we might have is dissipated by our hatred for Athalie and Mathan and our sympathy for Joad and his collaborators. And as in both early plays, the unsatisfactory nature of the plot structure prevents the development of any distinct, forceful, and dominating passion. From the start Racine found the making of character easy and the making of plot difficult; his progress from play to play brought constant improvement in the treatment of character but only occasional success in the construction of plot. *Athalie,* at the end of the series, stands as an additional triumph in the creation of character (not the greatest, however, and not involving the character of the protagonist); it is one of the least successful in the creation of dramatic plot. We must judge it as distinctly inferior to *Phèdre* in this regard, and hence of a much lesser general dramatic effectiveness.

Index